ERRATA

The following errors are the responsibility of the publisher. These as well as any minor typographical errors will be corrected in a second printing.

p. 25, line 4, should be etymology, not etiology

p. 25, last line, insert are before 'dependent'

p. 29, line 20, the sentence should begin as follows: It is useful to compare this eclectic grouping of semi-processed and processed goods...

p. 36, line 8, without should be within

p. 39, 20 lines from bottom, replaced should be placed

p. 60, Table 1. 1980 Foreign Non-financial Corporation Sales should read 31.6, Difference -4.4; 1980 Canadian, private sector sales should read 57.9, Difference +8.9.

p. 67, line 4, should be Royal Bank, not Bank of Montreal

p. 68, 13 lines from bottom, should be ensued, not ensured

p. 88, line 13, the sentence should begin as follows: John A. Macdonald's view of the American heresy was summed up by his aphorism that "the rights of the minority ought to be protected...

p. 91, 21 lines from bottom, should be 1759, not 1979

p. 97, line 3, should be footnote number 31, not 32

p. 101, delete the reference to Macpherson's (non-existent) *History...*

p. 114, the first paragraph of the Conclusions should read as follows: Since two different methodological approaches have allowed us to infer that nonfinancial corporate profitability is causally prior to the replacement of broken interlocks, we can arrive at the following conclusions.

p. 129, line 10, should read as follows: first, regulation of the economy as a whole, using fiscal and monetary policy, the regulation of foreign investment, and energy policy;

p. 136, line 13, the sentence should begin as follows: Third, the level of state expenditures influences...

p. 153, sectors should be added after state in the sentence at the foot of the Table.

p. 154, the sentence at the foot of the Table should read as follows: For example, a score of 125 indicates the standard deviation is 1.25 times the value for the state elites.

p. 164, item c. of section 6 should read as follows: c. Foreign-controlled firms do not act much differently from Canadian firms in the same industries.

Canadian Cataloguing in Publication Data

Main entry under title:
The Structure of the Canadian capitalist class

ISBN 0-920059-06-6

1. Capitalists and financiers—Canada—Addresses, essays, lectures. 2. Capitalism—Canada—Addresses, essays, lectures. I. Brym, Robert J., 1951—

HN103.5.S76 1985   306'.42'0971   C85-098668-0

Cover Design: Walter Augustowitsch
Typeset by Second Story Graphics
Printing by Hignell Printing Ltd.
Acknowledgements to Brad Wookey for the
original cover design concept

The Network Foundation for Educational Publishing has contributed towards the cost of publishing this book. Network is a voluntary membership foundation whose ojectives are:

1. To facilitate the development of a healthy and responsible Canadian-controlled post-secondary book publishing sector;
2. To assist in the production, dissemination and popularization of innovative texts and other educational materials for people at all levels of learning;
3. To develop more varied sources for critical works in the Humanities and Social Sciences.
4. To expand the readership for Canadian academic works beyond a select body of scholars.
5. To encourage the academic community to create books on Canadian topics for the community at large.
6. To develop works that will contribute to public information and debate on issues of historical and contemporary concern, thereby improving standards of education and public participation.

For further information, please contact Network Foundation, 163 Neville Park Blvd., Toronto, Ontario, M4E 3P7.

Network Foundation acknowledges the continuing support of the Canadian Studies Program, dept. of Secretary of State.

The Structure of the Canadian Capitalist Class

edited by **Robert J. Brym**

Garamond Press/Toronto

NOTES ON THE CONTRIBUTORS

KAREN ANDERSON lectures in sociology at King's College, University of Western Ontario. Her recent research focuses on the sexual division of labour among Canadian aboriginal peoples in the 17th century.

ROBERT J. BRYM is a Professor of Sociology at the University of Toronto. He has written several books and articles, and has edited, with R. James Sacouman, *Underdevelopment and Social Movements in Atlantic Canada,* (Toronto: New Hogtown Press, 1979). He has just finished a monograph on the development of Anglo-Canadian sociology since the Second World War.

WILLIAM K. CARROLL is Assistant Professor of Sociology at the University of Victoria. He is the author of several articles on the Canadian capitalist class, including "The Canadian corporate elite: financiers or finance capitalists?" *Studies in Political Economy* (8: 1982) and "The individual, class, and corporate power in Canada", *Canadian Journal of Sociology* (9: 1984). Aside from continuing his research on Canadian corporate power, he is studying class and socioeconomic status in the Canadian labour force.

DIANE CLARK is a PhD candidate in sociology at the University of Toronto. An SSHRCC fellow, her dissertation is a study of women's social welfare activities and their role in perpetuating upper class hegemony.

GORDON LAXER is Assistant Professor of Sociology at the University of Alberta. He is the author of "Foreign ownership and myths about Canadian development", *Canadian Review of Sociology and Anthropology* (22: 1985) and is currently writing a book on the roots of foreign ownership in Canada.

JORGE NIOSI is Professor of Sociology at the Université du Québec à Montréal. He has written many books and articles about the Canadian capitalist class, among the most important of which are *Canadian Capitalism: A Study of Power in the Canadian Business Establishment* (Toronto: James Lorimer, 1981), winner of the Canadian Sociology and Anthropology Association's John Porter Award; and *Canadian Multinationals* (Toronto: Garamond Press, 1985). He is currently researching the consequences for Canada of the decline of American industry.

MICHAEL D. ORNSTEIN is Associate Professor of Sociology and Associate Director of the Institute of Social Research at York University. His major articles on the Canadian capitalist class include "The boards and executives of the largest Canadian corporations: size, composition, and interlocks", *Canadian Journal of Sociology* (1: 1976); "The network of directorate links among the largest Canadian firms", with William Carroll and John Fox, *Canadian Review of Sociology and Anthropology* (19: 1982); and "Interlocking directorates in Canada: intercorporate or class alliance?" *Administrative Science Quarterly* (29: 1984). He is now working on studies of the political ideology of Canadians and the class structure of nineteenth century Ontario.

R.J. RICHARDSON is Assistant Professor in the Department of Administrative Studies at the University of Western Ontario in London. He is the author of "Merchants against industry: an empirical study of the Canadian debate", *Canadian Journal of Sociology* (7: 1982) and is currently doing research on intercorporate relationships and on formal organizations.

LORNE TEPPERMAN is Professor of Sociology at the University of Toronto. He is the author of many books and articles, including *Social Mobility in Canada* (Toronto: McGraw-Hill Ryerson, 1975). He is currently engaged in research on computer use in the social services.

TABLE OF CONTENTS

Preface

The essays in this book are based upon papers presented at a conference on "The Structure of the Canadian Capitalist Class," held at the University of Toronto in November 1983. Revised versions of some of the other conference papers will appear in Robert J. Brym, ed Regionalism in Canada (Toronto: Irwin, forthcoming 1985). The Social Sciences and Humanities Research Council of Canada funded the conference, and more modest financial contributions to its success were made by the Structural Analysis Programme, the Office of the Dean of Graduate Studies, and the Office of the President at the University of Toronto. The conference participants are greatly indebted to these agencies for their assistance; we hope that readers of this book will have reason to be thankful to them as well.

We are also happy to have the opportunity to publicly acknowledge the assistance of a number of individuals. Sylvia Wookey worked with efficiency and vigour in helping prepare for the conference. The representatives of Garamond Press displayed much good common sense, tolerance, and, when necessary, firmness, in all stages of this book's production. We are honoured to be among the first projects to be undertaken by this new publishing venture.

Although not all of the conference papers could be published, those which do appear in print have profited from the criticisms of all conference participants, whose efforts are reflected in the following pages.

ROBERT J. BRYM
TORONTO
MARCH 1985

I
Introduction

The Canadian Capitalist Class, 1965-1985
Robert J. Brym

A. From the Denial of Class to the Rise of Left Nationalism

I know of no more interesting subject of speculation, nor any more calculated to allow of a fair-minded difference of opinion, than the enquiry whether a professor has any right to exist . . . Apparently he has neither ideas nor enthusiasms, nothing but an elaborate catalogue of dead men's opinions which he cites with a petulant and peevish authority that will not brook contradiction . . . (S)ome explanation of the facts involved may perhaps serve to palliate, if not remove, demerits which are rather to be deplored than censured(:) . . . the professor more than any ordinary person finds himself shut out from the general society . . . Is it not possible, too, that when all is said and done the professor is performing a useful service in the world, unconsciously of course, in acting as a leaven in the lump of commercialism that sits so heavily on the world to-day? . . . (I)n these days, when money is everything, when pecuniary success is the only goal to be achieved, when the voice of the plutocrat is the voice of God, the aspect of the professor, side-tracked in the real race of life, riding his mule of Padua in competition with an automobile, may at least help soothe the others who have failed in the struggle.

—Stephen Leacock ''The apology of a professor:
an essay on modern learning'' (1910)

It is one of the more remarkable facts of Canadian intellectual life that, until some twenty years ago, few university professors or literary figures seem to have noticed that there are social classes in this country[1]. Or at least, if many intellectuals did notice they were not inclined to publicize the discovery. Thus, in 1963 a literary critic remarked that the theme of social class scarcely appears in Canadian literature (McDougall 1963). In 1965 an historian made an identical observation in a review of Canadian historical writing (Mealing 1965). And in that same year, John Porter, who was soon to be acknowledged as the outstanding sociologist in the country, wrote:

Even at times in what purports to be serious social analysis, middle class intellectuals project the image of their own class onto the social classes above and below them. There is scarcely any critical analysis of Canadian social life upon which a conflicting image could be based. The idea of class differences has scarcely entered into the stream of Canadian academic writing . . . (Porter 1965: 6).

At least in the context of the Canadian academic's contribution to class analysis as of two decades ago, Leacock's satire may therefore be worth taking seriously.

I would like to thank Michael Ornstein for helpful comments on an earlier draft.

His image of the professor—a person with "neither ideas nor enthusiasms"—seems particularly fitting. His assertion that the professor had little contact with the non-academic world also makes sense as a partial explanation for the state of class analysis in Canada prior to 1965 or so. So does his understanding of the academic's social function: "acting as a leaven in the lump of commercialism", helping "to soothe the others who have failed in the struggle". How better to contribute, even unwittingly, to social stability than deny the existence of class inequality altogether?

Since the mid-1960s the situation has, of course, changed a great deal, and the study of social class has even become something of a "growth industry". This development is a result of a number of factors, among the most important of which are the influence of Porter's work; the recruitment of Canadian professors from more diverse class and ethnic backgrounds than was once the case; the immigration, during the days of rapid university expansion, of scholars from the USA and England, where the study of social class was better developed; the strengthening of ties between the professoriate and what Leacock called "the general society", as academics came to serve more frequently as consultants and partisans of various class and political interests; and something which is perhaps best (if vaguely) labelled the changing "temper of the times".

This shift in the Canadian intellectual climate is worth reflecting upon. It is usually and, I think, justifiably ascribed mainly to the weakening role of the USA in international affairs from the mid-1960s on (Resnick 1977: 145-99). The United States suffered defeat in Vietnam. The post-Second World War recovery of the Japanese and West German economies threatened the competitiveness of American manufacturers. Increasingly, wealth flowed from the U.S.A. and other highly industrialized countries to the petroleum- and mineral-exporting nations as OPEC and other cartels secured enormous increases in the price of natural resources. The US government naturally reacted to these and other symptoms of decline through a series of defensive measures. For example, in the early 1970's special duties were placed on imports in order to protect jobs in the USA and lessen that country's balance of payments deficit—a measure which was bound to be viewed unfavourably in Canada, the United State's largest trading partner. Similarly, the American abandonment of the gold standard effectively exported inflation to Canada and other countries.

How did Canadians respond? Many became aware of some of the negative consequences of being so tightly bound, economically and politically, to the fortunes of the U.S.A. Also, the realization grew that new possibilities for economic growth were afforded by changing international circumstances, especially rising world market prices for Canada's abundant natural resources. This was as true of the federal government as it was more generally: throughout the 1970's and particularly with respect to energy, environmental, and maritime policies, a keen appreciation developed that American and Canadian interests are not necessarily the same. The National Energy Policy, the debate over acid rain, and negotiations concerning the Law of the Sea all reflect the growth of this more independent Canadian stance *vis-à-vis* the U.S.A.

Academics and university students tended to respond more radically to the American decline and Canada's expanded opportunities than did other segments of Canadian society. The most prominent manifestation of this trend was the formation, within the New Democratic Party, of a left-nationalist wing known as the "Waffle" (Hackett 1980). Supported by roughly one third of NDP activists at its height, the Waffle was dominated by intellectuals, and central to its platform was the view that Canadian "dependency" upon the United States was chiefly responsible for a whole range of economic and other ills.

The term dependency was intended to signify an unequal relationship in which the United States uses its superior power to secure a wide range of economic advantages over Canada. As the left-nationalist argument has been developed in academic circles (see especially Britton and Gilmour 1978; also Levitt 1970; Lumsden 1970; Rotstein and Lax 1974), it is held that one of the chief features of the Canada/U.S.A. relationship is the control of substantial portions of the Canadian economy by American-based multinationals. This control facilitates the outflow of a great deal of capital—in the form of profits, dividends, interest payments, royalties, and management fees—from the country. In the absence of foreign control, that capital would presumably be available for investment and job creation in Canada. The magnitude of the problem is indicated by the fact that Canada has had growing deficits on the "non-merchandise account" of its international balance of payments throughout the post-Second World War period. By 1977 the annual deficit amounted to over $7 billion. Nearly 75% of that deficit is a result of capital transfers such as those listed above.

Not only does American direct investment cause a net capital drain, but in addition (so the left-nationalist argument continues), the foreign capital which remains invested here creates fewer jobs than would an equal amount of domestic capital investment. This is the case because foreign capital is invested in Canada for two main purposes: to provide a secure source of raw materials for manufacturing plants in the U.S.A., and to produce manufactured goods for the Canadian market. Plants set up to produce only for the Canadian market are by definition prevented from trying to compete for international sales, from engaging in research and development, and in many cases from doing any more than assembling parts made outside the country. Thus, foreign direct investment seriously constrains growth in the manufacturing sector—which is one important reason why Canada imports substantially more manufactured goods than it exports ($11 billion more in 1977). Moreover, massive American direct investment in the resource sector is an inefficient creator of jobs: generally speaking, a unit of investment in resource extraction creates fewer employment opportunities than a unit of investment in manufacturing since resource extraction is generally more capital-intensive. Add to this the left-nationalists' fear that Canada's concentration on primary or extractive industries might soon lead to the depletion of oil, gas, and other natural resource reserves, and their conclusion becomes understandable: the long term economic prospects for Canadians are gloomy unless they rid themselves of U.S. economic domination.

B. Left-Nationalism and the Capitalist Class

Canada's dependency is a function not of geography and technology but of the nature of Canada's capitalist class.

—Jim Laxer, Leader of the Waffle (1973)

This corollary of the dependency thesis is particularly germane in the present context. It was first elaborated in a highly influential article by Tom Naylor (1972; see also Naylor 1975). According to Naylor, the whole sweep of Canadian economic history is characterised by Canada's role as a supplier of raw materials to, and a purchaser of manufactured goods from, a progression of imperial centres: first France, then Great Britain, and finally the U.S.A. Naylor allowed that out of this trade there emerged a Canadian capitalist class which specialized in the construction and operation of transportation facilities, as well as the provision of insurance, banking, and short-term credit services. But he further insisted that this class has historically had a vested interest in blocking the development of a vigorous and independent manufacturing sector in this country. After all, he reasoned, using raw materials here rather than shipping them abroad, and producing manufactured goods here rather than bringing them in from elsewhere, would undermine the trading and related activities upon which the prosperity of the Canadian capitalist class was founded. The high import tariffs on manufactured goods instituted by the Macdonald government in the National Policy of 1879, and eagerly backed by members of Canada's mercantile bourgeoisie, serve Naylor as an outstanding example of how the capitalist class stunted independent industrial growth in this country. The net effect of the tariff wall was to encourage the hothouse growth of foreign (mainly American) branch plants in Canada—plants designed to service only the local market and engage mainly in assembly and warehousing.

This argument, which came to be known as the "merchants against industry thesis", was widely accepted until the mid-1970s. Consider, for instance, the important studies undertaken by Wallace Clement (1975; 1977). One of the tasks Clement set himself was to analyze the density and pattern of ties among dominant corporations in Canada—ties formed by individuals sitting simultaneously on more than one corporate board of directors. According to Clement, the senior executives and members of the boards of directors of the country's dominant corporations, members of the "corporate elite", actually comprise two main groups. First, the "indigenous elite" consists of people, for the most part Canadian-born, who head corporations engaged mainly in commercial and transportation-related activities. Their business is conducted chiefly inside, but also to a degree outside, Canada. (An example of the latter is the case of Canadian banks setting up branches throughout the Caribbean region). Second, the "comprador elite" consists of people, only some of whom are Canadian-born, who merely operate or manage the Canadian branch plants of multinatonal corporations. The economic activities of these branch plants are also largely restricted to Canada itself, although in some cases they serve as intermediaries for American direct investment in third countries. (For example, the Ford Motor Co. in the U.S.A. holds 85% of the stock in the Ford Motor Co. of Canada, which in turn holds 100% of stock in the Ford Motor Co. of Australia, New Zealand, South Africa, and Singapore.) Most of the multinationals with branch plants in Canada have head offices in the USA, and most of them are engaged in manufacturing and resource extraction.

Clement does not suggest that the cleavage between indigenous and comprador "fractions" of the Canadian corporate elite implies conflict or rivalry between the two groups. Quite the contrary. The two groups play complementary roles in Canadian economic life, one basically financial, the other basically industrial and resource-related. Moreover, their boards of directors are highly interlocked, important financiers frequently serving on the boards of foreign-controlled companies engaged in manufacturing and resource extraction, and vice-versa. They also share a "continentalist" outlook on the nature of Canada/U.S. relations, as evidenced by their opposition to the growth of an indigenous Canadian manufacturing sector that could disrupt the existing pattern of economic relations between the two countries.

The left-nationalists maintain that members of the Canadian corporate elite have successfully transformed this continentalist vision into what is widely perceived as "the national interest". This is significantly evident in the behaviour of the two establishment political parties, Liberal and Progressive Conservative. These parties have, by and large, acted to stultify the growth of a vigorous manufacturing sector and have reinforced the liaison between indigenous commercial and foreign-controlled comprador elites. Two of the most frequently cited examples of the manner in which governments have acted in the interests of Canadian corporate leaders are the failure to enact a tough Foreign Investment Review Act limiting American takeovers of Canadian manufacturing and resource companies, and a readiness to introduce laws protecting Canadian banks, insurance companies, and transportation companies from foreign competition.

The theoretically important question is: How is it that the class interests of the corporate elite get translated into major government policies? Members of the left-nationalist school have differed in their answers to this question. Many of them have modified their opinions since the mid-1970's. While their views on other matters were, as I have noted, strongly influenced by the Canadian political climate, the same cannot be said in this case; their interpretation of the manner in which the Canadian capitalist class rules was shaped mainly by the state of neo-Marxist thinking on the subject in the early 1970's. There is thus no logical connection between left nationalism *per se* and the left nationalists' early views regarding the state in capitalist societies. With these qualifications in mind, I shall not distort matters greatly if I assert that the left nationalists' original answer to the question posed above, boiled down to essentials, went something like this: The corporate elite controls governments largely in a direct manner, that is by forging a wide variety of strong social ties to the state and to state personnel. These ties ensure that the people who occupy the command posts of economic institutions form a ruling class.

The implications of this viewpoint may by more fully appreciated if we contrast it with the earlier formulation of John Porter. Porter had discovered that members of various Canadian elites—the chief power holders in our economic, political, media, bureaucratic, and intellectual institutions—tend to be recruited from well-to-do families of British and Protestant origin in far greater proportions than their representation in the general population. Moreover, Porter sought to establish that members of the different elites come to share certain values and attitudes as they interact with one another. This cohesion enables them to achieve "the over-all co-ordination that is necessary for the continuity of the society" (Porter 1965: 523). Cohesion is attained informally by elite members attending private schools together, intermarrying, and forming strong friendship ties. In addition, a number of formal mechanisms reinforce this cohesion. For example, various commissions and advisory boards are set up by governments, and members of the economic elite are usually the favoured appointees. Similarly, funding for the establishment political parties comes almost exclusively from wealthy corporate patrons. A "confraternity of power" is thereby established among the various elite groups.

In Porter's opinion this does not, however, amount to saying that Canada's elites form a ruling class: "The elite groups remain separated and never become merged into one effective power group" (Porter 1965: 215). He emphasised that harmony among elites has limits, as is indicated by the fact that various elite groups come into conflict over a wide range of issues.

A decade later, Clement, a student of Porter, acknowledged the existence of such conflict. But he underscored the limits of this conflict, not the limits of elite harmony. Clement concluded that Canada's major institutional elites do indeed form a cohesive group which represents the country's capitalist class and makes it a ruling class. The members of this class are presumably united around the goals of protecting private property, preventing the spread of public sovereignty over economic resources, and preserving continentalism as the dominant Canadian way of life. Yet Clement based his conclusion largely on the same types of data which Porter used to come to the opposite conclusion: data showing the relatively similar class, ethnic, religious, and even family origins of members of different elites, and the effective operation of formal and informal mechanisms which bind together corporate and political elites in particular. In Clement's words:

What is interesting is the way these powers tend to come together, which classes are represented in the coalitions, and what the consequences of their actions are for the society. Using this approach can allow for a variety of historical combinations which can be empirically examined and evaluated . . . Miliband's work is a good example of this since he explicitly examines the state in liberal-democracies as part of capitalist society and not as some autonomous functioning apparatus . . . Common ideologies, class backgrounds, and relationships serve to solidify power holders, not bring them into opposition. Structured interlocks, combined with social ties, serve to create a system of mutual benefit and dependence between leaders of dominant corporations and other institutions (Clement 1975: 353, 359; cf Olsen 1980).

Even among these scholars inclined to accord the state greater independence of, or autonomy from, the corporate elite, it was common in the mid-1970's to remark upon "a particularly striking characteristic of the Canadian state—its very close personal ties to the bourgeoisie. Whatever the merits of Poulantzas' contention that the most efficient state is that with the least direct ties to the dominant class, it is a rather academic point as applied to Canada" (Panitch 1977: 11).

The crux of the discussion thus far may be summarised by follows. In the decade or so following the publication of Porter's pathbreaking *The Vertical Mosaic*, students of the Canadian capitalist class tried to establish the validity of several ideas, three of which I have emphasized here.[2] The first idea concerns the relationship between different segments of the Canadian capitalist class. That class was said to consist of two main groups: an indigenous commercial elite with deep historical roots in Canadian trade, transportation, banking, and insurance, and a more recently formed comprador elite whose role it is to manage manufacturing and resource-extracting branch plants to the principal advantage of head offices in the United States. These elites have allegedly conspired to block the growth of large Canadian-controlled manufacturing concerns.

The second idea concerns the boundaries of the Canadian capitalist class. According to the left nationalists, that class is not a wholly independent and indigenous entity. One of its two major subgroups is wholly controlled by American multinationals, and the orientation of both subgroups is not national but continental. To be sure, the business activities of the Canadian capitalist class are supposedly restricted for the most part to Canadian soil, but that restricted base of operations, insofar as it provides

American manufacturers with a secure supply of raw materials and a secure market for their products, favours American more than Canadian interests.

The third idea concerns the mechanisms that allow the capitalist class to rule, and especially the means by which it is able to shape at least the broad outlines of government policy. Direct ties between corporate leaders and powerful political figures were widely thought to transform wealthy capitalists into effective rulers; both formal and informal channels are supposedly used by members of the corporate elite to ensure their predominance.

These ideas, which together constitute the left-nationalist interpretation of Canadian capitalist class structure, are compelling in many respects. They were even more attractive ten years ago or so, when the Canadian political and intellectual climate was more congruent with their policy implications. But the left-nationalist interpretation has none the less been criticised on a number of grounds. These I should now like to review, partly in order to bring this sketch of the field up to date, partly to introduce the articles in this book by way of placing them in the context of ongoing debates.

C. Capitalist Class Cleavages

To us it seems somewhat extraordinary that, with raw materials near at hand, and every facility to manufacture, the bulk of the fabrics used in this country should continue to be imported . . . The aim to promote home industry embracing the erection of factories to give employment to a large number of work people, must ere long greatly benefit this country. However persistently politicians preach agriculture as the proper vocation for Canadians, it is being more fully recognized that while our money is sent elsewhere to employ others to manufacture our articles of consumption our progress cannot be satisfactory.

–Montreal *Journal of Commerce–Finance and Insurance Review*
(4 February 1881)

The "merchants against industry thesis" was the first aspect of the left-nationalist view to come under critical scrutiny. Adherents of this school were charged with an error of emphasis, another of definition, and yet another of fact. The thesis stands or falls partly on the degree to which indigenous manufacturers in Canada formed a relatively small, poor, and uninfluential segment of the capitalist class, constrained in its development during the latter part of the nineteenth and first part of the twentieth century by presumably more numerous, wealthy, and powerful commercial entrepreneurs. If, however, native industrialists were in fact not so insignificant, then a central element of the merchants against industry thesis is called into question.

Several historians of Canadian industrial growth have made precisely that point, and they have done so with a wealth of material attesting to the industrialization that began in the British North America colonies as early as the 1850's. There is no denying the predominance of "staple" production (especially lumber and wheat) in the pre-Confederation years, but this does not prevent Stanley Ryerson from making the following remark:

Together with a rise in the number engaged in "industrial employment" in the Province of Canada in the years 1851 to 1861 from 71,000 to 145,000, there was taking place at the top a consolidation of the new elite of railroad and factory owners; the shaping of that ruling class of industrial capitalists who were to be the real (not merely the titular) "fathers" of Confederation (Ryerson 1973 (1968): 269; see also Ryerson 1976).

By the 1880's and 1890's industrialization was certainly well under way, and by the early decades of the twentieth century Canadian manufacturing industry was well developed by international standards. Thus, according to data presented by Gordon Laxer (1983: 25 and *passim*), in 1913 Canada was the world's seventh largest manufacturing nation, outranked only by the U.S.A., Germany, the United Kingdom, France, Russia, and Italy. The great bulk of products manufactured in Canada were not semi-processed, but fully finished goods such as farm implements, footwear, furniture, and so forth. With only 0.4% of the world's population, Canada produced 2.3% of all manufactured goods in the world that year (compared to Japan's 1.2% and Sweden's 1.0%).

Moreover, Canada's commercial sector was not particularly "overdeveloped" in the first decades of this century, at least in comparison with that of the United States. Jack Richardson has computed ratios, for both Canada and the USA, in which the numerator is the amount of national income generated by commercial businesses and the denominator is the amount of national income generated by industrial activity. He discovered that the Canadian ratio is about the same, or lower than, the American ratio, depending on the precise definitions of "commercial" and "industrial" activity used. Yet this is exactly the opposite of what one would expect to find if the merchants against industry thesis were valid. (The ratios are for the years 1920-26; see Richardson 1982: 291).

In light of these facts it seems unjustified to speak of a tiny and influential manufacturing elite in late nineteenth and early twentieth century Canada. The current weakness of Canada's manufacturing sector is undeniable, but the twentieth century was well advanced before its frailty became obvious. Why Naylor and Clement none the less held otherwise is partly a result of a definitional quirk. They alluded to Marx's distinction between industrial or productive capitalists who engage in "the sphere of production" (i.e. manufacturing) and mercantile or non-productive capitalists who engage in the "sphere of capital circulation" (i.e. banking, insurance, and the like). According to Marx, only the economic activity organized by productive capital directly adds value to raw materials. Moreover, industrial capital is characterized by a comparitively high ratio of fixed to circulating capital—which is to say that manufacturers tend to invest relatively more in plant and equipment than do mercantile capitalists, who prefer short-term liquid investments. That is why, in Marx's view, sustained and substantial economic development depends upon the robustness of industry: only manufacturers organize the actual addition of value to raw materials by promoting the accumulation of long-term fixed investments.

The view that industry is generally the chief engine of economic development is unobjectionable. What is problematic is that Naylor and Clement classified entrepreneurs active in the railroad industry — one of the most important branches of the economy in late nineteenth century Canada — not as industrialists, but as financial or commercial capitalists engaged in trade. Yet, according to L.R. Macdonald (1975: 267, 268), "railways had much the highest proportion of fixed to circulating capital of any nineteenth-century enterprise" in Canada; and Marx himself "went out of his way in *Capital* to insist that the transportation industry was productive because it added value to commodities; for him, a railway was an industry, not a trade". If Naylor and Clement had characterized the railroad barons as productive, rather than financial, capitalists they might not so readily have jumped to the conclusion that productive capitalists were a minor force in

Canadian economic life. Neither do they seem to have been justified in positing a conflict of interest between financial and industrial capitalists. Not only was it the case that, by and large, financial capitalists in late nineteenth century Canada had nothing against the formation of domestic manufacturing concerns. In point of fact, as Macdonald (1975) has noted, many financial capitalists promoted the growth of manufacturing, and even became manufacturers themselves. Richardson (1982: 287-8) shows that this early tendency for merchants actually to become industrialists was clearly visible in the Brantford, Ontario, economic elite of the 1890's and in the Toronto economic elite of the 1920's. In Brantford, 55% of the 22 members of the economic elite were active in mercantile and in- dustrial firms at the same time. In Toronto, 53% of the 164 most powerful men in the economic elite simultaneously held directorships in both types of corporations. If the economic interests of financial and industrial capitalists were opposed one would not find such clear evidence of an identity of interest and personnel between these two groups.

Some analysts of the late twentieth century Canadian capitalist class have taken this last point a step further. They question whether it makes any sense at all to talk about two main groups in the Canadian capitalist class, and hold that it may be altogether more accurate to posit a merger of commercial and industrial interests, at least in contemporary times. The most important pieces of research which develop this theme are by William Carroll (1982), and by Carroll, John Fox, and Michael Ornstein (1982).

Carroll, Fox and Ornstein examined interlocking directorates among 100 of the largest financial, merchandising, and industrial firms in Canada in 1973. They discovered, first, that these firms are remarkably highly integrated by top cor- porate officials and managers serving simultaneously on more than one board of directors. Ninety-seven of the 100 firms were connected by single-director interlocks and 70 of the 100 by multiple-directorship ties. Their second important finding was actually a non-discovery: no evidence could be found in their interlock data to support the view that the largest Canadian firms are clustered in disconnected subgroups or cliques based on nationality of ownership or on sphere of economic activity. Such cliques would presumably have been discovered if the cleavages within the capitalist class posited by the left nationalists did in fact exist. Finally, Carroll, Fox, and Ornstein inferred from their data that non- financial corporations controlled by Canadians tend not to share directors with non-financial corporations controlled by non-Canadians; but both types of firms typically had multiple ties to Canadian-controlled financial firms. In other words, banks lie at the centre of the network of interlocking directorates, serving as the principal points of articulation and integration for the corporate elite.[3]

Some of these interpretations were confirmed and elaborated on in Carroll's (1982) study. He examined the boards of directors of the 100 largest Canadian indus- trial, financial and merchandising firms at five-year intervals over the period 1946-76, and discovered the existence of dense ties between Canadian-controlled financial firms and Canadian-controlled industrial firms, and markedly less dense ties between Canadian-controlled financials and US-controlled industrials operating in Canada. Moreover, the directorship ties among indigenous Canadian financial and non-financial firms have become more dense over time, while the ties between Canadian financials and American-controlled industrials have become less dense. This is the opposite of what the left-nationalist theory predicts.[4]

D. Capitalist Class Boundaries

All governments must bear in mind that when we protect uncompetitive industries or try to give an artificial edge to our own firms, we damage the international trade and payments system on which we all depend.

—Minister of External Affairs Allan MacEachen,
speaking at the 1984 annual meeting in Vancouver of the
Pacific Basin Economic Council (PBEC).

The Council should clearly indicate that it supports the GATT (General Agreement on Tariffs and Trade) . . . The basic thrust should be to reinforce market forces as the basic resource allocation mechanism.

—Hugh Stevens, Chairman Canada Wire and Cable Ltd.,
International President, PBEC, speaking at the same meeting.

The evidence just reviewed leads one to conclude that the cleavages in the Canadian capitalist class which the left-nationalists purported to detect were greatly overdrawn. Does the left-nationalist theory fare any better with regard to the second question it raised, concerning the boundaries of the capitalist class? Carroll (1982), for one, thinks not. He suggests that the Canadian capitalist class is now indigenous and independent, not continental and dependent. Steve Moore and Debi Wells (1975) come to much the same conclusion, and Jorge Niosi (1981 (1980); 1982; 1983) offers a more qualified assessment. Let us consider the evidence upon which they base their conclusions.

Carroll (1982:98) stresses the fact that the assets of top Canadian firms were overwhelmingly Canadian-controlled at the end of the Second World War and they exhibit the same characteristic today: in 1946 and in 1976 about 86% of such assets were Canadian-controlled (about 56% Canadian-controlled in the manufacturing sector alone) while roughly 11% were American-controlled (approximately 33% in the manufacturing sector). There was a period in the 1950's and 1960's when overall American control of assets in the largest Canadian firms nearly doubled, but that era began to fade into history after 1970. Similarly, Niosi (1981 (1980):32; 1983:132) cites government statistics showing that, among all non-financial companies in Canada, the value of assets under foreign control as a percentage of all assets has decreased from 36% in 1970 to 29% in 1978 to 26% in 1981. In manufacturing alone the decline was from 58% in 1970 to 52% in 1978. At the very least, these figures support the view that Canadian capitalism has become more indigenous and less controlled by non-Canadians over the past fifteen years.

It is also worth noting that this independence has been reflected in the propensity of Canadian companies to increase their foreign investments: the boundaries of the capitalist class's activities are, in other words, less and less circumscribed by the country's political borders. The ratio of foreign direct investment in Canada to Canadian direct investment abroad was 4.6 in 1970, 3.6 in 1975, and 2.7 in 1979, the latest year for which figures are available. Significantly, in 1969 nearly 62% of Canadian direct investment abroad was investment by Canadian-controlled companies; that figure increased to 83% by 1978. In absolute terms, Canada was the seventh largest overseas investor in the world by 1976 (after the U.S.A., the U.K., West Germany, Japan, Switzerland, and France). In relative terms, too, Canada's overseas investment record was impressive: in 1978 Canadian direct investment abroad amounted to $700 per capita—not much less than the American figure of $750; and by 1980 the annual rate of growth of Canadian investment abroad was 13.7%, compared to 9.0% for the U.S.A. (Moore and Wells, 1975:72; Niosi 1982:24, 25; 1983:132-3).

Some analysts are inclined, on the basis of these figures, to urge outright rejection of the view that the Canadian capitalist class is basically dependent and continentalist and largely constrained to Canadian territory in its business dealings. Carroll, Moore, Wells, and others tend to think of Canadian capitalists as having "come of age," engaging in their own economic ventures overseas and no longer subordinate to American interests.

However, these interpretations probably go rather farther than facts warrant. For, as Niosi (1982; 1983:133-4) points out, Canadian-controlled multinationals are still technologically dependent upon research and development in the U.S.A., and they are restricted to supplying only a narrow range of products and services abroad (utilities, engineering, mining, banking, real estate services). Furthermore, the decline in foreign control of the Canadian economy which we have witnessed over the past fifteen years has largely been confined to extractive and mineral processing industries (especially oil and gas, potash, coal, asbestos, and metals). The Canadian manufacturing sector is, as the left-nationalists stressed, still very weak. Most of it is still foreign-controlled, and because of the strict limits this places on its growth it still employs a smaller percentage of the labour force than is the case in any other industrialized country. It does not even come close to supplying Canadians with all the manufactured goods they need, and a large part of the manufacturing that takes places actually involves the mere assembly of parts made elsewhere (Williams 1983).

From all this, Niosi concludes—quite sensibly I think—that the Canadian capitalist class cannot at present be characterized either as purely continentalist and dependent or as purely independent of foreign interests; either as tightly constrained to engage in business almost exclusively in Canada or as freely able to engage in wide-ranging business ventures abroad. The Canadian capitalist class possesses aspects of all these features simultaneously because of the local and international economic and political conditions within which it has evolved.

E. Capitalist Class Rule

John Turner, a front-runner in the race for the leadership of the federal Liberal Party, was re-elected yesterday to the board of directors of Seagram Co. Ltd., the world's largest wine and liquor company.

"If we wins the leadership convention, and gets elected to Parliament, he would have to resign," Seagram President Edgar Bronfman told reporters . . . But he added with a smile that "From a Seagram standpoint it would not be a bad thing to have a future prime minister on our board."

Mr. Turner said recently he would resign his directorships of such corporate giants as Bechtel Canada Ltd., Canadian Pacific Ltd., MacMillan Bloedel Ltd. and Massey-Ferguson Ltd., if elected leader.

—Toronto *Globe and Mail* (24 May 1984)

There remains the vexing question of how the capitalist class rules, and especially of the relationship between the capitalist class and the state. The first post-Porter generation of class analysts has been faulted for taking too "instrumentalist" an approach to this problem. Instrumentalism refers to a school of Western neo-Marxism most closely associated with the early work of Ralph Miliband. Miliband (1973 (1969)) portrayed the various institutions which comprise the state—the government, legislature, judicial system, military, police, and public bureaucracy —as operating more to the advantage of the capitalist class than of other classes. He emphasized that this bias exists because the capitalist class directly controls state institutions. For example, top officials in all state institutions throughout the Western world are recruited substantially from the upper reaches of the class system. Therefore, he continued, they reflect the interests of the capitalist class. Similarly, state officials tend to rely upon members of the capitalist class for advice in policy formulation and, in the case of political parties, for material support in election campaigns. Thanks to the operation of these and other mechanisms the state allegedly serves as an *instrument* of the capitalist class's will (hence the school's name).

One of the main criticisms of this viewpoint is that, frequently, dominant segments of the capitalist class do not in fact rule in any direct sense. For example, in Canada the Liberal Party has been in power for most of the post-Second World War era, yet it has rarely been supported by the overwhelmingly Tory corporate elite. In addition, critics point out that even the capitalist class as a whole cannot be said to rule directly through its control of the state since to do so it would have to display much more cohesion and unity of purpose than is frequently the case. This is especially evident in Canada. Some critics of instrumentalism hold that major political conflicts in Canada reflect cleavages within the capitalist class— between, say, its different ethnic or national segments (notably Québecois versus English Canadian) or between its different regional components (such as Western versus Ontarian). These conflicts supposedly testify to the disunity of the capitalist class and its inability to rule the state directly and with the stability necessary to promote its overall best interests.

In light of these perceived shortcomings, many Canadian scholars have come to accept the ideas of the late Nicos Poulantzas (1975 (1968)) as an alternative to instrumentalism. His theory of the relationship between the capitalist class and the state is usually referred to as "structuralism". This name is derived from his insistence that it is the environing system of socio-economic relations that is responsible for the state serving the long-run interests of the capitalist class as a whole. This system (or structure) allegedly places certain restrictions upon the state's freedom of operation. For example, state officials are unlikely to take actions which offend capitalist interests too profoundly for fear of provoking an "investment strike". It is restrictions like these, not direct ties between the state and the capitalist class, that, according to Poulantzas, makes the state act with its characteristic bias. At times state officials may even find it necessary, in order to ensure the persistence of capitalist economic relations, to take actions opposed by one or more powerful segments of the capitalist class. In this sense the state must not be closely tied to, but rather "relatively autonomous" of, the capitalist class. Only then can it perform its functions effectively.

The work of Tom Traves (1979) serves as a good illustration of how this theory has been applied to the Canadian case (see also Craven 1980; van den Berg and Smith 1981). Traves sought to explain how the Canadian state came to play a more interventionist and regulatory role in the country's economic life during the period 1917-31. He argued that a variety of competing claims were placed on the state—for and against tariff protection, for and against direct financial assistance, and so forth—by different segments of the capitalist class and by industrial workers and farmers as well. The governments of the day did not heed only the demands of the most powerful subgroups in the capitalist class, nor only the demands of the capitalist class as a whole. Rather, they tried to mediate conflicts by working out compromises and maintaining "a delicate balance of power between contending classes and interest groups" (Traves 1970:156).

One might well ask how this analysis differs from the "pluralist" interpretations favoured by political analysts in the 1950s and 1960s, and now widely held in disrepute. Pluralists, too, thought of the state as performing certain "brokerage functions" and acting as a mediator of conflict between competing classes and other interest groups. But there is one critical difference between structuralism and pluralism. According to Traves (1979:158) the compromises worked out by governments are

not the equivalent of brokerage functions in pluralist theories of the state. For while the capitalist state does not directly represent the instrument for domination by a single class, it does assume the burden of perpetuating capitalism itself. In this sense it is not a value-free broker, but rather the protector and promoter of a specific set of rules and social relationships founded upon capitalist property relationships . . .

This may seem like functionalist reasoning, and indeed it is. Structuralists like Traves think that, fundamentally, it is the "needs" of the socio-economic system which compel state officials to adopt policies that appear to satisfy all interests but actually have the effect of perpetuating existing class relations, and therefore benefiting capitalists more than others.

However, this introduces a number of serious conceptual and empirical problems, some of which have been raised with reference to functionalist reasoning in general. In the first place, imputing needs to socio-economic systems makes it seem as if these systems have human attributes, including the ability to engage in goal-directed behaviour. Of course, people have needs and goals, and powerful people are often able to convince, pay, or coerce others to act in ways which serve their needs and goals. Socio-economic systems do not, however, have needs and goals other than those which people, including entire classes of people, impose upon them. A capitalist system's "need" to perpetuate capitalist class relations is no more than a desire on the part of people who benefit from those relations to see things continue pretty much as they are. The teleological and anthropomorphic tendencies of structuralism obscure this simple fact.

Second, the argument made by Traves and other structuralists is circular. Why, they ask, is a particular government policy adopted? Because, they answer, it is functional for the capitalist system, i.e. it has certain salutary consequences for existing class relations. But how does one know that a given policy is functional? By virtue of the fact that it was adopted: in the structuralist view all existing state policies are functional. In other words, policies are enacted because they are functional, and they are functional because they are enacted. One is bound to admit that this provides little enlightenment for those genuinely interested in the important question of how particular state policies evolve.

Third, structuralists interpret the introduction of unemployment insurance, public health care, laws recognizing the right of workers to form unions, strike, and engage in collective bargaining, and all other reforms associated with the growth of the welfare state as "fundamentally" irrelevant to the long-term well-being of employees. Typically, Carl Cuneo (1980:38), in a study of the introduction of unemployment insurance in Canada during the 1930's, writes:

The implementation of (unemployment insurance) schemes in virtually every developed Western capitalist state has been accompanied by a legitimizing myth of a fundamental redistribution of wealth from the capitalist class to the working class. According to this the working class is seen as the chief beneficiary of contributory unemployment insurance. Accepting such legitimation as reality masks the way these plans reinforce the dominance of the capitalist class and its support by capitalist states.

What this wholly ignores, however, is that reformist changes may have a cumulative effect on the distribution of income in society. Thus, there is considerably less economic inequality in Sweden than in Canada, largely because Sweden has a better developed welfare system that provides universal public daycare and other benefits unknown in this country. This may indeed increase the longevity of capitalism, but one must remember that this more mature capitalism is not the same capitalism that existed in Dickensian England; and that, as Marx and Engels argued, it is at least possible that in the most advanced capitalist societies socialism may evolve through electoral politics. Electoral politics can matter, and hard-won reforms, including unemployment insurance, may indeed add up to "fundamental" change (cf Hibbs 1978; Shalev 1983a; 1983b; Stephensl 1979).

The fact that these reforms are hard-won suggests a fourth and final criticism of the structuralist viewpoint. By claiming that state policies are automatic responses to the "needs" of the capitalist system, structuralism plays down the fact that farmers and workers often endure bitter struggles in order to have these policies implemented. Structuralists also imply that workers and farmers are gullible or irrational to do so since they are "fundamentally" just contributing to a legitimizing myth which enables the process of capital accumulation to continue. It is especially ironic that some Marxists should minimize the significance of class (and other group) conflict and assume such an attitude towards working people. These people may, after all, frequently elect to engage in "mere" reformist action because that strategy assures them of more certain benefits and fewer likely costs than other possible strategies.

Despite these untenable functionalist assumptions, the idea that the state is relatively autonomous of the capitalist class nevertheless amounts to a useful insight. It seems to me to overcome the major weaknesses of instrumentalism and enables us to portray more accurately the relationship between capitalist classes and states.[5]

The state's relative autonomy derives partly from the mundane fact that state officials want to keep their jobs. Thus, the occupational (if not class) interests of state officials demand that they not offend any class or group to such a degree that their re-election or re-appointment is jeopardized. It is thus a matter of survival for the political elite to remain somewhat removed from the will of the capitalist class.

Normally, members of this elite will be able to remain in office if they succeed in sustaining conditions which promote economic growth, i.e. if they are able to facilitate both capital accumulation and increases in the real incomes of workers and others. Satisfaction with government will be widespread in such a situation. However, a variety of conditions—such as a sharp and prolonged downturn in the business cycle or sustained pressure on government by well organized and effectively mobilized lower classes—may make it difficult to achieve both or either of these goals.[6] This may heighten class and other forms of group conflict, as different classes and other groups make incommensurable claims on the state.

The outcome of such conflict depends on the distribution of power in society and the strategies adopted by the various political actors. It may result in sufficient pressure being placed on the state to effect reforms that benefit disadvantaged classes and groups. But even so, the more highly advantaged classes and groups are in a position to limit the gains of the disadvantaged and minimize their own losses: the outcome is analogous to the resultant of two or more vectors, with one vector having a greater magnitude than any of the others. For example, state medical care has historically been supported by labour unions and workers' political parties and opposed by business leaders and physicians. Pressured by the former, governments in Canada and all other Western countries have enacted legislation which has increased the minimum level of health care available to all citizens. But pressured by the latter, many governments have not sought to achieve equity in health care: the quality of medical services available seems still to be highly structured along class, regional, ethnic, and racial lines in Canada, the United Kingdom, and the U.S.A. (Manga and Weller 1980).

The fact that progressive laws and institutions may result from such episodes of class and other forms of group conflict suggests a second, and more profound, source of the state's relative autonomy. This derives from the frequently overlooked fact that state policies and institutions are no more than long-lasting legal resolutions of historically specific conflicts among classes and other groups. Put differently, states are social structures which reflect the distribution of resources, organization, and support—in short, of power—among classes and other groups at given points in time. These structures, once created, usually pattern political life for many years—specifically, until power is significantly redistributed, at which time new conflicts arise to cause change.

Laws regulating election procedures illustrate the point. These laws have a profound effect on who gets represented in parliaments, and how well they are represented. Thus, constituency-based electoral systems such as those in Canada ensure that parliamentary representation often reflects actual party support in a highly attenuated manner. This comes about because people who vote for unsuccessful candidates have no representative in the legislature. In the 1980 federal election this included, among others, the roughly 20% of Atlantic Canadians who voted for the New Democratic Party, the nearly 20% of Westerners who voted for the Liberal Party, and the 15% or so of Quebecers who voted Progressive Conservative: these voters, perhaps a million or more, were represented by a total of only three or four parliamentarians. Is it any wonder that groups which suffer most from under-representation in the Canadian parliament are most in favour of adopting a system of proportional representation, such as exists, with variations, throughout continental Europe? In that part of the world, class and religious conflicts, often bitter, produced electoral systems which now represent major collectivities more equitably than does the Canadian system. Underrepresented groups in this country may be able to win similar changes, but only if they become sufficiently numerous, organized, and have enough material and other resources to force the hand of overrepresented groups. Meanwhile, the electoral system, a resolution of past conflict, continues to affect the party composition of our parliaments. Canadian political life is thus no simple reflection of the current will of the capitalist class or of the country's present class structure as a whole. Electoral laws—and other state institutions and policies which remain relatively autonomous of the class system—also have a major impact on political life.

I suspect that when enough research has been done on the relationship between the state and the capitalist class in Canada, it will be possible to conclude, as did Robert R. Alford and Roger Friedland (1975:472) in a comprehensive review of relevant American studies, that the Canadian state structure has

(a) bureaucratically insulated dominant interests from political challenge; (b) politically fragmented and neutralized nondominant interests; (c) supported fiscal and policy dependence on private economic power; and (d) therefore resulted in a lack of legislative or electoral control over the structure of expenditure and revenues.

But it is to be hoped that, if such conclusions indeed hold for the Canadian case, no functional imperatives will be invoked to explain them. The second generation of class analysts in Canada has forced us to discard the merchants against industry thesis and substantially qualify our interpretation of the boundaries of the Canadian capitalist class. So iconoclastic a group can surely perform an equally enlightening job on structuralism.

F. About This Book

The following essays are highly representative of recent debates and innovations in the study of the Canadian capitalist class. In Section II, William Carroll and Jorge Niosi depart from some of the main orthodoxies of a decade ago. Carroll rejects the view that the Canadian capitalist class is weak and dependent. He begins with a useful summary of a large body of literature which argues against the concept of dependency on both conceptual and empirical grounds. He then applies to the Canadian case an alternative framework, which is more indebted to classical Marxism than is dependency theory.

Niosi synthesizes his previous work on the subject, and reacts to dependency theory in a more qualified fashion. Although he also maintains that the reach of the Canadian capitalist class has now extended well beyond Canada's borders, and that its members have become bigger players at home over the past fifteen years or so, he none the less recognizes that there are some important respects in which this class, and the Canadian socio-economic system as a whole, retain the marks of dependency.

The significance of the relationship of the financial segment of the capitalist class to the industrial segment is taken up in Section III by Gordon Laxer, Jack Richardson, and Karen Anderson. Anderson disputes the left-nationalist contention that the Canadian capitalist class at the end of the last century consisted of a group of conservative St. Lawrence merchants who helped create the Canadian state to serve their interests—interests which held back the country's economic development. By examining the financing of the Canadian Pacific Railway, she shows how Canadian capitalists were at the forefront of the latest developments in mobilizing capital internationally. In this, Canadian financiers were anything but conservative. Anderson also contends that the Canadian state was created not as an instrument of the will of Canadian financiers, but as a means of providing favourable conditions for the operation of international capital.

Gordon Laxer borrows some ideas from Weber, Marx, and the economic historian Alexander Gerschenkron, in order to show that Canada's industrialization was not retarded simply because a strong financial elite held a weak industrial elite in check. He notes that Sweden and Japan also had weak industrial elites, and began to industrialize late. Counterintuitively, Laxer argues that the industrial success of these "late-follower" countries was a result of the strength of their agrarian classes. Where politically strong agrarian classes existed, certain state policies were enacted which, quite incidentally, facilitated independent industrialization. In Canada, by contrast, farmers were politically weak and disunited. The French-English conflict occupied such a prominent place in the life of the nation that the farmers' impact on politics was minimal and the inadvertently beneficial effect they had elsewhere on the growth of manufacturing was absent.

Jack Richardson analyzes the functions of directorship ties between financial and non-financial corporations. Using contemporary data on patterns of directorship replacement, he tests a number of available interpretations (proferred by Hilferding, Lenin and Selznick) of the relationship between these two sectors. His findings broadly suport the Leninist interpretation—that modern capitalist economies are dominated by a financial-industrial complex in which neither segment dominates—but he usefully qualifies that theory and renders it more sophisticated.

The two papers in Section IV are concerned with the question of how the capitalist class rules. Almost all studies of the Canadian capitalist class emphasize economic and political domination, but very few works pay much attention to domination in other institutions, despite its acknowledged importance. Diane Clark and Lorne Tepperman depart from this traditional emphasis by analyzing data on the economic affiliations of members of the board of directors of the Toronto General Hospital from 1879 to 1982. The T.G.H. was (and still is) a focus of the business community's social welfare interest in the commercial and industrial centre of the country. The social composition of the capitalist class has of course changed markedly over the past century, and Clark and Tepperman demonstrate how the T.G.H. board has served as a mechanism of class consolidation throughout that period. In the process they also cast serious doubt on the validity of the merchants against industry thesis.

Michael Ornstein criticizes the sort of instrumentalist thinking that has been so influential in Canadian discussions of the relationship between the capitalist class and the state. In an analysis of the first Canadian survey of its kind, he shows that ideological conflict, not harmony, prevails between state personnel and members of the capitalist class, contrary to the instrumentalist prediction. He also reports on the type and degree of ideological differentiation within the Canadian capitalist class, and finds that big businessmen are indeed class conscious.

Overall, these essays testify to the fact that the study of Canadian social classes in general, and research on the capitalist class in particular, have come a very long way indeed since academics first turned their attention to the subject some twenty years ago. Few of the controversies surrounding the subject have been resolved in a definitive manner, but more sophisticated methods of study, together with refined theoretical debate, have just as certainly ensured that considerable progress has been made.

Notes

1. The major exceptions include (Creighton 1956 (1937); Lipset 1968 (1950)); Macpherson 1962 (1953); Marsh 1940; Pentland 1981 (sections published in 1948, 1950, and 1959); and Scott *et al.* 1975 (1935)). Among non-academics, see the work of (Irvine 1976 (1920); King 1973 (1918); Myers 1972 (1914); and Park and Park 1973 (1962)).

2. A Fourth idea which has been proposed by students of the Canadian capitalist class, concerning the relationship between that class's regional cleavages and major political conflicts in the country, is discussed in (Brym, forthcoming 1985).

3. However, as Jorge Niosi (1978: 14-67; 1981 (1980): 5-10; 1983: 135) shows, this last point cannot be taken to mean that the banks actually control industry.

4. See also Ornstein's (1976) relevant finding that foreign-controlled corporations have fewer directorship ties than Canadian-controlled corporations.

5. This discussion draws mainly on (Alford and Friedland 1975; Brym 1979; 1984; Esping-Anderson, Friedland and Wright 1976; Skocpol 1980).

6. American analysts of the state tend to stress crises as preconditions for progressive reform since nearly all American welfare state legislation has its roots in the New Deal. In Canada, however, progressive legislation has generally been passed earlier and on a more incremental basis (Kudrle and Marmor 1981; Leman 1977). My sense is that this difference is probably a result of the fact that the Canadian electoral system allows more sustained pressure to be placed on governments by disadvantaged classes and groups. In contrast, the American electoral system, which militates against the formation of third parties, allows such pressure to build up to the point of explosion.

Bibliography

Alford, Robert R. and Roger Friedland (1975)—"Political participation and public policy," *Annual Review of Sociology* (1) 429-79.

Britton, J. and J. Gilmour (1978)—*The Weakest Link: A Technological Perspective on Canadian Industrial Development* (Ottawa: The Science Council of Canada).

Brym, Robert J. (1979)—"Political conservatism in Atlantic Canada," in *Underdevelopment and Social Movements in Atlantic Canada,* Robert J. Brym and R. James Sacouman, eds (Toronto: New Hogtown Press) 59-79.

Brym, Robert J. (1984)—"Social movements and third parties," in *Models and Myths in Canadian Sociology,* S.D. Berkowitz, ed (Toronto: Butterworths Canada) 29-49.

Brym, Robert J. (forthcoming 1985)—"An introduction to the regional question in Canada" in *Regionalism in Canada,* Robert J. Brym, ed (Toronto: Irwin).

Carroll, William (1982)—"The Canadian corporate elite: financiers or finance capitalists?" *Studies in Political Economy* (8) 89-114.

Carroll, William K., John Fox and Michael D. Ornstein (1982)—"The network of directorate interlocks among the largest Canadian firms," *The Canadian Review of Sociology and Anthropology* (19) 44-69.

Clement, Wallace, 1975—*The Canadian Corporate Elite: An Analysis of Economic Power* (Toronto: McClelland and Stewart).

Clement, Wallace (1977)—*Continental Corporate Power: Economic Linkages Between Canada and the United States* (Toronto: McClelland and Stewart).

Craven, Paul (1980)—*'An Impartial Unpire': Industrial Relations and the Canadian State, 1900-1911* (Toronto: University of Toronto Press).

Creighton, Donald (1956 (1937))—*The Empire of the St. Lawrence* (Toronto: Macmillan of Canada).

Cuneo, Carl J. (1980)—"State mediation of class contradictions in Canadian unemployment insurance, 1930-1935," *Studies in Political Economy* (3) 37-65.

Esping-Anderson, Gosta, Roger Friedland and Erik Olin Wright (1976)—"Modes of class struggle and the capitalist state," *Kapitalistate* (4-5) 186-220.

Hackett, Robert (1980)—"Pie in the sky: a history of the Ontario Waffle," *Canadian Dimension* (15, 1-2) 2-72.

Hibbs Jr., Douglas A. (1978)—"On the political economy of long-run trends in strike activity," *British Journal of Political Science* (8) 153-75.

Irvine, William (1976 (1920))—*The Farmers in Politics* (Toronto: McClelland and Stewart).

King, William Lyon Mackenzie (1973 (1918))—*Industry and Humanity: A Study in the Principles Underlying Industrial Reconstruction* (Toronto: University of Toronto Press).

Kudrle, Robert T. and Theodore R. Marmor (1981)—"The development of welfare states in North America," in P. Flora and A. Heidenheimer, eds *The Development of Welfare States in Europe and America* (New Brunswick, New Jersey: Transaction Books) 81-121.

Laxer, Gordon (1983)—"Foreign ownership and myths about Canadian development," Working Paper No.50, Structural Analysis Programme (Toronto: Department of Sociology, University of Toronto).

Laxer, Jim (1973)—"Introduction to the political economy of Canada," in *(Canada) Ltd.: The Political Economy of Dependency,* Robert M. Laxer, ed (Toronto: McClelland and Stewart) 26-41.

Leacock, Stephen (1973 (1910))—"The apology of a professor: an essay on higher education," in *The Social Criticism of Stephen Leacock,* Alan Bowker, ed (Toronto: University of Toronto Press) 28-39.

Leman, Christopher (1977)—"Patterns of policy development: social security in the United States and Canada," *Public Policy* (25) 261-91.

Levitt, Kari (1970)—*Silent Surrender: The Multinational Corporation in Canada* (Toronto: MacMillan of Canada).

Lipset, Seymour Martin (1968 (1950))—*Agrarian Socialism: The Cooperative Commonwealth Federation in Saskatchewan,* rev edn (Berkeley and Los Angeles: University of California Press).

Lumsden, Ian, ed (1970)—*Close the 49th Parallel: The Americanization of Canada* (Toronto: University of Toronto Press).

Macdonald, L.R. (1975)—"Merchants against industry: an idea and its origins," *The Canadian Historical Review* (56) 263-81.

Macpherson, C.B. (1962 (1953))—*Democracy in Alberta: Social Credit and The Party System,* 2nd edn (Toronto: University of Toronto Press).

Manga, Pranial and Geoffery R. Weller (1980)—"The failure of the equity objective in health: a comparative analysis of Canada, Britain, and the United States," *Comparative Social Research* (3) 229-67.

Marsh, Leonard (1940)—*Canadians In and Out of Work: A Survey of Economic Classes and Their Relation to the Labour Market* (Toronto: Oxford University Press).

McDougall, Robert L. (1963)—"The dodo and the cruising auk: class in Canadian literature," *Canadian Literature* (18) 6-20.

Mealing, S.R. (1965)—"The concept of class and the interpretation of Canadian history," *The Canadian Historical Review* (46) 201-18.

Miliband, Ralph (1973 (1969))—*The State in Capitalist Society* (London: Quartet).

Moore, Steve and Debi Wells (1975)—*Imperialism and The National Question in Canada* (Toronto: privately published).

Myers, Gustavus (1972 (1914))—*A History of Canadian Wealth* (Toronto: James Lewis & Samuel Ltd.).

Naylor, Tom (1972)—"The rise and fall of the third commercial empire of the St. Lawrence," in *Capitalism and The National Question in Canada,* Gary Teeple, ed (Toronto: University of Toronto Press) 1-41.

Naylor, Tom (1975)—*The History of Canadian Business,* 1867-1914, 2 vols (Toronto: James Lorimer).

Niosi, Jorge (1978)—*The Economy of Canada: A Study of Ownership and Control,* Penelope Williams and Hugh Ballem, trans (Montreal: Black Rose Books).

Niosi, Jorge (1981 (1980))—*Canadian Capitalism: A Study of Power in The Canadian Business Establishment,* Robert Chodos, trans (Toronto: James Lorimer and Co.).

Niosi, Jorge (1982)—"The Canadian multinationals," *Multinational Business* (2) 24-33.

Niosi, Jorge (1983)—''The Canadian bourgeoisie: towards a synthetical approach,'' *Canadian Journal of Political and Social Theory* (7) 128-49.

Olsen, Dennis (1980)—*The State Elite* (Toronto: McClelland and Stewart).

Ornstein, Michael D. (1976)—''The boards and executives of the largest Canadian corporations: size, composition, and interlocks,'' *Canadian Journal of Sociology* (1) 411-36.

''Pacific Basin Council urges support of free trade'' (1984)—Toronto *Globe and Mail* (24 May) B13.

Panitch, Leo (1977)—''The role and nature of the Canadian state,'' in *The Canadian State: Political Economy and Political Power,* Leo Panitch, ed (Toronto: University of Toronto Press) 3-27.

Park, Libbie and Frank (1973 (1962))—*Anatomy of Big Business* (Toronto: James Lewis & Samuel).

Pentland, H. Clare (1981)—*Labour and Capital in Canada, 1650-1860,* Paul Phillips, ed (Toronto: James Lorimer & Co.)

Porter, John (1965)—*The Vertical Mosaic: An Analysis of Social Class and Power in Canada* (Toronto: University of Toronto Press).

Poulantzas, Nicos (1975 (1968))—*Political Power and Social Classes,* Timothy O'Hagan, trans (London: New Left Books).

Resnick, Philip (1977)—*The Land of Cain: Class and Nationalism in English Canada, 1945-1975* (Vancouver: New Star Books).

Richardson, R.J. (1982)—''Merchants against industry'': an empirical study of the Canadian debate,'' *The Canadian Journal of Sociology* (7) 279-95.

Rotstein, Abraham and Gary Lax, eds (1974)—*Getting It Back: A Program for Canadian Independence* (Toronto: Clarke Irwin & Co.).

Ryerson, Stanley (1973 (1968))—*Unequal Union: Roots of Crisis in the Canadas, 1815-1873* (Toronto: Progress Books).

Ryerson, Stanley (1976)—''Who's looking after business?'' *This Magazine* (10, 5) 41-6.

Scott, F.R. *et al.* (1975 (1935))—*Social Planning for Canada* (Toronto: University of Toronto Press).

Shalev, Michael (1983a)—''Class politics and the Western welfare state,'' in S. Spiro and E. Yuchtman-Yaar, eds *Evaluating the Welfare State: Social and Political Perspectives* (New York: Academic Press) 27-50.

Shalev, Michael (1983b)—''The social democratic model and beyond: two generations of comparative research on the welfare state,'' *Comparative Social Research* (6) 315-51.

Skocpol, Theda (1980)—''Political response to capitalist crisis: neo-Marxist theories of the state and the case of the New Deal,'' *Politics and Society* (10) 155-201.

Stephens, John D. (1979)—*The Transition From Capitalism to Socialism* (London: Macmillan).

Traves, Tom (1979)—*The State and Enterprise: Canadian Manufacturers and the Federal Government, 1917-1931* (Toronto: University of Toronto Press).

''Turner re-elected Seagram director'' (1984)—Toronto *Globe and Mail* (24 May) 11.

van den Berg, Axel and Michael Smith (1981)—''The Marxist theory of the state in practice,'' *Canadian Journal of Sociology* (6) 505-19.

Williams, Glen (1983)—*Not for Export: Towards a Political Economy of Canada's Arrested Industrialization* (Toronto: McClelland and Stewart).

II
Capitalist Class Boundaries

Dependency, Imperialism and The Capitalist Class in Canada
William K. Carroll

A. Introduction

In the past two decades of western scholarship the concept of dependency has served as an enormously influential root metaphor in analyses of international and interregional political economy. Stemming originally from the radical structuralism of Prebisch (1950) and the seminal analysis of backwardness offered by Paul Baran (1957), and extending to the more recent theories of accumulation on a world scale (Amin, 1974; Wallerstein, 1974; Frank, 1979), "dependency" has permeated discussions of contemporary world capitalism.

Within Third World discourse, the concept has generally carried a directly political connotation as the focus of a critique of foreign capitalist domination. But, as Howe and Sica (1980) have noted, in American academic circles dependency theory has been largely "consumed" in two politically anaesthetized forms: (1) a grand totalizing theory, that portrays world capitalism as a juggernaut governed by natural laws (as in Wallerstein, 1974) and (2) a raft of quantitative, cross-national studies in which "significant advances in the theory of imperialism and the world economy become hidden from view under a mass of contradictory and misdirected empirical 'evidence '" (Portes and Walton, 1981:18).

In Canada, the palpable hegemony of American imperialism in the 1960s and the availability of a complementary account of Canadian history in Innis' staples thesis were the social premises for the politically motivated acceptance of dependency theory, along similar lines to those discernible in Latin America. Since Kari Levitt popularized the concept in her influential *Silent Surrender,* "dependency" has claimed dual status as both a scientific construct purporting to *explain* the Canadian quandary and a political slogan rallying Canadians to the cause of national self-determination[1] By 1977 a sufficient body of research and argumentation had emerged around the theme of Canadian dependency to form the basis of "a Canadian Marxist school of political economy" (Drache, 1977: 26) whose major strength has been described as "its ability to situate Canada's dependency within the world system and the power of this to account for internal development" (Clement, 1983a: 142).

It was on the basis of this sort of reasoning that Robert Laxer (1973:25) predicted that the 1970's and 1980's would be "the decades when Canada's future will be pointed either towards continentalism and a final lament, or toward

I wish to thank Rick Ogmundson, Michael Ornstein, Anne Preyde, and Rennie Warburton for their comments and encouragement, and Robert Brym for his editorial suggestions.

socialist independentism and a new birth.'' A third possibility – the relative re-surgence of Canadian capital in the face of declining U.S. hegemony and deepening world economic crisis – was not articulated by Laxer, nor could it have been easily predicted from the logic of Canadian dependency. Notwithstanding Watkin's (1981:27) claim that ''the essentially dependent quality of the Canadian economy, and the comprador quality of its bourgeoisie, will surely survive the '80's,'' the strong evidence for what Niosi (1981) has termed a *renaissance* of Canadian capitalism should give pause for thought about the adequacy of the Canadian dependency framework. In addition, at least two other reasons provide grounds for caution in this regard.

Several critics have argued that, political rhetoric aside, there is little basis for 'dependency' as a coherent explanatory construct in the political economy of world capitalism. To the extent that these criticisms impeach the dependency framework *in general,* its capacity to inform studies of Canadian capitalism is likewise undercut. On the other hand, the Canadian dependency school has not been without its own critics, and several of them have presented very cogent arguments questioning the particular relevance of dependency analysis in Canada (cf Macdonald, 1975; Moore and Wells, 1975; Ryerson, 1976; McNally, 1981; Panitch, 1981; Schmidt, 1981). In these works, however, the critical literature on 'dependency theory in general' has not been systematically brought to bear on the Canadian case, nor has much attention been devoted to the articulation of a theoretical alternative capable of integrating the raw material of Canadian capitalist development within a qualitatively different perspective on world capitalism.[2]

This article, then, has two purposes. First, I review the general critiques of de-pendency theory and attempt to establish their relevance to our understanding of Canadian capitalism. Second, I examine some recent formulations which situate phenomena formerly subsumed under the rubric of dependency within a Marxist theory of modern imperialism; and I suggest how the latter perspective might inform an alternative account of capitalist development in Canada.

Dependency Theory: A Critical Review

One of the first things one notices in surveying the literature on dependency theory is the eclecticism that predominates in most analyses. Due to their mixed lineage in the structuralist economics of Prebisch and the neo-Marxism of Baran, the core concepts of dependency and underdevelopment are often given different meanings according to the user's beliefs about the nature of underdevelopment and the processes that have caused or are maintaining it (Lall, 1975; cf. Chinchilla and Dietz, 1981). As a consequence, any attempt to draw out the ''implicit core'' of dependency theory risks the charge of distorting the work of each particular author (Weeks and Dore, 1979:67-8). The same sort of eclecticism has been noted by critics of the Canadian dependency school[3], yet the tendency for several Canadian dependency analysts to embrace Frank's (1967; 1972) version of dependency theory as the complement of Innis' staples thesis simplifies somewhat the tasks of summarization and critique.[4]

In Frank's (1967:30-8) original formulation, underdevelopment on the periphery was attributed to three contradictions of capitalism: (1) the hierarchical chain of metropolis-satellite relations, (2) the extraction of surplus from the satellite and its movement to the metropolis, and (3) historical continuity in change, conserving basic structures of dependency in spite of such apparent transformations as the winning of political independence. Frank has in more recent accounts injected a class element into his analysis with the claim that the metropolis-satellite relation transforms the class structure of the periphery, creating a close alliance between the metropolitan power (e.g., the colonial administration, transnational corporations) and the local reactionary interests (composed of merchants and landowners; Frank, 1972, 1979). This depiction has much in common with Baran's (1957) earlier account of underdevelopment: for Frank, as for Baran, the peripheral bourgeoisie is essentially dependent on external forces, and therefore unable to play a progressive role in national development (Angotti, 1981:127).

Dependency in Canada

The core theses of dependency theory are in large part reproduced within the Canadian dependency tradition. The purported contradiction between metropole and satellite is evident in Levitt's (1970) notion of the "new mercantilism" in which Canada supplies the American metropole with raw material for its industries and provides a market for manufactured goods from the metropole or its branch plants (cf. Naylor, 1972:36). This neo-mercantilist system is said to have emerged on the basis of a peculiar bourgeois class formation, and to have the effect of reinforcing that formation. The Canadian bourgeoisie, or more properly its dominant fraction, has been overwhelmingly *commercial* in its orientation, eschewing an interest in domestic industry (Naylor, 1975; Clement, 1975, 1977; Drache, 1977; Marchak, 1979). By implication, an essential element in Canada's dependency is the deeply-rooted *disarticulation* of indigenous financial and industrial capital, which has engendered an *uneven* pattern of capitalist accumulation by 'overdeveloping' the financial and service sectors and allowing or even encouraging the underdevelopment of domestic industry (Naylor, 1972; Clement, 1975, 1977). Concomitantly, the dominant commercial fraction has allied with foreign industrial interests, represented by the "comprador fraction," and become dependent for its own wealth on these surplus-producing clients (Clement, 1977). The branch plant economy contains the seeds of economic stagnation, as research and development are conducted in the parent firm (Levitt, 1970), capital in the form of repatriated profits leaks across the border (Gonick, 1970; Drache, 1977), and the manufacturing sector declines in the face of de-industrialization (Jim Laxer, 1973).

In both its general and Canadian version, "dependency" ultimately refers to an external relation of international (or interregional) dominance, which is held to distort the internal functioning of the dependent social formation (Browett, 1981:14). Dependency is observable as a syndrome of economic conditions in the hinterland, including the predominance of foreign capital, the use of foreign, capital-intensive technologies in a relatively small industrial sector, and export specialization in primary products (Lall, 1975:803). The argument is that these features have an inner coherence, allowing one to speak of dependence on foreign capital, foreign technology or trade as interrelated aspects of "dependent capitalism," implying that this dependence acts as a break on development and *distorts* whatever development occurs. The explanatory value of dependency theory consequently rests on the extent to which the symptoms of dependence are systematically interrelated in the empirical world as well as on the posited link between dependence as a specific condition, and blocked or distorted development as a dynamic tendency. On these issues, critics have pointed to both conceptual and empirical difficulties that seem inherent in the theory of dependency itself.

B. Conceptual Problems
Heterogeneity in the World System

The first major problem that one encounters in attempting to apply the concept of dependency to concrete national economies is the tremendous heterogeneity with which the purported symptoms of dependency are actually distributed within the world system. As a result, many of the general characteristics of peripheral capitalism made by *dependentistas* cannot be sustained by systematic empirical description (Little, 1975:226). In particular, the diversity of conditions among the less developed economies is so great that in order to be adequately inclusive concepts such as dependency and underdevelopment must be framed so broadly as to have little meaning in empirical analysis (Leys, 1977:95; Cypher, 1979a). According to Lall (1975), attempts to form a general category of dependency do not seem to have been successful; some countries classified as non-dependent inevitably show some characteristics of dependence, and vice versa. Foreign capital, for instance, is massively present in many less developed countries (LDCs), but this appears to be part of a more general phenomenon in which all countries within the capitalist ambit are becoming increasingly penetrated by international capital. Thus, Canada and Belgium are more "dependent" on foreign investment than India or Pakistan, yet in Lall's view are not among the dependent countries. Similarly, on the matter of technological dependence, it is clear that LDCs obtain most of their technology from abroad, but so do a number of advanced capitalist countries; indeed the whole concept of "technological independence" is rapidly growing obsolete as advanced economies such as Denmark become as reliant on foreign technology as Colombia and Taiwan (Lall, 1975:804).

These empirical inconsistencies subvert the rigour of dependency analyses, since "it is ultimately to draw a line between dependence and non-dependence ... without falling into the basic error of *defining* underdevelopment to constitute dependence only when found in underdeveloped countries" (Lall, 1975: 802-3). This resolution, of course, is unsatisfactory due to its logical circularity. But the alternative — arguing that the same features constitute dependence *wherever they are found* — is no more satisfactory, since in practice it eliminates the possibility of discriminating dependent from non-dependent countries.

Studies of Canadian dependency have followed this second course: they have *assumed* the internal coherence of dependency as a construct and proceeded — on the basis of observations about foreign investment, trade patterns, etc. — to subsume Canada under the same rubric of dependency as supposedly applies to LDCs. But in light of the stubborn refusal of many countries to conform to the neat categories of "dependency" and "autonomous capitalism" an alternative interpretation can be suggested. It may well be the case that Levitt's (1970) description of Canada as a "rich dependency," attests less to a unique condition in need of special explanation than to the analytic incoherence of dependency as a general construct.

The Inversion of Modernization

A second conceptual problem arises from dependency theory's etiology as a radical, "Marxified" structuralism which developed through a series of revisions of orthodox economic analysis. This began with Prebisch's critique of international trade theory and his advocacy of import substitution as a means of overcoming structural barriers to development (Leys, 1977:97). In the course of its development, dependency theory never broke decisively from the problematic or orthodox development theory: it simply inverted the latter's core concepts and propositions to arrive at the diametrically opposed conclusion that capitalist penetration engenders underdevelopment. This innovation might seem to mark a radical departure toward a qualitatively different understanding of world capitalism, but in a deeper sense, however, dependency analysis remains squarely within the same domain assumptions and conceptual structure as the diffusionist paradigm (cf. Cueva, 1976; Brenner, 1977; Leaver, 1977; Browett, 1981; Henfrey, 1981): the "polemical inversions" of developed/underdeveloped, centre/periphery, and dominant/dependent are merely substituted for analogous pairings within bourgeois development theory, such as traditional/modern, rich/poor, and advanced/backward (Leys, 1977:95). As such, the two approaches present a false dialectic, with the strengths of one appearing as the weaknesses of the other. *Both* occupy the same metatheoretical terrain of non-Marxist political economy.

In the Canadian context this "dialectic" is at work in R.T. Naylor's (1972) seminal attempt to "stand Creighton on his feet" by reversing his eulogy to the progressiveness of Canada's dominant commercial capitalists, yet retaining the idea that they were the driving force in Canadian development/underdevelopment. While giving the appearance of radical departure, Naylor remains trapped within Creighton's problematic of a Canadian development as he substitutes for Creighton's eulogy a "moralistic apportionment of blame" for Canada's blocked development (Schmidt, 1981:76).

Idealism, Teleology, Moralism

The example of Naylor brings up a third ground on which dependency theory has been challenged, namely the extent to which its core concepts are imbued with such moralistic and ideological content that empirical analysis is inevitably distorted. At the heart of the theory is a contrast between the ideal types of autonomous development and dependent underdevelopment. Numerous critics have pointed out the difficulties in the empirical use of these categories.

Consider first the term "autonomous development," which attempts to encapsulate the course followed by advanced capitalist countries. By turning the variety of Western historical experiences into an ideal type, this concept disregards the fact that capitalism grew up in the various countries in a variety of ways, under different historical settings, and with varying degrees of world market integration. To the extent that development in the peripheral economies does not correspond to this model, countries are judged to lack an 'autonomous capacity' and hence 'dependent' (Marcussen and Torp, 1982: 144-5 cf. Swainson, 1977: 55; Henfrey, 1981: 44; Johnson, 1981:73). "Autonomous development" is thus set up as a normative, teleological category which serves as an abstract standard by means of which dependent underdevelopment can be recognized (Phillips, 1977:11). Autonomous development implies a fully independent national capitalist class, a full range of manufacturing industries, an indigenous capacity to develop and implement technologies — in short an ideal state of economic well-being and national autonomy, carrying a strong positive moral connotation (Chinchilla and Dietz, 1981:142; Johnson, 1983:90-1). "Dependent underdevelopment" provides just the opposite idealization and carries an appropriately negative connotation. Dependent countries are bound to core countries by economic and political relations such that the structures and movements of the latter determine those of the former in a fashion detrimental to their own economic progress (Warren 1980:59).

The polar opposites of autonomous development and dependent underdevelopment give rise to curious distortions when one attempts to deploy them empirically (Angotti, 1981:134; Henfrey, 1981:37). A clearer idea of how these problems occur can be gained by examining the concepts of dependency and underdevelopment.

Little attempt has been made to define the term "dependency" in a rigorous way. In light of this, several authors have argued that "dependency" is a poorly-formed *descriptive* concept that masquerades as an *explanation* of underdevelopment. Leaver, for instance, holds that

... the notion of dependence really implies nothing more or less than the lack of some factor. Technological dependence is simply the lack of technology, financial dependence the lack of finance, etc. ... But to invoke dependence as an explanation for underdevelopment seems to me to be profoundly mystifying; all that we are doing is stating what we already know in a different way. The task of naming should not be confused with that of explanation (Leaver, 1977: 113).

For Colin Leys the question arises whether the concept of dependency is not "a fairly arbitrary way of sensitizing us to one set of relationships at the cost of anaesthetising us to others — i.e. sensitizing us only to one dimension of a more complex *inter*dependency" (1977:95). This argument has been made quite succinctly by Carlos Johnson (1981:73), who notes that the very superficiality of dependency as an interrelationship makes it inherently bidirectional. Against the arbitrary claim that "Latin America is dependent on the United States" one could just as defensibly substitute the reverse (Johnson, 1983:87). For Johnson it is not a question of "who depends on whom" but of concrete social relationships and their contradictions (1983:89). In contrast, by setting up "autonomous development" as an ideal type to be politically realized in the LDCs through gaining independence from a particular class's or country's dominance, dependency theory obscures the important reality that "... social relations precisely mean specific kinds of relationships, independent, and interdependent at specific moments" (Johnson, 1981:73).

The concept of "underdevelopment" has fared no better than "dependency" when subjected to critical scrutiny. "Underdevelopment" in the hinterland is said to have occurred in tandem with "autonomous development" in the metropolis. Rarely, however, is underdevelopment assigned a precise definition. Instead, Lall

(1975:808) is able to recount three quite distinct usages: (1) underdevelopment as immiseration, (2) underdevelopment as market constriction, and (3) under-development as marginalization and subservience. What ultimately unites these disparate themes are the undesirable conditions such as lack of domestic inno-vation and subjection to international market fluctuations, which are seen as inherent consequences of dependency.

At the core of "underdevelopment," then, is not a scientific concern with the concrete process of social and economic reproduction in LDCs but a *moral* con-demnation of capitalism's inability to "fully" develop its periphery (cf. Lall, 1975:808). The problem with proceeding from such a moral premise is that there is in the final analysis no *scientific* way to distinguish "normal" from "distorted," or "under"-development (Phillips, 1977:12). As a result, "under-development" becomes "an empty concept into which any subjective-normative criterior may be fitted so as to expound an apparent historical alternative, or even more important, a *better* alternative" (Warren, 1980:169).

In Canadian studies, the concept of dependency has been applied in a variety of ways, each emphasizing the lack of indigenous industrial capital and technolo-gical innovation, but especially the absence of effective capitalist entrepreneur-ship. In the twentieth century, the symbiotic combination of a commercial bour-geoisie with no interest in participating in local industry, and a foreign-controlled industrial sector geared to production of raw materials for export and manu-factured goods for domestic consumption has resulted in a pattern of "distorted development" (Clement, 1977, 1983b), "advanced resource capitalism" (Drache, 1977), "truncated development" (Britton and Gilmour, 1978; Ehrensaft and Armstrong, 1981), "de-industrialization" (Jim Laxer, 1973), and so forth.

In these various descriptions, the concept of underdevelopment is applied meta-phorically to encapsulate the undesirable effects of Canadian dependency. The tacit comparison is always with an idealized condition of autonomous develop-ment, often represented concretely by the metropoles of Britain and the United States. A serviceable example is provided by the notion that Canada's bour-geoisie "caused economic distortions" by overdeveloping the sphere of circu-lation and services while underdeveloping indigeous industry, especially manufacturing (Naylor, 1972; Clement, 1977, 1983a:151; Marchak, 1979; cf. Drache, 1970:9). This characterization borrows significantly from orthodox development theory (Fisher, 1935, 1952) in assuming a "normal" transition from primary through secondary to tertiary economic activities. It therefore *appears* anomalous that

no clear progression from primary to secondary to tertiary activities took place in Canada as it had in the United States. In Canada the economy changed from primary to tertiary without developing the area of secondary production. Here again can be seen the uneven nature of Canada's development and the effects of external control (Clement, 1977:96).

Singelmann's comparative study of the labour force distributions of seven advanced capitalist economies makes clear the pitfalls of this approach to the specificity of Canadian capitalism. According to Singelmann, "the early industrialized countries themselves do not follow one common pattern of labour force transformation" (1978:14), but can be described in terms of three distinct types of sectoral change. Singelmann's (1978:145-153) data show that the U.S.

had by 1970 the most "overdeveloped" circulation and service sector while Italy, Japan and France were saddled with especially "overdeveloped" primary sectors (cf. Panitch, 1981: 21-2; Richardson, 1982: 290-1). In short, the hypothetical ideal of "normal," "balanced" capitalist development just does not exist in concrete history. Given this, Canada's slightly smaller manufacturing sector is no more indicative of "distorted," "truncated" or "arrested" development than are France's or Italy's large primary agricultural sectors and their associated agrarian petty bourgeoisies (see Burris, 1980).

Empiricism

A fourth conceptual criticism of dependency theory focuses on the empiricist tendency to mistake the *appearance* of social reality for its essential relations and dynamics. The basic issue for dependency theory is not how fundamental class relations are reproduced within concrete social formations, but how immediately observable phenomena such as multinational corporations and international trade patterns have distorted or blocked development. The perspective is empiricist in that it displaces theorization of capitalism "from the abstract realm of capital and value in a commodity system to the more concrete and empirical realm of 'nations', 'agriculture', 'industry'', and 'international relations' '' (Howe and Sica, 1980:247). Rather than penetrating these immediately perceivable forms of empirical reality to reveal real relations such as class (Mepham, 1979:147-8), dependency theory appropriates *as real* the superficial categories of capitalism and proceeds to erect explanations that account for some categories (e.g., the unemployment rate, growth rate, size of manufacturing sector) in terms of others (e.g., domination by MNCs, importation of technology, international trade relations). By remaining primarily at this empiricist level of discourse, dependency analyses inevitably pursue "the common features of conjunctures rather than the structural features of generic systems" (Howe and Sica, 1980:249; cf. Warren, 1980:157).

Two particularly telling instances of this empiricism are an overwhelming concern with spatial relations and a view of production relations as defined by exchange relations (Brenner, 1977; Browett, 1977). The former entails a "fetishism of space" (Anderson, 1973:3) as relations between social groupings and classes are depicted in terms of antagonistic metropolis-hinterland linkages between nation-states or regions (Brenner, 1977:91; Howe and Sica, 1980:240; Szymanski, 1981:15-16). The latter tends to reduce classes from active historical agents to passive *"categories* resulting from the structural evolution of under-development or dependent development" (Leys, 1977:95; cf. Henfrey, 1981; Schmidt, 1981:77).

The thesis that Canada's economic development has comprised a succession of "staple trades" with more advanced metropolitan economies (Innis, 1970: Watkins, 1973; Drache, 1977) in which the dominant fraction of Canadian merchants and bankers has stultified local industry while allying with foreign interests (Naylor, 1972, 1973; Clement, 1973, 1977; Marchak, 1979) presents an especially instructive example of empiricist analysis in the Canadian dependency tradition. By equating capitalism with exchange, the staples thesis attends mainly to phenomenal appearances in the sphere of commodity circulation, failing to consider the specific manner in which labour and means of production are combined within concrete modes of production. These analyses "abstract the market, the sphere of circulation, from the total circuit of capital and treat it as the general determinant of economic and social phenomena" (McNally, 1981:41; cf. Cuneo, 1982:61-2; Clement, 1983c:175-7). The particular *things* produced and exchanged in the economy are held to have conditioned development in peculiar ways, such that "the history of Canada … is the history of its great staple trades: the fur trade, the cod fisheries, square timber and lumber, wheat, and the new staples of this century – pulp and paper, minerals, oil and gas" (Watkins, 1973:116). As McNally (1981) emphasizes, it is this fetishism of commodities, of materialized labour circulating on the world market and analytically abstracted from the social relations in which labour is appropriated, that provides the empiricist premise for a view of Canadian capitalist development as a process of "staple-ization" (Drache, 1977). For

various writers of the Canadian dependency school the "new staples" include forest products, base metals, minerals, energy products, electricity, and even aluminum (cf. Easterbrook and Airken, 1956:520; Gonick, 1970:59; Levitt, 1970:127; Drache, 1977:19; Marchak, 1979:107), all of which are produced within capitalist relations using sophisticated technologies. Only at the most superficial level can the fur trade of the seventeenth century be compared to the "new staples" of modern Canada. It is useful to compare processed goods with Marx's concept of industrial capital. For Marx, industrial capital is capital engaged directly in the generation of surplus value. It is "not a thing, but rather a definite social production relation" (Marx, 1967, Vol. III: 814) which is continually reproduced as a "circuit describing process" involving the successive metamorphosis of value across money, productive and commodity forms, and resulting in the expansion of value (Marx, 1967, Vol. II: 48). Industrial capital, then, refers to *any* process in which wage labour is purchased and consumed in the production of new use-values, whose exchange brings to the industrialist a reflux of surplus value realized as profit. This includes capitalistically organized farming, resource extraction, manufacturing, as well as tranportation (Marx, 1967, Vol. II: 149-50).

The empiricism of the Canadian dependency school is evident in the superficial and eclectic grounds on which its exponents have defined industrial and commercial capital. In Naylor's view, for instance, under the National Policy "industrial capital formation was retarded relative to investment in staple development and the creation of the commercial infrastructure necessary to extract and move staples" (Naylor, 1975 I: 15). Guided by the image of a staple-producing hinterland Naylor equates industrial capital with the manufacture of finished products (Naylor, 1975, Vol. II: 78). All other forms of industry in the Marxist sense of capitalist production of use-value – resource extraction, the transportation industry, public utilities – are eclectically defined as part of the dominant "commercial bloc" which is supposed to have stultified industrial development. But if we are to take Marx's analysis of capitalism seriously, we must conclude that the notions of "industrial underdevelopment" and "commercial domination" so central to the Canadian dependency school betray a profound misunderstanding of what capitalist industrialization is and resulting in a serious underrating of Canada's industrial development (Ryerson, 1976:42).

The confusion surrounding the meaning of industrial capital spills over into the notion, also promulgated initially by Naylor (1972), that Canada's commercial bourgeois fraction has remained historically detached from indigenous industrial interests, thereby stultifying domestic industrialization. As we have seen, Canadian dependency analysis interprets railway investments in the nineteenth century as a drain of funds from industrial development to mercantile pursuits (Naylor, 1972, 1975; Clement, 1977; Marchak, 1979). If, however, we accept the Marxist analysis of capitalistically-operated railways and other means of transportation as *industrial* capital

then, on the distinction between parasitic merchants and productive industrialists, we are forced to admit that a mass of mercantile funds was really flowing into production as industrial capital. The prominent men associated with railways would be industrialists. And since railways were such a large part of the economy the general complexion of nineteenth-century Canada would not be mercantile at all but, if anything, over-invested in industry (Macdonald, 1975: 267).

Nor are the problems of the dependency thesis confined to its misconstrual of the railway's economic significance. Naylor, for instance, (1975a, Vol. I: 108-9) entirely misreads the significance of the ties that emerged in the late nineteenth century between Canadian financial capital and indigenous manufacturing. He describes in some detail the close relations between the banks and manufacturers of cotton, sugar, and steel. Yet, instead of recognizing in these examples an *intermingling* of financial and industrial interests, Naylor sees only a commercial elite, refusing to fund small-scale industry in southern Ontario and diversifying into industries such as cotton manufacturing, sugar refining, and iron and steel, which become "stamped" with the same mercantile character (Naylor, 1975a, Vol. I: 109). Eschewing an historical conception of capital, Naylor continues to "detect" his commercial elite well into the twentieth century — long after Canadian bankers have actively intervened in circuits of industrial capital in transportation, resource extraction, and manufacturing.

Nor does the subsequent history of Canadian capitalism lend support to the disarticulation of indigneous commerce and industry posited by the dependency school. Several studies have documented the close connection and interpene-tration of financial and industrial interests in Canada, most decisively since the industrial merger movement that preceded the First World War (Piedalue, 1976; DeGrass, 1977; Richardson, 1982), and continuing throughout the post-Second World War era (Sweeny, 1980; Carroll, 1982, 1984; Carroll, Fox and Ornstein, 1982).

To summarize, the dependency approach is hampered by an empiricism that confines it to the realm of superficial and misleading appearances. In the Canadian case, the formulation is empirically suspect. This observation raises the wider issue of the empirical adequacy of dependency theory in general.

C. The Problem of Empirical Fit

Bill Warren has provided perhaps the most resolute empirical criticism of the dependency perspective. He accepts the *fact* of uneven world development of the forces of production, but disputes the "fiction of underdevelopment" as a *process*. In terms of concrete productive forces there is in Warren's view no evidence of any systematic process of underdevelopment on the periphery since

Western contact, but of capitalist development, especially since the Second World War. Consequently, as Warren puts it, the quality of postwar literature on dependency has suffered from "ascribing rising significance to a phenomenon of declining importance" (Warren, 1980: 114-15).

To begin, consider the postwar records of economic growth among LDCs. Per capita Gross Domestic Product has in general grown at a faster rate than in the prewar period, and often faster than the rates for advanced capitalist economies (Warren, 1980: 190-9). Even excluding the oil-producing countries, in the 1960's and 1970's the economies of all other LDCs grew much faster than those of the most advanced capitalist countries (Cypher, 1979a; Szymanski, 1981). The same period has witnessed the rapid growth of manufacturing in these countries, again faster than in the advanced capitalist countries (Warren, 1980:241). For all LDCs the proportion of GDP devoted to manufacturing has grown from 14.5 percent in 1950-1954 to 20.4 percent in 1973; for developed capitalist economies the figure in 1973 was 28.4 percent. The implication of these trends lies in the rapidly diminishing significance of a world division of labour between primary production in the periphery and manufacturing in the core.

Ironically, one of the major forces propelling capitalist industrialization in LDCs has been foreign investment by "core" capitalists. From the mid-1960's to the late 1970's the U.S.A. transferred twice as much total wealth to LDCs as it repatriated, a trend also evident for other advanced capitalist countries (Szymanski, 1981:292). Between 1970 and 1977 LDCs with the highest ratio of service payments to GDP grew at faster rates than LDCs less afflicted by such "surplus drainage." Contrary to the predictions of dependency theory, "within the parameters of capitalist imperialism (i.e., the logic of the world capitalist system) the more foreign investment, the more rapid the rate of growth ..." (Szymanski, 1981:335; cf. Barone, 1983).

These empirical tendencies, and the numerous conceptual inadequacies reviewed earlier, seriously call into question the interpretations of world capitalism that have been cast within the problematic of dependency. The implications for political-economic analysis in Canada are, I think, unavoidable. If we are not to be continually overtaken by "unpredictable" developments such as the "coming of age of Canadian capital" (Resnick, 1982) or even the "Latin-Americanization of the United States" (Barnet and Muller, 1974) we shall have to break decisively with the problematic of dependency, and situate Canadian capitalism and its bourgeoisie on the basis of an alternative conceptualization of the world capitalist system.

D. Toward Reconceptualization

Any theory of world economy adequate to this task need have two elements: (1) a model of accumulation, and (2) "a theory of the relevant division of the world for purposes of considering that accumulation as international" (Weeks, 1981:118). The historical-materialist theory of modern imperialism incorporates a model of accumulation based on the extended reproduction of a capital-labour relation, whose motion is subject to certain objective tendencies. Capitalist accumulation occurs as both an exploitative and a competitive process which compels individual capitalists to concentrate and centralize their capital while they develop the productive forces of society. Capital also expands in a spatial sense, first in the form of trade but later as the export of money capital and productive capital. This formulation then

converts its theory of accumulation into a theory of the world economy by locating it explicitly in the context of *countries*. What makes a political territory a "country" is that the territory is controlled by a distinct ruling class, the vehicle for such rule being the state. Materialists identify their theory of the world economy as "the theory of imperialism," which can be defined as the theory of the accumulation of capital in the context of the struggle among ruling classes (Weeks, 1981:121).

Apart from the capital-labour relation itself, the dominant focus here is not on bilateral relations between the "core" and "periphery" but on the internationalized process of accumulation and the relations it engenders (a) among capitalist ruling classes (inter-imperialist rivalry/cooperation), (b) between advanced capitalist ruling classes and ruling classes in backward countries (the articulation of modes of production), and (c) between ruling classes and oppressed peoples (national oppression/liberation; Weeks, 1981:121-2; cf. Brewer, 1980:80; Howe and Sica, 1980:241).

Above all, modern imperialism is the historical culmination of the tendencies of capitalist concentration, centralization and internationalization identified by Marx. The phenomenon arose around the turn of the century as capital in the advanced countries became reorganized in the monopoly form of "finance capital" and exported to the most profitable outlets (Lenin, 1970; Bukharin, 1973; Hilferding, 1981).

Essentially, finance capital integrates the specific forms of capital – industrial, merchant, and loan – into articulated circuits of accumulation (Thompson, 1977; Clairmonte, 1982) controlled by "financial groups" of allied capitalists who own or manage giant firms (Aglietta, 1979:252-3). Depending on particular historical circumstances, this *coalescence* of capitals is attained and sustained by means of a series of relationships, including the intertwining of share capital through invest-ment banks, holding companies, etc., the institutionalization of long-term credit relations, the interlocking of corporate directorates, and familial ties (Menshikov, 1969: 158-84; Lenin, 1970: 706; Bukharin, 1973: 71-3; Overbeek, 1980: 102-3).

The formal circuit of finance capital, shown as Figure 1, also to some extent characterized the competitive capitalism of the nineteenth century, allowing Marx (1967, Vols. II and III) to dissect and analyze its constituent parts. Under advanced capitalism, however, it is important to note the following points:

(a) Much of the total social capital has been concentrated into a relatively few large units.

(b) Since large scale production requires enormous amounts of financing, the provision and control of financial capital (whether as bank loans, bond purchases or stockholding) take on great strategic importance.

(c) These developments imply that the few capitalists owning large blocks of corporate shares or controlling major financial institutions—typically organized into groups of associated capitalists – comprise the most powerful bourgeois fraction: an elite of finance capitalists.

(d) In the earlier era the process of internationalization occurred within circuits of commercial capital (M-C-M) as the export of commodities. Under imperialism these circuits continue to internationalize as trade relations are extended and the world market broadened, but in addition, capital exports occur on a large scale, first as financial capital in the form of loans and stock (portfolio and direct investments: M-M'), more recently as productive capital (the internationalization of the production process itself; Palloix, 1977; Cypher, 1979a; cf. Bukharin, 1973).

FIGURE 1
The Formal Circuit of Finance Capital*

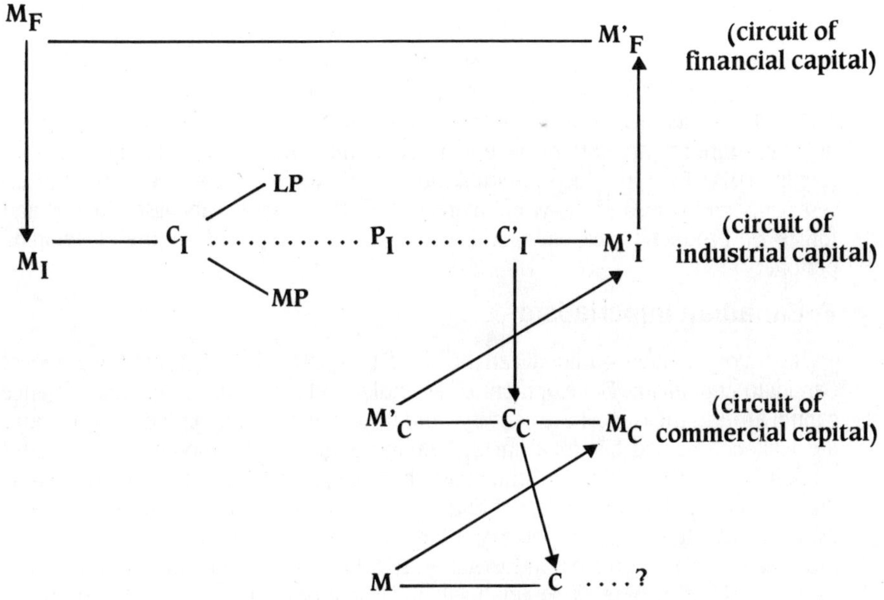

*After Thompson (1977: 249)

Legend
M=money capital
C=commodity capital
LP=labour power
MP=means of production
P=productive capital
' =capital containing newly-produced
    surplus value

The reasons for this capital export encompass both the opportunities and the exigencies that emerge as capital becomes monopolized. On the one hand, as it develops, finance capital breaks down institutional barriers to international capital mobility. The corporate form of organization and close links between industrial and financial capital allow foreign subsidiaries to be established and financed without the capitalist having to migrate. On the other hand, tariffs erected by other capitalist states discourage the expansion of domestic production for export while encouraging establishment of branch plants behind tariff walls (Hilferding, 1981), a fact of recognized significance in the Canadian case (Naylor, 1975; Clement, 1977). Also, to a considerable extent, monopolized price structures in the domestic economy can only be maintained through reinvestment of profits in nonmonopolized sectors where there is no danger of eroding monopoly positions through overproduction in the home market (Szymanski, 1981:38; Bukharin, 1973:122-3). Thus, a portion of the surplus value produced within large domestic enterprises is capitalized elsewhere. The low wages and rent on land in less developed countries and colonies serve as a particularly strong magnet for investment as capital gains the capacity to become fully internationalized (Lenin, 1970:716; Hilferding, 1981). All these constraints and opportunities give rise to an "international network of dependence on and connections of finance capital" (Lenin, 1970:715) in which national monopoly fractions jostle for spheres of investments and shares of the world market while they export capitalist relations and forces of production to each other's home markets, and to the developing periphery.

E. Canadian Imperialism

The theory I have outlined can be used to good advantage on the issue of Canadian capitalism. Development of an indigenous fraction of Canadian finance capital around the turn of the century, and its subsequent expanded reproduction, are well-established historical facts. Leaving aside for the moment the issue of foreign investment in Canada, the period from 1870 to 1910 can be recognized as one of very rapid accumulation of financial and industrial capital, marked in 1881 by the coalescence of the country's largest financial institution − the Bank of Montreal − and its greatest industrial undertaking, the Canadian Pacific Railway (Niosi, 1978:87). The close financial and directorate relations between these major monopolies were to form an axis for a financial group of corporations and capitalists that may still be fairly described as the bedrock of Canadian finance capital.[5] Following on the heels of this coalescence came a progressive centralization of manufacturing capital, first with the combination movements of the 1800's and 1890's and ultimately in the intense merger movement of 1908 through 1913 (Stapells, 1927; McLennan, 1929; Bliss, 1974) An indigenous financial-industrial elite composed of a few dozen highly interlocked capitalists in control of major banks, railways, steamship lines, manufacturing plants, mining firms, stock brokerages, and insurance companies consolidated in this period (Degrass, 1977:115-23). Nor did the concrete manifestation of this finance capital remain confined to the Bank of Montreal − CPR interests. In Toronto, concentration of industry and finance gave rise to a financial group around George A. Cox's Canada Life Assurance Co. and the Canadian Bank of Commerce (Drummond, 1962:211).

By the second decade of this century, an advanced form of indigenously-controlled capitalist production, circulation and finance was in place in Canada. At the apex of this finance capital stood the dominant fraction of the Canadian bourgeoisie, a small elite of monopoly capitalists whose interlocking investments and corporate positions effectively fused big industry with high finance. The subsequent reproduction of this dominant fraction has been abundantly documented in a host of corporate network analyses (e.g., Park and Park, 1973; Piedalue, 1976; Sweeny, 1980; Richardson, 1982; Carroll, 1982, 1984).

But the historical hallmarks of imperialism have been evident not simply in the internal structure of the Canadian bourgeoisie. As it attained monopoly form at the turn of the century, a portion of Canadian capital began to search for profitable outlets on an *international* basis. During the course of its development international expansion of Canadian finance capital has taken a variety of forms, from the monopolization of banking and insurance in Cuba and of infrastructural industries in several Latin American countries (Park and Park, 1973:126-8, 136-55; Naylor, 1975, Vol. II 252-64) to the multinational enterprises—and international in-banking consortia — of the post-war era (Neufeld, 1969; Moore and Wells, 1975; Litvak and Maule, 1981; Rush, 1983:282-4).

The theory of imperialism together with the fact of Canadian monopoly capital provide grounds for reconsideration of two issues that bear closely upon Canadian political economy. On the one hand, what dependency theorists mistook to be a universal process of "underdevelopment" in the Third World can be recognized as a *conjunctural* phenomenon in the broader history of imperialism; on the other hand, the *specificity* of Canadian capitalism can be distinguished from the more general features that Canada has actually shared with most other imperialist powers.

Let us consider each of these points in turn. It is generally held that the era of modern imperialism can be periodized into an *early* phase, in which financial capital exported to the periphery spurred the limited production of infrastructure and of raw materials for export to advanced capitalist economies; and a *late* phase which, in the wake of the long crisis of 1914-1945, has brought a broad range of industrial production and a predominance of capitalist production relations to an increasing number of LDCs (Howe, 1981; cf. Brewer, 1980; Szymanski, 1981).

In the former period capitalist development of the periphery occurred at a slow pace, due to a conjunction of conditions both internal to peripheral social formations and integral to the imperialist powers' regimes of accumulation.[6] The period since the Second World War, and especially from about 1960, may be characterized as one of unrelenting capitalist internationalization. Having attained political independence, many LDCs have successfully encouraged industrial development through state capitalism, subsidies, tariffs, and international cartels, as industrial capital has flowed from advanced capitalist countries to take advantage of cheaper labour and expanding Third World markets (Cypher, 1979a:39; Szymanski, 1981). Transnational production, now made feasible by a new wave of technology such as air cargo, containerized shipping, and commercial satellites (Cypher, 1979b:521) and generating in its turn a supranational banking system, has brought a qualitatively new level of international interdependence, a world economy characterized by global corporations and banks (Hawley, 1979:80-1).

This post-war movement toward internationalized production carries several important implications for our understanding of Canadian capitalism and the Canadian bourgeoisie. If "underdevelopment" was not primarily a *cumulative* process organically rooted in the metropolis-satellite relation but a *conjunctural* phenomenon in an era of monopolization and capitalist internationalization, it follows that relations between countries cannot be adequately comprehended with the use of its theoretical complement, "dependency." To appreciate the position of Canadian capital without an increasingly *interdependent* imperialist system, we must begin not from an abstracted bilateral relation conceptualized by means of the metropolis-hinterland metaphor, nor even with a single agency, as in the multinational corporation, but from the totality of international capitalism and its dynamic tendencies.

F. Canada and the Internationalization of Capital

The Tendency Toward Capitalist Cross-Penetration

Initiated by the massive American expansion into Canada and Europe, the postwar internationalization of capital has engendered a multilateral cross-penetration: circuits of national finance capital quite often cross political boundaries, whether as merchant capital (foreign trade), financial capital (loans, interest, dividends) or industrial capital (transnational production). From 1960 to 1972 among member countries of the Organization for Economic Co-operation and Development (OECD), the average annual growth rate of total foreign direct investment was nearly 12% or one-and-a-half times the same countries' average growth in Gross Domestic Product (GDP). At present, about three-quarters of world foreign direct investment is concentrated in the advanced capitalist countries, compared with two-thirds in the 1960's (Portes and Walton, 1981:142; Marcussen and Torp, 1982:25).

The result of this interpenetration has been a general tendency toward increased foreign control in the *advanced* economies. In Britain, U.S. subsidiaries' sales alone accounted for 22% of the GDP in 1976, up from 13.5% nine years earlier. In France, more than 50% of sales in the petroleum, agricultural equipment, electronics and chemical industries are presently attributable to foreign-controlled firms. In West Germany, foreign investment predominates over German capital in oil refining, glass, cement and brick production, food, electrical machinery and iron and metals. As in Canada, foreign investment in Europe tends to concentrate in large companies, reflecting its character as internationalized monopoly capital. For example, "among West Germany's 30 largest corporations are nine foreign subsidiaries, including Exxon, GM, Ford, IBM, Texaco, and Mobil Oil" (Syzmanski, 1981:502). By way of comparison, a recent listing of the largest corporations in Canada also reveals the presence of nine foreign subsidiaries in the top 30, among them GM, Exxon, Ford, and Texaco (*Financial Post 500*, June 1983).

Although the overall levels of foreign, particularly American, investment in Canada are definitely higher than those in other imperialist countries, this example does put what is often depicted as a unique Canadian situation into a proper international perspective. Moreover, since most capital flows have occurred between monopoly capitalist countries it is doubtful that the *importation* of capital—

abstracted from the totality of intercapitalist relations—can provide an unambiguous indication of any country's position in the world system. In this respect we can begin to understand the problems in Levitt's (1970:25) depiction of Canada's post-war importation of U.S. capital as a "regression" to dependence and under-development at the hands of the American transnational corporation.

Forms of Capitalist Internationalization

Analysis of the dynamics of foreign direct investment does not, however, tell the whole story of post-Second World War accumulation. Studies of world capital-ism tend to focus exclusively on transnationals, and this results in an oversimpli-fied analysis in which large, international and apparently uncontrollable com-panies are identified as "the objective enemy of the people" (Barkin, 1981:159). This motif of "domination by the multinationals" is a central element in Canadian dependency studies (Panitch, 1981:9).

However, transnational corporations represent only one form of internationalized finance capital (Nabudere, 1979:50; Portes and Walton, 1981:140), and, depending on the internal character of the host society, need not necessarily be the most pernicious. Levitt (1970) and others have contrasted the beneficial developmental effects of portfolio investment with the regressive ramifications of foreign direct investment, destroying indigenous entrepreneurship, closing off opportunites for accumulation by the national bourgeoisie, and culminating in the "appropriation in perpetuity of the economy's surplus" (Watkins, 1970:xii). To the contrary, several recent analyses of international capitalism stress the similar effects of *both* these forms of foreign investment in social formations where capitalist production relations are, or are becoming, predominant. Direct and portfolio investment both bring a local accumulation of capital and return flow of wealth to the capital-exporting country. Although direct investment implies a form of multinational control and a flow of repatriated profit, if the investment is to be maintained, a share of the profit must be kept in the country. In the final analysis, the rate of re-production of this capital "depends on conditions of accumulation in the receiving country relative to the returns on capital that might be obtained by redeployment" (Friedman, 1978:143). Warren has pursued the larger implications of this rather basic fact of modern capitalist accumulation:

To the extent that political independence is real, private foreign investment must normally be regarded not as a cause of dependence but rather as a means of fortification and diversi-fication of the economies of the host countries. It thereby reduces "dependence" in the long run (Warren, 1980: 176).

Warren's point is especially well taken *vis-à-vis* the Canadian case, where the capacity has existed not simply to *transpose* foreign investment into indigenous circuits of accumulation, but more recently to *reclaim* much of the foreign-controlled capital that contributed to Canada's economic growth during the post-war boom. On one hand, the existence in Canada of an advanced capitalist economy with an extensive and integrated domestic market for both capital and consumer goods has allowed domestic industries to reap multiplier effects as foreign investments cross the circuits of domestic capital in associated economic sectors (cf. Amin,

1974; Palloix, 1975:76; Williams, 1983:4). The excellent post-war growth record of the Canadian steel industry, for example, is related in part to the expansion and emergence of such major steel consumers as the automobile makers and pipeline companies, just as the full development of an oil and gas sector has supplied industrial and residential consumers with an abundant source of fuel at relatively low prices. Similarly, increases in the size of the work force, resulting from capital accumulation under both foreign and domestic control, have increased demand for products such as automobiles and food and beverages (cf. Warren, 1980:142).

However, as we have seen in recent years (Niosi, 1981; Carroll, 1982:106; Resnick, 1982), the advanced form of Canadian capitalism renders foreign direct investment less than permanent. In fact, between 1970 and 1981 foreign control of all capital employed in non-financial Canadian industries fell from 36 to 26 percent (Niosi, 1983:132). Because they possess the independent financial power that accrues to an advanced economy, capitalists in Canada (as well as crown corporations) have been able to patriate foreign-controlled companies through share purchases, just as they have been able to expand their investments abroad.

It is instructive here to take note of the recent shift in imperialist investments on the periphery, from equity participation (portfolio and direct investment) to the use of loans and credits (Marcussen and Torp, 1982:26-7). As the global economic crisis had deepened in the past decade, international banking capital, often through such institutions as the IMF, has shifted its emphasis from supplying multinational corporations with working capital to providing enormous amounts of long-term credit to LCDs with balance of payments deficits (Hawley, 1979:86). Unlike portfolio and direct investment, such internationalized loan capital does not necessarily entail local investment, at least not at a rate adequate for repayment of the principle. Rather, as the historical example of British imperialism in Egypt shows (Luxemburg, 1951:429-39), "the debt-service implied by massive loans can greatly outweigh the local accumulation of capital" (Friedman, 1978:142), especially when growth is trade-related and when protectionism is on the rise in the advanced capitalist countries (as is presently the case; Hawley, 1979: 88).

The desperate need for lenders, in order to avoid the dire consequences of national bankruptcy in a growing number of countries has now led to the re-establishment of an extreme form of neocolonialism: institutions such as the International Monetary Fund require Third World governments to submit their economic policies to surveillance by international finance capital (Kolko, 1977:14-15; Phillips, 1980; Szymanski, 1981:250-2). The proud participation of Canadian bankers with other monopoly capitalist powers in these relations of imperialist domination is well known.

Inter-Imperialist Relations in the Post-Second World War Era

In sorting out the *specificity* of Canadian capitalism, we should bear in mind the crucial difference between the generally stimulative, relatively atomized, and increasingly cosmopolitan form of foreign investment that predominates in Canada and the wholly parasitic and highly centralized economic relation that has been imposed upon large sectors of the Third World.

To appreciate this difference it is necessary to examine the character of relations not simply between centre and periphery, but *among imperialist powers themselves.* In particular, U.S.-Canada ties need to be viewed against the backdrop of American hegemony which provided essential direction in reconstituting world capitalism after the Second World War. In this period, inter-imperialist relations were not marked by the rivalry which had spawned both world wars, but by the hegemony of one power acting to enhance and preserve the unity of the entire capitalist system in the face of internal and external threats.[7]

After the Second World War, the potential for socialist revolutions in Western Europe and in South East Asia gave the United States—which enjoyed enormous financial and technological advantages over its competitors—a compelling interest in reconstructing European capitalism and converting Japan from a defeated nation to a junior partner in containing communism in the East (Nabudere, 1977:156-8). These objectives were accomplished under the formal aegis of the Bretton Woods Agreement and Marshall Plan (Arrighi, 1978:96) with the willing consent of the old pre-war bourgeoisies of Europe and Japan, who were for the most part restored to their positions as ruling classes (Dann, 1979:70).

America's role as a state above states had appeal not merely by virtue of its contribution to the viability of world capitalism as a whole. With the reconstruction of Europe, U.S. capitalists secured an increasing demand for American goods, without which the U.S. economy probably would have stagnated (Marcussen and Trop, 1982:18). At the same time, through its Open Door strategy, the U.S. effectively dismembered many of the colonial relations that had benefitted its rivals, replacing them by a system of open trade and investment more congenial to American interests. The new regime of post-Second World War imperialism would witness the eclipse of particular "spheres of influence," as formal colonial ties of classical imperialism were replaced by informal multilateral relations with "client states" (Nabudere, 1977:145-6).

In this period of hegemony, most world capital exports emanated from the booming U.S. economy and were replaced internationally on the basis of long-term comparative profits prospects. During the Korean War years, dominated by U.S. fears of a shortage of strategic raw materials, Canada received half of all U.S. foreign direct investment (Levitt, 1970:163). U.S. capital remained skeptical of the economic and political viability of European capitalism, and reluctant to expand across the Atlantic, despite the exhortations and incentives of the U.S. government (Tugendhat, 1973:50). Confirmation of Europe's recovery as a reliable and lucrative locus for U.S. capital came with the creation of the Common Market in 1957. Thereafter, Europe attracted an enormous flow of U.S. direct investment (Nabudere, 1977:156; Castells, 1980:105-6).

The legacy of post-war American world hegemony gave rise in the 1970's to serious concern in other imperialist countries about the "American challenge." Ironically, this was coupled with an eroding basis for that concern, as the period of unrivalled American dominance was drawing to a close. Canadian expressions of consternation about "Americanization" (e.g., Levitt, 1970; Lumsden, 1970; Robert Laxer, 1973) need to be viewed, again, against the broader pattern of inter-imperialist relations. In Europe, U.S. direct investments, concentrated especially in basic industries, brought the same sorts of dominance relations in the areas of technology and marketing as have been observed in post-war Canada (Poulantzas, 1974:162; Dann, 1979:72; Marcussen and Trop, 1982:21). The tremendous amount of U.S. direct investment flowing to Europe was perceived by some fractions of European national capital as a definite threat; however "in the longer perspective this view was probably an exaggeration, and the importance today of U.S. investments is partly that of an external pressure contributing to a fast concentration and centralization process among the national capital groups in Western Europe" (Marcussen and Torp, 1982:22)—an insight that was not lost on Canada's Royal Commission on Corporate Concentration (Canada, 1978:408).

The international dominance relations that grew up under the wing of American hegemony, however, were ultimately to erode the U.S. position in world capitalism by fostering revitalized national economies capable of competing directly with American capital (Camilleri, 1981:141). The very high wage rates and strong dollar that characterized the American imperial state presented opportunities to the high-skill but low-wage economies of Western Europe and Japan, whose post-war expansion, like Canada's, was built on a massive outflow of exports (Barnet, 1980:240). These same countries welcomed American direct investment as a means of expanding and strengthening domestic capitalist production (Warren, 1975:139; cf. Frank, 1979:121; Castells, 1980:105-6). Because the European and Japanese economies had relatively little capital tied up in ageing and obsolete equipment, they were able to realize the "merits of borrowing" while the financially and technologically stronger U.S. paid the "penalty of taking the lead." U.S. companies often found it more costly to introduce technology, since they had to take into consideration the book value of existing fixed capital (Cypher, 1979b:521). Moreover, as the leading economy, the U.S. bore much of the costs of *developing* new technology, which could then be incorporated into the productive structures of competing economies, allowing them to grow more rapidly (Szymanski, 1981:517; cf. Warren, 1980:180; Niosi, 1983:132).

The ironic effects of international accumulation under the hegemony of American imperialism became visible in the 1970's, in two respects. First, parts of the formal structure of *Pax Americana*—such as the dollar standard—were jettisoned (Arrighi, 1978:102-3) as the competitive position of American capital visibly deteriorated. The decline of the United States from unrivalled dominance is evident across a range of indicators, from per capita wealth (Szymanski, 1981: 495) and the shrinking U.S. share of the world market in such industrial goods as steel and machine tools (Barnet, 1980: 273-5) to the decreasing number of the world's largest firms based in the U.S. (Frank, 1978; Syzymanski, 1981: 496; Droucopoulas, 1981) and the declining U.S. share in the world capital exports (Nabudere, 1977: 203; Szymanski, 1981: 504).

Secondly, as a regime of multilateral capitalist internationalization emerged, several of the socio-economic problems interpreted by dependency theory as consequences of foreign direct investment actually came to characterize the American metropole, only to spread to other advanced economies as the crisis of the 1970's and 1980s deepened. Massive capital exports from the U.S. led to a relative *stagnation* of internal production, as the foreign operations of U.S.-based multi-national corporations (MNC's) effectively competed with domestic American establishments (Baran and Sweezy, 1966:23; Friedman, 1978:134; 138-9; Castells, 1980:109; Portes. and Walton, 1981:146). Developments such as deindustrialization in the American northeast have, ironically, been linked by Portes and Walton (1981: 154-61) in the American case to U.S. direct investment *abroad* (cf.

Barnet, 1980:275; Siedman and O'Keefe, 1980; Bluestone and Harrison, 1982). Similarly on the matter of foreign trade, Barnet and Muller (1974: 217) had described the "Latin-Americanization of the United States," as the American economy "becomes increasingly dependent on the export of agricultural products and timber to maintain its balance of payments and increasingly dependent on imports of finished goods to maintain its standard of living".

The story, of course, does not end with an American "regression to dependence," recalling Levitt's description of post-war Canada. With a devalued dollar, rising costs of production in Europe, and an ineffectual trade union movement at home, U.S. exports have recently become more competitive in world markets, and U.S. as well as foreign capital has been returning to the American economy (Barnet, 1980: 275; Portes and Walton 1981: 184). As a consequence of investment flow to the U.S., the pattern of unilateral American investments in Canada, Western Europe and Japan is in the process of being superseded by a tendency toward *cross-penetration* of capital. Again, the recent Canadian experience simply reflects this broader trend: whereas in 1970 there were $6.6 of U.S. foreign direct investment in Canada for $1 of Canadian direct investment in the U.S., by 1979 the ratio was 3.5 to 1 (Niosi, 1983: 133).

The International Formation of the Bourgeoisie

Capitalist internationalization has also had an impact on the formation of the bourgeoisie. With growth of an international capital market and cross-penetration of investments, and with development of supracapitalist institutions such as the World Bank, the IMF, and the Trilateral Commission, the "contours of an international capitalist class are emerging" (Portes and Walton, 1981: 174; Frieden, 1977; Goldfrank, 1977; Sklar, 1980), a fraction of internationalized finance capital conscious of the manner in which transnational capitalist production divides labour against itself while enabling the freest flow of capital (Hymer, 1972: 99-103; DeCormis, 1983).

This nascent class formation is evident in the international network of corporate interlocks studies by Fennema and De Jong (1978; summarized in Fennema and Schijf, 1979: 319-20). These researchers investigated interlocking directorates among 176 large corporations from twelve countries—including Canada—and found one large connected network of European and North American companies and a smaller network of Japanese corporations, detached from the first. The existence of an international network of the largest companies in Europe and North America puts into a broader perspective Clement's notions of a Canadian economic elite that is "distorted" by the presence of foreign-affiliated compradors (Clement, 1975: 117), and a "continental elite" that expresses the symbiotic but ultimately dependent ties of Canadian capitalists to the American metropole (Clement, 1977: 179-80). Canada's bourgeois formation certainly appears distorted in comparison with an autarkic ideal type in which "the economic elite would be contained within a national economy and controlled by citizens and residents of the nation" (Clement, 1975: 123). But relative to other capitalist classes that are being similarly restructured by the process of internationalization, the "comprador" elements within the bourgeoisie in Canada are not particularly exceptional, especially since they tend to occupy relatively peripheral positions in the structure of Canadian corporate power (Carroll, Fox and Ornstein, 1981, 1982; Carroll, 1982,

1984). By the same token, while there is no doubt that a "continental elite" of leading Canadian and American capitalists exists, it can perhaps be most fruitfully viewed as a segment of a larger, international network that has developed with capitalist cross-penetration in the post-Second World War era.

The Legacy of Capitalist Internationalization

Lastly, the internationalized capitalism that has matured in the period since the Second World War has brought important changes to the manner in which capital accumulates within national boundaries. The upshot of a transnational network of capitalists and their finance capital is that " . . . increasingly the dynamics of the world capitalist economy cannot be understood with reference to a single nation or group of nations. Productive decisions are now made on a global scale" (Barkin, 1981: 156).

With the development of internationalized monopoly capital an increasing disjuncture appears between the big bourgeoisie's accumulation base and the state's national boundaries, making it hazardous at best to assign "nationalities" to financial groups. According to Friedman, "it is just as serious an error to reduce international capital to its place of origin as to assume that all capital belongs to the place where it is employed" (Friedman, 1978: 141). As Rowthorn's (1975) discussion of post-war British capital illustrates, there is no simple relation between the strength of a "national fraction" of monopoly capital and the vitality of a national economy or the "independence" of a national state. Indeed, in Rowthorn's view it was the very international *strength* of British big capital in the post-Second World War era that led to a *weakening* of the domestic economy and state: " . . . as the British economy became more integrated into a global capitalism over which the British state had no control, it became increasingly vulnerable internationally and the potential benefits to big capital of a straightforwardly aggressive nationalist development have dwindled accordingly" (Rowthorn, 1975: 174-5).

Rowthorn's analysis of the "denationalization" of British monopoly capital and its contribution to that country's industrial decline, together with the example of diminishing American hegemony, provides an important lesson in the dynamics of capitalism and nation-states in the present era. Simply put, all transnational enterprises, irrespective of their "nationality", have the flexibility to play one set of workers off against another. On these grounds, given the strength of Canada's "own" multinationals, it is very misleading to attribute the problems that beset Canadian workers to the dominance of "foreign" capital. By reconceptualizing Canada as an imperialist power in an era of internationalized capitalism we can avoid the error, common in Canadian dependency analyses, of imputing to capitalists a voluntaristic capacity to do business on the basis of such patently noncapitalist considerations as patriotism. Ideological chimeras aside, the accumulation process is in fact highly constrained by competitive struggles around class-structured prospects for producing, appropriating and realizing surplus value at a given time and place (Walker, 1978: 30; Brewer, 1980: 276). Indeed, to the extent that imperialism has integrated the entire non-socialist world around capitalist relations of production and exchange, the logic of allocative decisions is now global even when transnational capital is not involved in a given activity (Barkin, 1981: 158).

The ultimate implication of capital's internationalization is a strong tendency for the law of value to operate more directly than ever on a world scale, producing in the present moment uneven patterns of economic fragmentation, truncation, and state-imposed "austerity" in imperialist countries such as Canada, the United States and Britain as well as in the Third World, as the international division of labour is violently restructured under the weight of global crisis (cf. Kolko, 1977: 20-1; Walker, 1978: 32, Portes and Walton, 1981: 16). In these circumstances, criticizing foreign firms for "disregarding the needs of the national economy," or blaming indigenous capitalists for "selling out the country" and "stultifying industrial development," or lamenting the "relative dependence" of the state on foreign capital can only obscure the structural bases of contemporary capitalism in Canada behind an exaggerated concern with the peculiarities of Canadian "dependency."

There is of course a pressing need to grasp the *specificity* of Canadian capitalism. The great contribution of the Canadian dependency school has been to direct critical attention to that specificity and, in the process, to create the space for a resurgence of radical scholarship that has had some success opposing the received ideology of liberal continentalism. But although the dependency approach has placed the issue of specificity on the agenda of Canadian scholarship it seems that the very problematic of dependency has tended to hamper understanding in at least two ways. There has been a certain "insularity of focus" (Panitch, 1981: 28) on imputed political and economic effects of Canada's particular relationship with the United States. This has obscured the fact that many "symptoms" of Canadian dependency are, as we have seen consequences of the international-ization of capital in the post-Second World War period, evident in all or most advanced capitalist societies. Related to this first problem has been a tendency to impose *qualitative* distinctions between Canadian capitalism and other advanced capitalist economies, where differences are perhaps better viewed as matters of degree.

A concept that holds promise as a means of capturing the specificity of various capitalist societies, whilst avoiding the problems outlined above, is that of the *regime of accumulation:* the manner in which labour power and means of pro-duction have been concretely configured into a functioning social economy (cf. Aglietta, 1979; Therborn, 1983: 42). As I shall now seek to establish, the strong presence in Canada of U.S. monopoly capital, especially since the Second World War, furnishes a good example of how a feature of Canadian capitalism previously explained in terms of the peculiarly dependent logic of Canadian development can be fruitfully analyzed by considering Canada's specific regime of capitalist accu-mulation.

G. Canada's Regime of Accumulation and U.S. Direct Investment

The issue of U.S. direct investment in Canada ultimately turns on the way in which capital became monopolized and internationalized in the early phase of modern im-perialism. It is crucial to note in this connection that the difference between Canada and Europe is essentially one of the *timing* of American capital exports to particular countries. As Schmidt (1981: 92) points out and as we have seen above, Canada simply presents the first case of a more general phenomenon in the international-ization of capital. Nevertheless, in Canada the extent of U.S. control in sectors such as automobiles, petroleum, and electrical equipment has been especially great.

The question is: What class-structured conditions made these investments more attractive to American capitalists than possible investments elsewhere, while limiting the extent to which Canadian capitalists could directly compete in the same industries? These conditions can perhaps be best comprehended as a conjuncture of interrelated features, several of which have been recognized by Canadian dependency writers. In the early decades of the twentieth century, for instance, surplus American capital was attracted both because of Canada's proximity—in light of the technical limits on intercontinental enterprise (cf. Clement, 1977: 6)—and because of the protected and expanding market that Canada provided as a high-growth capitalist economy in its own right *and* as a member of the British Commonwealth (cf. Drache, 1970; Clement, 1977; Williams, 1983). By the same token, for a number of reasons which Panitch (1981) has incisively analyzed, Canada's working class developed in the late nineteenth century as a relatively high-wage proletariat, placing constraints on the extent to which Canadian capitalists could compete with the large and technologically advanced U.S. firms that concentrated their Canadian investments in what were to become the growth industries of the second industrial revolution (McNally, 1981: 55; cf. Clement, 1977: 59; Hutcheson, 1978: 95).[8]

In conjunction with this first constraint on indigenous capitalists was the tying up of enormous amounts of finance capital in the construction and operation of a domestic transport industry. Again, the differences between Canada and other capitalist countries in this regard should not be overdrawn. In general, the development of railways has been a fundamental aspect of capitalist industrialization (Singelmann, 1978: 17), a fact well documented in the Canadian case by Pentland (1981: 145-8; cf. Palmer, 1983: 60-2). The importance of the transportation industry to modern regimes of accumulation has been explained by Richard Walker (1978: 31):

A general aim of capital is to lower its time of circulation, i.e., the speed of self-expansion of capital. Geographic movement of capital is one aspect of the circulation problem as a whole, the most specifically *geographic* problem for capital is in overcoming the barriers which (absolute) space presents, and the primary way capital overcomes this barrier is by what Marx called "the annihilation of space by time"—i.e., speeding up physical movement, especially through the development of transportation and communication systems.

In Canada the vast expanse of space to be annihilated, relative to the size of the home market, necessarily entailed a proportionately very large outlay of capital to the transportation sector, leaving a relative scarcity of indigenous finance capital for the rising industries in which American capital came to predominate. Thus, by 1923, 60% of the total assets of the 100 largest non-financial corporations—and nearly 40% of all industrial and merchant capital in Canada—was claimed by just two indigenous enterprises—the CPR and CNR (Canada, 1937: 21-2, 330). In the meantime, subsidiaries of U.S. corporations had become well entrenched in several expansive branches of Canadian manufacturing.[9]

In short, a regime of monopoly capitalism emerged in Canada at the turn of the century on the *dual* premises of (a) international concentration and centralization (U.S. direct investment) and (b) domestic monopolization (formation of indigenous financial groups such as the CPR—Bank of Montreal interests). The post-Second World War period of American economic and political hegemony in the capitalist world culminated in the late 1950's in the enlarged presence of U.S.-controlled monopoly capital in Canada, together with an intermingling of powerful U.S. financial groups with Canadian finance capital (Park and Park, 1973: 15).

These facts have been interpreted by Levitt and others as symptoms of a cumulative regression to dependence, but a more meaningful issue to explore in light of post-Second World War developments in the imperialist system is the *rate* at which the accumulation base of the Canadian bourgeoisie has been internationalizing, compared with the rate at which other imperialist class fractions have been expanding their circuits of accumulation within Canada. Considering direct investment only, these comparisons are made in Table 1. The three decades seem to divide evenly into two periods. Between 1946 and 1961—the era of unrivalled American international hegemony—foreign direct investment grew at a rate faster than that of Canadian direct investment abroad. In the 1960's, and especially the 1970's, however, the opposite pattern came to prevail. From 1950 to 1965, U.S.-controlled capital in Canada accumulated more rapidly than Canadian-controlled capital in the U.S., but by the mid-1970's Canadian capitalists were augmenting their U.S. investments at a rate more than twice that of U.S. direct investment in Canada. Moreover, since 1966 there has been a clear tendency for Canadian capital to internationalize beyond the economies of the United States and the British Commonwealth.

On balance, Canada seems to present the example of a middle-range imperialist power in an era of thoroughly internationalized monopoly capitalism. The post-Second World War pattern of accumulation makes it clear that a focus on Canadian dependency ascribes increasing significance to a phenomenon that has been in decline. This decline is both *relative* to other advanced capitalist economies, as monopoly capital has further internationalized, and *absolute,* as the proportion of Canadian industrial capital under U.S. control has dropped while indigenous capital exports have continued to expand. The resilience and recent consolidation of Canadian finance capital is further underscored by findings from studies of corporate interlocking that the network of large Canadian companies is increasingly focussed around predominantly indigenous interests (Carroll, Fox, and Ornstein, 1981; Carroll, 1982, 1984).

This is not to deny that Canadian finance capital, along with other imperialist fractions, is beholden to the American military machine in order to protect its substantial investments in the Third World and keep the Soviet Union in check. These same capitalist fractions also yearn to share in the stimulative benefits of the current U.S. economic recovery, even as they resent the American attempt to recover lost economic space by projecting its political power (Petras and Morley, 1982: 6, 30-1). Canadian monopoly capital, while presently more *independent* of singularly American interests than it has been in several decades, is deeply involved in a complex structure of international politico-economic relations in which the largest imperialist power necessarily plays a focal role.

TABLE 1
Annual Rates of Growth of Foreign Direct Investment in Canada and Canadian Direct Investment Abroad, 1946-1977

Year	Foreign Direct Investment in Canada Controlling Country				Canadian Direct Investment Abroad Host Country				
	United States	United Kingdom	Other	Total	United States	United Kingdom	Other Commonwealth Countries	Other	Total
1946-1949	8.9	8.3	-1.1	8.6	12.2	2.2	2.4	-16.2	6.5
1950-1953	15.3	9.4	28.0	14.9	11.6	15.2	15.0	14.7	12.4
1954-1957	13.5	15.9	32.0	14.5	6.7	13.4	15.3	15.5	8.8
1958-1961	7.4	8.4	19.5	8.1	4.4	13.8	4.4	9.1	5.8
1962-1965	4.4	7.0	10.7	5.1	4.3	13.8	12.9	12.8	7.5
1966-1969	8.7	6.2	13.4	8.8	9.9	5.4	12.5	16.6	10.7
1970-1973	6.6	7.1	11.9	7.2	7.1	7.6	12.7	20.8	10.7
1974-1977	6.6	5.7	9.2	6.8	15.7	15.3	2.5	17.6	14.5
1946-1977	9.0	8.5	15.7	9.3	8.9	10.7	9.6	10.7	9.6

Source: Statistics Canada, Canada's International Investment Position 1977 (Ottawa, 1981), pp. 22, 63.

Included in Canadian direct investment abroad are the investments of foreign-controlled Canadian companies. Since the proportion of such 'go-between' investment has fallen dramatically in recent years (Litvak and Maule, 1981: 8-9), the table underestimates the real rate at which indigenous capital has been expanding abroad.

References

Aglietta, Michel, 1979—*A Theory of Capitalist Regulation.* London: New Left Books

Amin, Samir, 1974—*Accumulation on a World Scale.* New York: Monthly Review Press, 2 Vols.

Anderson, J. 1973—"Ideology in geography: An introduction" *Antipode* 5 (3), 1-16

Angotti, Thomas, 1981—"The political implications of dependency theory." *Latin American Perspectives* 8 (3/4), 124-37

Arrighi, Giovanni, 1978—*The Geometry of Imperialism.* London: New Left Books

Ashley, C.A., 1957—"Concentration of economic power." *Canadian Journal of Economics and Political Science* 23, 105-8

Baran, P.A., 1957—*The Political Economy of Growth.* New York: Monthly Review Press

Baran, P.A., and P.M. Sweezy, 1966—"Notes on the theory of imperialism." *Problems of Economic Dynamics and Planning: Essays in Honour of Michal Kalecki.* New York: Pergamon Press

Barkin, David, 1981—"Internationalization of capital: an alternative approach." *Latin American Perspectives* 8 (3/4), 156-61

Barnet, Richard J., 1980—*The Lean Years.* New York: Simon & Schuster

Barnet, Richard J. and Ronald E. Mullen, 1974—*Global Reach.* New York: Simon & Schuster

Barone, Charles A., 1983—"Dependency, Marxist theory, and salvaging the idea of capitalism in South Korea." *Review of Radical Political Economics* 15 (1), 41-70

Bluestone, B. and B. Harrison, 1982—*The Deindustrialization of America.* New York: Basic Books

Bliss, Michael, 1970—"Canadianizing American business: The roots of the branch plant." In Ian Lumsden (ed.) *Close the 49th Parallel Etc., the Americanization of Canada.* University of Toronto Press, 26-42

Bliss, Michael, 1974—*A Living Profit.* Toronto: McClelland and Stewart

Brenner, Robert, 1977—"The origins of capitalist development: A critique of neo-Smithian Marxism." *New Left Review* 104, 25-92

Brewer, Anthony, 1980—*Marxist Theories of Imperialism.* Boston: Routledge & Kegan Paul

Britton, J.N.H. and J.M. Gilmour, 1978—*The Weakest Link: A Technological Perspective on Canadian Industrial Underdevelopment* Science Council of Canada Background Study No. 43. Ottawa

Browett, John, 1981—"Into the cul de sac of the dependency paradigm with A.G. Frank." *Australian and New Zealand Journal of Sociology* 17, 14-25

Bukharin, Nikolai, 1973—*Imperialism and World Economy.* New York: Monthly Review Press

Burris, Val, 1980—"Class formation and transformation in advanced capitalist societies: A comparative analysis." *Social Praxis* 7 (3/4), 147-79

Camilleri, Joseph, 1981—"The advanced capitalist state and the contemporary world crisis." *Science and Society* 45, 130-58

Canada, 1937—*Report of the Royal Commission on Price Spreads.* Ottawa: King's Printer

Canada, 1978—*Report on the Royal Commission on Corporate Concentration.* Ottawa: Minister of Supply & Services

Canada, 1980—Corporate and Labour Unions Returns Act *Annual Report 1978 Part I: Corporations.* Ottawa: Statistics Canada

Cardoso, F.H. and E. Faletto, 1979—*Dependency and Development in Latin America.* Los Angeles: University of California Press

Carroll, William K., 1982—"The Canadian corporate elite: Financiers or finance capitalists?" *Studies in Political Economy* 8, 89-114

Carroll, William K., 1984—"The individual, class, and corporate power in Canada." *Canadian Journal of Sociology* 9 (3), 245-68

Carroll, William K., John Fox and Michael D. Ornstein, 1981—"Longitudinal analysis of directorate interlocks." Paper presented at the annual meetings of the Canadian Sociology and Anthropology Association. Halifax, May

Carroll, William K., John Fox and Michael D. Ornstein, 1982—"The network of directorate links among the largest Canadian firms." *Canadian Review of Sociology and Anthropology* 19, 44-69

Castells, Manuel, 1980—*The Economic Crisis and American Society* Princeton: Princeton University Press

Chinchilla, Norma S. and James L. Dietz, 1981—"Toward a new understanding of development and underdevelopment." *Latin American Perspectives* 8 (3/4), 138-47

Chodos, Robert, 1973—*The CPR: A Century of Corporate Welfare.* Toronto: James Lewis and Samuel

Clairmonte, Frederick, 1982—"Dynamics of finance capital." *Journal of Contemporary Asia* 12 (2), 158-67

Clawson, Patrick, 1976—"The internationalization of capital and capital accommodation in Iran and Iraq." *Insurgent Sociologist* 6 (2), 64-73

Clement, Wallace, 1977—*Continental Corporate Power.* Toronto: McClelland and Stewart

Clement, Wallace, 1983a—"Canadian class cleavages: An assessment and contribution." In Wallace Clement, *Class, Power and Property.* Toronto: Methuen, 134-71

Clement, Wallace, 1983b—"Uneven development: A mature branch-plant society." In Wallace Clement *Class, Power and Property.* Toronto: Methuen, 172-43

Clement, Wallace, 1983c—"Transformations in mining: A critique of H.A. Innis." In Wallace Clement, *Class, Power and Property.* Toronto: Methuen, 172-43

Cliffe, Lionel and Peter Lawrence, 1977—"Editorial." *Review of African Political Economy* 8, 1-6

Craven, Paul and Tom Traves, 1979—"The class politics of the national policy 1872-1933." *Journal of Canadian Studies* 14 (3), 14-38

Cueva, Agustin, 1976—"A summary of 'Problems and Perspectives of Dependency Theory.'" *Latin American Perspectives* 3 (4), 12-16

Cuneo, Carl J., 1982—"The politics of surplus labour in the collapse of Canada's dependence on Britain, 1840-49." *Studies in Political Economy* 7, 61-87

Cuneo, Carl J., 1983—"Transition in Canada's class structure 1901-81." Paper presented at the Marx Centenary Conference, University of Manitoba, March

Cypher, James M., 1979a—The internationalization of capital and the transformation of social formations: A critique of the Monthly Review School. *Review of Radical Political Economics* 11 (4), 33-49

Cypher, James M., 1979b—"The transnational challenge to the corporate state." *Journal of Economic Issues* 13, 513-42

Dann, James, 1979—"U.S. hegemony over the three worlds." *Review of Radical Political Economics* 11 (4), 64-77

Davis, Arthur K., 1971—"Canadian society and history as hinterland versus metropolis." In Richard J. Ossenberg (ed.), *Canadian Society: Pluralism, Change and Conflict.* Scarborough: Prentice-Hall, 6-32

De Cormis, Anna, 1983—"So much for 'the American way' in auto and steel." *Guardian* (New York) 35 (32), 11

De Grass, Richard P., 1977—*Development of Monopolies in Canada from 1907-1913.* Masters Thesis, University of Waterloo

Drache, D., 1970—"The Canadian bourgeoisie and its national consciousness." In Ian Lumsden (ed.), *Close the 49th Parallel etc.: The Americanization of Canada.* Toronto: University of Toronto Press, 3-25

Drache, D., 1977—"Staple-ization: A theory of Canadian capitalist development." In Craig Heron (ed.) *Imperialism, Nationalism, and Canada.* Toronto: New Hogtown Press and Between the Lines, 15-33

Drache, D., 1983—"The crisis of Canadian political economy: Dependency theory versus the new orthodoxy." *Canadian Journal of Political and Social Theory* 7 (3), 25-49

Droucopoulos, Vassilis, 1981—"The non-American challenge: a report on the size and growth of the world's largest firms." *Capital and Class* 14, 36-46

Drummond, Ian, 1962—"Canadian life insurance companies and the capital market, 1890-1914." *Canadian Journal of Economics and Political Science* 27, 204-24

Drummond, Ian, 1978—"Review of R.T. Naylor, History of Canadian Business." *Canadian Historical Review* 59, 90-93

Easterbrook, W.T. and H.G.J. Aitken, 1956—*Canadian Economic History.* Toronto: Macmillan

Ehrensaft, P., and W. Armstrong, 1981—"The formation of dominion capitalism: economic truncation and class structure." In A. Moscovitch and G. Drover (eds.), *Inequality: Essays on the Political Economy of Social Welfare.* Toronto: University of Toronto Press, 99-155

Emmanuel, Arghiri, 1972—*Unequal Exchange.* New York: Monthly Review Press

Fanon, Frantz, 1966—*The Wretched of the Earth.* New York: Grove Press

Fennema, Meindert and P. De Jong, 1978—"Internationale vervlechting van industire en bankwezen." In A. Tevlings (ed.), *Herstrukturering van de Nederlandse Industrie.* Alphen a/d Rijn: Samson

Fennema, Meindert and Schijf, Huibert, 1979—"Analysing interlocking directorates: theory and methods." *Social Networks* 1, 297-332

Fisher, A.G.B., 1935—*The Clash of Progress and Security.* London: Macmillan

Fisher, A.G.B., 1952—"A note on tertiary production." *Economic Journal* 62, 820-34

Frank, Andre G., 1967—*Capitalism and Underdevelopment in Latin America.* New York: Monthly Review Press

Frank, Andre G., 1972—*Lumpenbourgeoisie. Lumpendevelopment.* New York: Monthly Review Press

Frank, Andre G., 1979–*Dependent Accumulation and Underdevelopment*. New York: Monthly Review Press

Franko, Lawrence G., 1978–"Multinationals: the end of U.S. dominance." *Harvard Business Review* (Nov-Dec), 93-101

Frieden, Jeff, 1977–"The Trilateral Commission: Economics and politics in the 1970s." *Monthly Review* 29 (7), 1-18

Friedman, Jonathan, 1978–"Crises in theory and transformations of the world economy." *Review* 2, 131-46

Godfrey, Dave and Mel Watkins (eds.), 1970–*Gordon to Watkins to You*. Toronto: New Press

Goldfrank, Walter L., 1977–"Who rules the world? Class formation at the international level." *Quarterly Journal of Ideology* 1 (2), 32-7

Gonick, C.W., 1970–"Foreign ownership and political decay." In Ian Lumsden (ed.) *Close the 49th Parallel etc.: The Americanization of Canada*. University of Toronto Press, 43-73

Halliday, J. and G. McCormack, 1973–*Japanese Imperialism Today*. London: Penguin

Harding, Timothy F., 1976–"Dependency, nationalism and the state in Latin America." *Latin American Perspectives* 3 (4), 3-11

Hawley, Jim, 1979–"The internationalization of capital: banks, Eurocurrency and the instability of the world monetary system." *Review of Radical Political Economics* 11 (4), 78-90

Henfrey, Colin, 1981–"Dependency, modes of production, and the class analysis of Latin America." *Latin American Perspectives* 8 (3/4), 17-54

Hilferding, R., 1981–*Finance Capital*. London: Routledge and Kegan Paul

Howe, Gary N., 1981–"Dependency theory, imperialism, and the production of surplus value on a world scale." *Latin American Perspectives* 8 (3/4), 82-102

Howe, Gary N. and A. Sica, 1980–"Political economy, imperialism, and the problem of world system theory." In S.G. McNall and G.N. Howe (eds.), *Current Perspectives in Social Theory*, Vol. I. Greenwich, Connecticut: JAL Press, 235-86

Hutcheson, John, 1978–*Dominance and Dependency*. Toronto: McClelland and Stewart

Hymer, Stephen, 1972–"The internationalization of capital." *Journal of Economic Issues* 6 (1), 91-111

Innis, Harold A., 1970–*The Fur Trade in Canada*. Revised Edition. Toronto: University of Toronto Press

Johnson, Carlos, 1981–"Dependency theory and the processes of capitalism and socialism." *Latin American Perspectives*, 8 (3/4), 55-81

Johnson, Carlos, 1983–"Ideologies in theories of imperialism and dependency." In R.H. Chilcote and D.L. Johnson (eds.), *Theories of Development*. Beverly Hills: Sage, 75-106

Johnson, Leo A., 1972–"The development of class in Canada in the twentieth century." In Gary Teeple (ed.), *Capitalism and the National Question in Canada*. Toronto: University of Toronto Press, 141-84.

Kay, Geoffrey, 1975–*Development and Underdevelopment: A Marxist Analysis*. New York: St. Martin's Press

Kealey, Gregory S., 1982–"Toronto's industrial revolution, 1850-1892." In Michael S. Cross and Gregory S. Kealey (eds.), *Canada's Age of Industry, 1849-1896*. Toronto: McClelland and Stewart, 20-61

Kemp, Tom, 1978–*Historical Patterns of Industrialization*. London: Longman Canada

Kolko, Joyce, 1977–"Imperialism and the crisis of capitalism in the 1970s." *Journal of Contemporary Asia* 7 (1), 9-21

Kotz, David M., 1978–*Bank Control of Large Corporations in the United States*. Berkeley: University of California Press

Laclau, Ernesto, 1971–"Feudalism and capitalism in Latin America." *New Left Review* 67, 19-38

Lall, S., 1975–"Is 'dependence' a useful concept in analyzing underdevelopment?" *World Development* 3 (11-12), 799-810

Landsberg, Marty, 1976–"Multinational corporations and the crisis of capitalism." *Insurgent Sociologist* 6 (3), 19-33

Laxer, Jim, 1973–"Canadian manufacturing and U.S. trade policy." In R.M. Laxer (ed.), *(Canada) Ltd.* Toronto: McClelland and Stewart, 127-152

Laxer, Robert (ed.), 1973–*(Canada) Ltd., The Political Economy of Dependency*. Torontod: McClelland and Stewart Limited

Leaver, Richard, 1977–"The debate on underdevelopment: 'On Situating Gunder Frank.'" *Journal of Contemporary Asia* 7 (1), 108-15

Lenin, V.I. 1970 (1917).–"Imperialism, the highest stage of capitalism." In V.I. Lenin, *Selected Works*, Vol. 1. Moscow: Progress Publishers, 667-768

Levitt, Kari, 1970–*Silent Surrender*, Toronto: Macmillan of Canada

Leys, Colin, 1977—"Underdevelopment and dependency: critical notes." *Journal of Contemporary Asia* 7 (1), 92-107
Leys, Colin, 1978—"Capital accumulation, class formation and dependency—the significance of the Kenyan case." *Socialist Register,* 241-66
Lindsey, C.W., 1982—"Lenin's theory of imperialism." *Review of Radical Political Economies* 14 (1), 1-9
Little, I.M.D., 1975—"Economic relations with the Third World—old myths and new prospects." *Scottish Journal of Political Economy* 22, 223-35
Litvak, I.A. and C.J. Maule, 1981—*The Canadian Multinationals.* Toronto: Butterworths
Lumsden, Ian, 1970—"American imperialism and Canadian intellectuals." In Ian Lumsden (ed.), *Close the 49th Parallel etc.: The Americanization of Canada.* Toronto: University of Toronto Press, 321-36
Luxemburg, Rosa, 1951—*The Accumulation of Capital.* New York: Monthly Review Press
Macdonald, L.R., 1975—"Merchants against industry: an idea and its origins." *Canadian Historical Review* 56, 263-81
McLennan, J.L., 1929—*The Merger Movement in Canada Since 1880.* Masters Thesis, Queens University
McNally, David, 1981—"Staple theory as commodity fetishism: Marx, Innis and Canadian political economy." *Studies in Poltical Economy* 6, 35-63
Mandel, E, 1968—*Marxist Economic Theory,* London: Merlin Press
Markusen, Ann R., 1978—"Class, rent and sectoral conflict: uneven development in western U.S. Boom-World.* London: Zed Press Ltd.
Markusen, Ann R., 1978—"Class, rent and sectoral conflict: Uneven development in western U.S. Boom-towns." *Review of Radical Political Economics* 10 (3), 117-129
Marx, Karl, 1967—*Capital.* New York: International Publishers, 3 vols.
Matthews, Ralph, 1983—*The Creation of Regional Dependency.* Toronto: University of Toronto Press
Menshikov, S., 1969—*Millionaires and Managers.* Moscow: Progress Publishers
Mepham, John, 1979—"The theory of ideology in *Capital.*" In John Mepham and D.H. Ruben (eds.), *Issues in Marxist Philosophy.* Vol. III. Brighton: Harvester, 141-74
Moore, Steve and Debi Wells. 1975. *Imperialism and the National Question in Canada.* Toronto: privately published
Nabudere, D.W., 1977—*The Political Economy of Imperialism.* London: Zed Press Ltd.
Nabudere, D.W., 1979—*Essays on the Theory and Practice of Imperialism.* London: Onyx Press Ltd.
Naylor, R.T., 1972—"The rise and fall of the third commercial empire of the St. Lawrence." In Gary Teeple (ed.) *Capitalism and the National Question in Canada.* Toronto: University of Toronto Press, 1-41
Naylor, R.T., 1975a—*The History of Canadian Business 1867-1914.* Toronto: James Lorimer and Company Publishers, 2 vols.
Naylor, R.T., 1975b—"Commentary." *Our Generation* 11 (1), 17-24
Neufeld, E.P., 1969—*A Global Corporation: A History of the International Development of Massey Ferguson Ltd.* Toronto: University of Toronto Press
Niosi, Jorge, 1978—*The Economy of Canada.* Montreal: Black Rose Books
Niosi, Jorge, 1981—*Canadian Capitalism.* Toronto: Lorimer
Niosi, Jorge, 1983—"The Canadian bourgeoisie: towards a synthetical approach." *Canadian Journal of Political and Social theory* 7 (3): 128-149
Overbeek, Henk, 1980—"Finance capital and the crisis in Britain." *Capital and Class* 2, 99-120
Palloix, Christian, 1975—"The internationalization of capital and the circuit of social capital." In Hugo Redice (ed.), *International Firms and Modern Imperialism.* Markham: Penguin, 63-88
Palloix, Christian, 1977—"The self-expansion of capital on a world scale." *Review of Radical Political Economics* 9 (1), 1-28
Palmer, Bryan D., 1983—*Working-Class Experience.* Toronto: Butterworth
Panitch, Leo, 1981—"Dependency and class in Canadian political economy." *Studies in Political Economy* 6, 7-33
Park, Libbie and Frank Park, 1973 (1962)—*Anatomy of Big Business.* Toronto: James Lewis and Samuel
Penner, Norman, 1977—*The Canadian Left.* Scarborough: Prentice-Hall of Canada Ltd.
Pentland, H.C., 1981—*Labour and Capital in Canada 1650-1860.* Toronto: Lorimer
Petras, James and Morris Morley, 1982—"The new cold war: Reagan's policy towards Europe and the Third World." *Studies in Political Economy* 9, 5-44
Phillips, Anne, 1977—"The concept of development." *Review of African Political Economy* 8, 7-20
Phillips, James, 1980—"Renovation of the international economic order: Trilateralism, the IMF, and Jamaica." In Holly Sklar (ed.), *Trilateralism: The Trilateral Commission and Elite Planning for World*

Management. Boston: South End Press, 468-91

Phillips, Paul, 1979—"The national policy revisited." *Journal of Canadian Studies* 14, 3-13

Piedalue, Gilles, 1976—"Les groupes financiers au Canada 1900-1930." *Revue d'Histoire de l'Amerique Francaise* 30 (1), 3-34

Portes, Alejandro, and John Walton, 1981—*Labor, Class, and the International System.* Toronto: Academic Press

Poulantzas, Nicos, 1974—"Internationalization of capitalist relations and the nation-state." *Economy and Society* 3, 145-79

Prebish, R., 1950—*The Economic Development of Latin America and its Principal Problems.* Lake Success, New York: U.N. Department of Economic Affairs

Resnick, Philip, 1977—*Land of Cain.* Vancouver: New Star Books

Resnick, Philip, 1982—"The maturing of Canadian capitalism." *Our Generation* 15 (3), 11-24

Reuber, Grant L. and Frank Roseman, 1969—*The Take-Over of Canadian Firms, 1945-61.* Economic Council of Canada Special Study No. 10. Ottawa: Queen's Printer

Richardson, R.J., 1982—"Merchants against industry: an empirical study." *Canadian Journal of Sociology* 7, 279-96

Rosenblum, Simon, 1975—"Economic nationalism and the English-Canadian socialist movement." *Our Generation* 11 (1), 5-15

Rowthorn, B., 1975—"Imperialism in the 1970s—unity or rivalry?" In Hugo Radice (ed.), *International Firms and Modern Imperialism.* Markham, Ontario: Penguin, 158-80

Rush, Gary B., 1983—"State, class and capital: demystifying the westward shift of power." *Canadian Review of Sociology and Anthropology* 20, 255-289

Ryerson, Stanley B., 1973—*Unequal Union.* Toronto: Progress Books

Ryerson, Stanley, 1976—"Who's looking after business?" *This Magazine* 9, 41-6

Schmidt, Ray, 1981—"Canadian political economy: a critique." *Studies in Political Economy* 6, 65-92

Seidman, Ann and Phil O'Keefe, 1980—"The United States and South Africa in the changing international division of labour." *Antipode* 12 (2), 1-16

Singelmann, Joachim, 1978—*From Agriculture to Services.* Beverly Hills: Sage

Sklar, Holly (ed.), 1980—*Trilateralism: The Trilateral Commission and Elite Planning for World Management.* Boston: South End Press

Smout, T.C., 1980—"Scotland and England: Is dependency a symptom or a cause of underdevelopment?" *Review* 3, 601-30

Stapells, H.G., 1927—*The Recent Consolidation Movement in Canada.* Masters Thesis, University of Toronto

Statistics Canada, 1983—Corporations and Labour Unions Returns Act. *Annual Report Part 1—Corporations.* Ottawa

Swainson, Nicola, 1977—"The rise of a national bourgeoisie in Kenya." *Review of African Political Economy* 8, 39-55

Sweeny, Robert, 1980—*The Evolution of Financial Groups in Canada and the Capital Market Since the Second World War.* Masters Thesis, Universite du Quebec a Montreal

Szymanski, Albert, 1981—*The Logic of Imperialism.* New York: Praeger

Therborn, Goran, 1978—*What does the Ruling Class do When it Rules?* London: New Left Books

Therborn, Goran, 1983—"Why some classes are more successful than others." *New Left Review* 138, 37-55

Thompson, Grahame, 1977—"The relationship between the financial and industrial sector in the United Kingdom economy." *Economy and Society* 6, 235-83

Tugendhat, C., 1973—*The Multinationals.* London: Penguin

Walker, Richard A., 1978—"Two sources of uneven development under advanced capitalism: spatial differentiation and capital mobility." *Review of Radical Political Economics* 10 (3), 28-38

Wallerstein, Immanuel, 1974—*The Modern World System: Capitalist Agriculture and the Origins of the European World Economy in the Sixteenth Century.* New York: Academic Press

Warren, Bill, 1975—"How international is capital?" In Hugo Radice (ed.), *International Firms and Modern Imperialism: Pioneer of Capitalism.* London: New Left Books

Watkins, M.H., 1970—"Preface." In Kari Levitt, *Silent Surrender.* Toronto Macmillan of Canada. ix-xvii

Watkins, M.H. 1973—"Resources and underdevelopment." In Robert M. Laxer (ed.) *(Canada) Ltd: The Political Economy of Dependency.* Toronto: McClelland and Stewart, 107-26

Watkins, Mel, 1981—"Perspectives on nationalism." *This Magazine* 15 (4), 26-8

Watkins, Mel, 1981—"Perspectives on nationalism." *This Magazine* 15 (4),m 26-28
Weeks, John, 1981—"The differences between materialist theory and dependency theory and why they matter." *Latin American Perspectives* 8 (3/4), 118-123
Weeks, John, and Elizabeth Dore, 1979—"International exchange and the causes of backwardness." *Latin American Perspectives* 6 (2), 62-87
Wilkens, Mira, 1974—*The Maturing of Multinational Enterprise: American Business Abroad from 1914 to 1970.* Cambridge: Harvard University Press
Williams, Glen, 1983—*Not for Export: Toward a Political Economy of Canada's Arrested Industrialization* Toronto: McClelland and Stewart

NOTES

1. On the latter see, for instance, Godfrey and Watkins (1970), Penner (1977: 240) and Resnick (1977)
2. See, however, Moore and Wells (1975).
3. Notably Ryerson (1976: 46); Panitch (1981: 7); Schmidt (1981: 66).
4. Among those who have explicitly applied Frank's model to Canadian capitalism are Davis (1971), Watkins (1973), Clement (1977), and Marchak (1979). On the other hand, Drache (1970) is inspired by Fanon's (1965) analysis of colonialism in Africa in describing Canadian capitalists as a colonial bourgeoisie, while Naylor (1975b:23) has denied any intellectual connection with Frank or Baran.

5. (cf. Ashley, 1957; Johnson, 1972; Chodos, 1973; Park and Park, 1973: 104-7). It is worth pointing out that this initial fusing of financial capital with industrial capital invested in means of transportation was by no means a phenomenon unique to Canada, but reflected the enormous financing requirements of railways everywhere. See, for example, David Kotz's (1978) account of the similar course followed by finance capital in the United States.
6. Discussion of these conditions is well beyond the scope of this paper, but can be found in Kay (1975). Brenner (1977), Phillips (1977). Cypher (1979a) and Szymanski (1981).

7. Camilleri, 1981: 141; cf. Arrighi, 1978d: 96-103; Cardoso and Faletto, 1979: 182; Castells, 1980: 104-9; Szymanski, 1981: 492.
8. Panitch's account has recently been challenged by Drache (1983), who notes that from 1870 through 1930 American wage rates were consistently higher than Canadian wage rates. This observation, however, has no relevance to Panitch's central claim that the Canadian working class developed as a high wage proletariat "not only relative to the Third World but relative to the capitalisms of Europe" (1981: 16). More fundamentally, Drache grievously misrepresents the thrust of Panitch's argument, which is not that "the relatively high wage levels of the Canadian working class at the end of the nineteenth century retarded the rate of capital accumulation" (Drache, 1983: 27), but that "industrial production in Canada had to expand on the basis of *relative* surplus value, the application of extensive fixed capital to the production process to expand labour productivitiy" (Panitch, 1981: 19)—an undertaking for which large American corporation were favoured.
9. We ought not to push this account beyond its limited purpose in explaining the relatively large share of U.S. Direct investment in certain Canadian industries. One legacy of the very extensive involvement of Canadian capitalists in the manufacturing sector from Canada's industrial revolution on (Phillips, 1979: 11) is the list of Canadian MNCs engaged principally in manufacturing: Seagrams, Northern Telecom, Massey-Ferguson, Moore Corporation, Bata Shoe Company, Canada Packers, etc. (Moore and Wells, 1975: 79-90; Litvak and Maule, 1981).

Continental Nationalism: The Strategy of the Canadian Bourgeoisie

Jorge Niosi

What then does the ruling class do when it rules? Essentially it reproduces the economic, political and ideological relations of its domination. This rule is exercised through state power, that is to say, through the interventions or policies of the state and their effects upon the positions of the ruling class within the relations of production, the state apparatus and the ideological arena. The class character of state power is thus defined by the effects of state measures on class positions in these three spheres (Therborn, 1978: 161).

This article deals with two different but related subjects. The first concerns the identification of the ruling class in Canada or, more precisely, of the ruling fraction of that class and its social basis. The second involves determining the business strategy of this ruling fraction, a set of corporate policies I call "continental" or "rentier" nationalism. My main hypotheses are that the Canadian indigenous bourgeoisie is the ruling class, and that its main business strategy involves Canadianization, and the extension of Canadian multinationals into the United States in particular. I argue as well that this policy has been shaped by the interaction of Canadian corporate leaders and the top bureaucrats of the Canadian state. In other words, the state has played a key role in the formation of these corporate policies.

Marxist theories and empirical methods provide the tools for such an analysis. However, some theoretical clarification is required from the outset. There are many currents of thought and debates on the state and the ruling class within Marxism, but Marxist theories — with their high level of abstraction and their emphasis on long-term trends — have rarely dealt with business strategy as a key question.

I will start by outlining and trying to clarify some recent debates within Marxism concerning the state and the ruling class. I will also look at how business strategies are developed and adopted, and try to connect this question to the debates within neo-Marxism.

The next part of this article will briefly analyze the internal composition of the Canadian capitalist class and shed some light on the typical alliances which its various fractions forge with different groups among the subordinate classes. Some major characteristics of the Canadian state will also be reviewed.

The third part will present some critical evidence to support the thesis that the Canadian indigenous bourgeoisie is the ruling class of our society and that continental nationalism is its reproductive strategy. I will conclude with some hypotheses on the limits and likely future evolution of this development strategy.

The State, the Ruling Class and Business Strategies

Several years ago David Gold, Clarence Lo and Erik O. Wright tried to classify different Marxist perspectives on the capitalist state in a much-quoted and very stimulating article (Gold, Lo and Wright, 1975). They noted that Marx, Engels and Lenin did not build any systematic theory of the state. On the basis of this incomplete and fragmentary legacy, these scholars identified three currents of thought in the post-Second World War evolution of Marxist thought: "instrumentalism", "structuralism" and "Hegelian-Marxism". On the basis of more recent work, two new perspectives have to be added to their classification: "reproductivism" and "state autonomism". My own theoretical framework borrows different dimensions from most of these lines of thought, whose key elements I will very briefly review.

"Instrumentalism" is the oldest and most common Marxist perspective on the relationship between the state and the ruling class. It builds upon some classic works such as Marx's *The 18th Brumaire of Louise Bonaparte,* Engels' *Revolution and Counter-Revolution in Germany,* and Lenin's *State and Revolution.* A variety of state policies are explained as the outcome of direct control exercised by the ruling capitalist class. Modern instrumentalists such as Ralph Milibrand and G.W. Domhoff conceive of the state as a set of institutions, and try to discover links between those who occupy positions of power in the state and members of the capitalist ruling class who control private corporations. They have succeeded in demonstrating significant links and a high degree of ruling class control, through the supply of political personnel, the activity of pressure groups and long-term planning organizations, and political party financcing. (Miliband, 1969; Domhoff, 1967, 1971, 1979)

These contributions notwithstanding, some major deficiencies in this method have been pointed out by those who adhere to other approaches. These include the limited autonomy instrumentalism grants to the state, the excessive emphasis it puts on individuals and social or political groups rather than classes, and its lack of analysis of structural restrictions (including state restrictions) on the strategies and activities of the ruling classes. Another problem is the inability of instrumentalism to account for facts such as the acceptance by large segments of the business community of some reformist economic policies (like the New Deal in the U.S.A.) and the control of many state apparatuses by non-capitalist middle-class groups, especially in the spheres of culture, education, and health and welfare.

I would add another criticism of instrumentalism: its very definition of the state as an institution (or set of institutions) precludes any possible generalization of the theory to all capitalist societies. In most of the dependent, underdeveloped countries, for example, we see military dictatorships and naked repression. The institutions of state and government—the Parliament and executive and judiciary along with the provincial and municipal administrations—are often circumvented or destroyed almost entirely so that the ruling class can maintain its power. In such cases the actions of the military are not determined by the existing institutions; instead the rule of law and the application of the Constitution is simply suspended.

Instrumentalism, then, is a highly empirical method which provides a useful perspective for the analysis of the state and the ruling class and for the study of the origins and development of *some* state policies within business groups *outside* the state. It is a perspective that emphasizes (and, indeed, over-emphasizes) the conscious domination and hegemony of the ruling class and its intellectuals.

Opposed to this first approach is "structuralism", most closely associated with the name of Nicos Poulantzas. It defines the state as an objective set of social relations underlying institutions, and regards the direct participation of business-men and business lawyers in governmental and other state institutions as un-important. Economic conflicts, market competition, and the atomizing effect of bourgeios law make social classes — in Poulantzas' view — highly divided groups, barely conscious of their own interests. The state must therefore provide unity and consciousness *for* the ruling class and initiate development strategies and policies, irrespective of the social composition of its political personnel. The emphasis of this perspective is on the *relative autonomy* of the state, (Poulantzas, 1968, 1974, 1978).

The structuralist viewpoint includes economic structuralism in both its American form (Baran and Sweezy, 1966, 1970) and the European state monopoly capitalist tradition espoused by Poulantzas. Both versions argue that state policies respond to the overall long-term economic needs of the entire ruling class. The structuralist perspective leads to a less "individualistic" and institutional analysis of the state, but fails to show empirically how the ruling class rules or to clarify the concrete relationships between (economic) classes and political structures. Poulantzas even argues that the state bureaucracy is as divided into social classes as civil society. This implies an even greater reduction in the relative autonomy of the capitalist state, an autonomy that Poulantzas had previously postulated but failed to demonstrate.

Structuralism is therefore a barely empirical and highly speculative theory of the state. Its main contribution is the definition of the state as a set of apparatuses or social relations, often sanctified by institutions but not synonymous with them.

The "Hegelian-Marxist" approach is based on the early writings of Marx and Engels and on some of Engels' later writings. It treats the state as an idea, a pure mystification. The Frankfurt school of J. Habermas, H. Marcuse and other very philosophical writers has adopted this perspective and contributed somewhat to understanding the problem of legitimacy. But they have not provided a definition of the state, nor an understanding of the mechanisms and varieties of ruling class domination, not any clarification as to how economic and social strategies are formed in either private business or the state (Habermas, 1975; Marcuse, 1968).

The fourth perspective may be referred to as "reproductivism" and appears in the works of James O'Connor, Pierre Bourdieu and Göran Therborn. This pers-pective sees the state as a set of apparatuses ensuring the economic, political or ideological reproduction of capitalist society. Therborn follows in the tradition of Marx and Lenin, defining classes as economic groups determined by the relations of production. Since classes in any existing capitalist society are linked to different modes of production and since the different economic and social fractions of the bourgeoisie are based on different economic sectors and regions, the state has the means by which to endow one class or one fraction of a capitalist class with power over the other classes or class fractions. It can do so by either ensuring the expanded reproduction of that class or class fraction, or by intensifying the ex-traction of surplus value (the rate of exploitation) in favour of that class or class fraction. How then does the ruling class rule? By reproducing the economic, political and ideological relations of domination. Which class fraction then rules? The fraction that uses state policies to guarantee the expanded reproduction of its dominance within society.

Therborn keeps his distance from instrumentalism. He notes that in some cases — the absolutist state being one example — the governing class is not the ruling class. On this issue he sides with the structuralists:

From the perspective of reproduction, the dominant question of all subjectivist approaches to the study of power — "Who rules: a unified elite or competing leadership groups? Is the economic elite identical with or in control of the political one?" — is displaced by the interrogation: "What kind of society and what basic relations of production are being reproduced?" (Therborn, 1978: 137-8).

Reproductivism is a useful empirical perspective. Its analysis of accumulation (O'Connor) and social reproduction (Therborn, Bourdieu) contributes to an understanding of the dynamics of capitalist society, to the study of key dimensions of state functions, and to identifying the ruling class.

Since the 1970's neo-Marxism has come a long way towards elaborating a theory of the state that treats the political arena seriously. Various but converging perspectives now consider the sphere of politics as an autonomous structure with its own history and laws of development, with its own personnel, and with various types of relationships to the economy. I call these viewpoints "state autonomism". One of the most noteworthy contributions to this all-embracing theoretical work comes from Hal Draper, who has shown (contrary to the views of Poulantzas) that the works of Marx and Engels treat the state bureaucracy as a specific social group, one distinct from economic classes (Draper, 1977 and 1978).[1] Other contributions to this body of work are the Latin American writings of J.H. Cardoso, L.C. Bresser Pereyra, G. O'Donnell and C.E. Martins, showing the autonomous role of the bureaucracy (mainly the military) in the state policies adopted in that region (Cardoso, 1975; Bresser-Pereyra, 1977; Martins, 1977; O'Donnell, 1982); Bob Jessop's neo-institutional analysis from England (Jessop, 1977 and 1982); and the works of P. Evans, T. Skocpol and F. Block in the U.S.A. (Evans, 1979; Skocpol, 1979; Block, 1977).

These writers share the view that the bureaucracy is neither a class not a set of class fractions, but a social group with no direct relationship to the means of production. Normally the behaviour of the bureaucracy as a whole is determined by the hierarchical decisions of its top leaders, both civilian and military. The state is a collection of apparatuses organized according to two main institutional categories: bureaucracy and state enterprises.

For those who share this perspective, the question as to whether or not the ruling capitalist class actually *governs* is one open to empirical observation. Historical evidence shows different patterns of control by the ruling class over state institutions. In some cases the top state managers can achieve a high level of autonomy from parts of or even the entire ruling class. Whether they actually do so depends on a wide variety of characteristics and processes in the political sphere, the economy and the state itself. The deep fragmentation of the ruling class observed in dependent societies is often associated with a large degree of state autonomy.

Although the state takes different social and institutional forms in relation to different types of class struggle and domination, the general trend is towards increasing complexity, bureaucratization and autonomy. The state's ever-growing intervention in the economy is a response not only to the ruling class's own financial imperatives but also to "internal" pressure from the top bureaucracy, which has its own electoral constraints along with the need for economic stability and growth. Nevertheless, the degree and specific forms of state intervention vary from one society to another. The Canadian state, for example, is much more interventionist than the American, much less so than the French or Japanese; while the resort to state enterprises as a solution to particular industrial problems is more widespread in Canada than Japan, and in France than in Canada.

In concluding this review of theoretical perspectives I want to stress the fact that my own point of departure is one close to "state autonomism" with elements borrowed as well from "reproductivism" and "instrumentalism". I consider these three approaches to be more complementary than contradictory, and I define the state as a set of social relations consolidated by institutions and sub-divided into bureaucracy and public enterprises. Bureaucratic institutions represent a specific social group that should not be confused with a social class. The bureaucracy is an autonomous group within society with its own rules governing mobility, its specific forms of revenue, and its particular lines of command and promotion. Members of the bourgeoisie *can* occupy the top bureaucratic positions, as well as the administrative positions within state enterprises. The instrumentalists argue that this happens frequently whilst the structuralists promote the opposite view. The frequency with which this occurs is open to empirical research.

These approaches have ignored one essential problem: the analysis (mainly at the micro-economic level) of state intervention in the economy. Some Marxists cling to the model of perfect competition found in *Das Kapital* while others have built highly abstract macro-economic models of monopolistic competition, like the state monopoly capitalist theories from France and Italy and the American version of monopoly capitalism. But there are no theses to be found concerning the methods by which the capitalist state can effect business strategies at the corporate or industrial level.

This neglect forces us to turn to the economics literature on oligoplistic behaviour and strategy. One extremely useful source to fill the theoretical gap is the work of the Canadian economist Stephen Hymer (Hymer, 1976). Hymer has adopted Alfred Chandler's definition of business strategy, which is as follows:

Strategy can be defined as the determination of the basic long-term goals and objectives of an enterprise, and the adoption of courses of action and the allocation of resources necessary for carrying out these goals. Decisions to expand the volume of activities, to set up distant plants and offices, to move into new economic functions, or become diversified along many lines of business involve the defining of new basic goals.

Business strategies, therefore, are micro-economic phenomena that occur only in oligopolistic markets. (In a situation of perfect competition, business behaviour would be completely controlled by the anonymous and fragmented market). Several aspects of business strategy are worth noting here:

1) Strategies come into being in a business environment which includes large enterprises, trade unions, foreign competition and (increasingly) state

intervention. Decisions to multinationalize, to take over another firm or to expand operations are made more and more frequently as a response to state policies and guidelines, such as tariff and non-tariff barriers, tax incentives, and government subsidies. The capitalist state has become one of the most important factors shaping the strategies of big business (Chandler, 1962; Channon, 1973).

2) Even when the strategies adopted involve decisions at the micro-economic level, changes in the economic environment (such as a new tariff barrier) often affect all the firms in a given industry. Furthermore, the interaction among competing oligopolies usually dictates that their business strategies be similar. One example of this is the local purchasing laws adopted by the American federal state and the various American state governments, laws which have prompted many Canadian firms to invest in the United States over the past twelve years. Oligopolistic firms also tend to follow their industry leaders by copying their national and multinational strategies, as has often been pointed out (Knickerbocker, 1973). In both cases the business strategies of many firms tend to be similar.

3) The concept of business strategy does not imply any particular degree of social or collective consciousness among the bourgeoisie. These strategies are actual patterns of behaviour, rather than merely symbolic expressions of corporate sttitudes. They are not ideologies, even economic ideologies; they are observable activities with long-term goals and consequences.

The Canadian Bourgeoisie

As a social group the Canadian bourgeoisie is deeply divided. With so many large foreign multinational corporations present in Canada, there is a comprador counterpart to the autochthonous Canadian bourgeoisie whose job is to manage these foreign subsidiaries. In 1980, nearly 27% of the Canadian economy was under foreign control.

The regional character of the Canadian economy provides a second basis for cleavage within the bourgeoisie. Most of the large corporations (both autochthonous companies and foreign subsidiaries) operate on a pan-Canadian basis, while most small and medium-sized enterprises serve specific regional markets. During the period since the Second World War, Quebec and Alberta have provided the most fertile ground for the development of regionally-based fractions of the capitalist class.

Ethnicity is a third source of cleavage. Historically, the Canadian bourgeoisie has been white Anglo-Saxon, and Protestant, but the post-Second World War period has seen new ethnic groups rising to positions of ownership and control in large corporations. The Canadian capitalist class is now deeply divided along linguistic and ethnic lines, with the Anglophone/Francophone split the single most important cleavage.

The high level of concentration in the Canadian economy ensures that most of the assets are owned by a very small number of corporations. In 1977, for example, 77% of all non-financial industries were owned by only 4,404 corporations (1.7%). Most of these corporations were part of conglomerates like Canadian Pacific, Argus Corporation or Power Corporation. These giant conglomerates are led by a Canadian "haute bourgeoisie", while small and medium-sized capitalists own and control the remaining 250,000 corporations. (Statistics

Canada, 1983: 2).

These divisions within the Canadian bourgeoisie are only partially reflected in the political sphere. The new French-Canadian bourgeoisie along with the bourgeoisies of other rising ethnic groups tend to be more interventionist; they need public support to consolidate their market positions. The older established WASP enterprises are much more conservative. While the non-WASP capitalists (possibly 20% of all large corporations) tend to support the Liberal Party, most of the traditional Anglo-Saxon establishment supports the Progressive Conservatives. The foreign subsidiaries hire Anglo-Saxon managers almost exclusively, and thereby increase the conservative bias of the Anglophone bourgeoisie.

Although 80% of the Canadian business milieu is Conservative, it is the Liberals who have held power for almost the entire post-Second World War period. This situation is a result of the voting patterns among the two main ethnic groups. The Anglophone vote is divided, with the middle and upper classes voting mainly Conservative, and the working class vote (both blue and white collar) split between Conservatives, Liberals and New Democrats. The Francophone vote, on the other hand, has been massively Liberal. It would appear that in the total absence of a labour tradition, the French-Canadian upper classes are able to maintain their ethnic social base, while the Anglophone capitalists, contending with a working class political tradition imported by British and other immigrants, are not.

The Canadian political scene is therefore far from being a simple mirror image of the class system. The specific characteristics of the Canadian political structure mean that neither the largest ethnic fraction of the bourgeoisie (Anglo-Saxon) nor the most important linguistic group (Anglophone) are capable of governing alone. A simple instrumentalist model does not fit Canadian reality.

At the socio-economic level the Canadian bourgeoisie is a highly-organized group. There are hundreds of industrial, sectorial and multi-sectional employers' associations like the Canadian Bankers Association, the Canadian Manufacturers Association and the Canadian Chamber of Commerce. Along with their role as pressure groups (helping to push legislation through Parliament) these associations also produce and distribute business information and ideology. More long-range and global economic policies are taken up by private non-profit and "non-political" organizations like the Canadian-American Committee, the Conference Board of Canada, the continentalist C.D. Howe Research Institute and the nationalist Canadian Institute for Economic Policy. All these organizations provide effective centres for the development of consciousness and political activity within the capitalist class.

The Canadian state is a complex and divided but robust set of institutions. Behind its most visible institutions of government, education and the judiciary lies hidden a second level of much more important structures: the state corporations. The first level is controlled by a state elite (Olsen, 1980) while the state enterprises at both the Federal and Provincial levels are firmly controlled by the Canadian autochthonous bourgeoisie (Niosi, 1981; Fox and Ornstein, 1983).

Traditionally, these crown corporations have provided infrastructure, energy and services; examples of this role include the Canadian National Railway (CNR), the Canadian Commercial Corporation, the Export Development Corporation, and the various provincial hydro electric companies. But state corporations are no longer confined to this traditional role. They are increasingly active in the more profitable mining industries such as oil and gas, potash, coal, asbestos, and uranium, and in sophisticated manufacturing enterprises like pharmaceutical products, copy machines, petrochemicals, aircraft production, and oil rigs. Nearly 20% of the assets of all Canadian non-financial industries are owned by crown corporations. The initiative behind the creation of these public ventures has come from either state managers, as in the cases of Polysar, Petro-Canada, and the Saskatchewan Potash Corporation, or from the Canadian indigenous bourgeoisie, as happened with the Canada Development Corporation and the Quebec General Investment Corporation (Niosi, 1981).

Continental Nationalism as a Reproductive Strategy

The development strategy of large indigenous Canadian firms has been characterized over the past decade and a half by two main elements: Canadianization, and multinational expansion (chiefly in the United States). These twin dimensions of business strategy are strongly conditioned by the policies of the Canadian state.

The process of Canadianization began in 1970. The latest report from CALURA (Corporate and Labour Union Returns Act) says that "foreign control of Canadian corporations reached its peak in the early 1970's. Since then, as a result of mainly government and private acquisitions, foreign control has declined" (Statistics Canada, 1983: 19).

Some of the government acquisitions, such as those by Petro-Canada, the Saskatchewan Potash Corporation, the Quebec National Asbestos Corporation, and the Canada Development Corporation, have received much public attention,

TABLE I: Sales, All Non-financial Corporations, 1970 and 1980 (%)

	1970	1980	Difference
Foreign	36	36.5	+0.5
Canadian, private sector	49	51.9	+2.9
Canadian, government sector	5	5.6	+0.6
Unclassified	10	5.0	-5.0
Total	100	100	

Sources: Statistic Canada (1970: 158-9; 1983: 42)

TABLE II: Assets, All Non-financial Corporations, 1970 and 1980 (%)

	1970	1980	Difference
Foreign	36	27.3	-8.7
Canadian, private sector	40	52.3	+12.3
Canadian, government sector	18	17.2	-0.8
Unclassified	6	3.2	-2.8
Total	100	100	

Sources: Statistics Canada (1970: 21; 1983: 43)

but private acquisitions have actually been more important. Government enterprises have only maintained their share of sales and assets of all non-financial corporations, but the decade from 1970 to 1980 saw Canadian enterprises increase their share of sales by almost 9% and their share of assets by more than 12%. During the same period foreign control declined by 4.5% in terms of sales and 8.7% in terms of assets. This information is detailed in tables I and II.

Government policies have played a key role in this process of Canadianization, with the oil and gas industry one of those most affected by initiatives from the Federal and Provincial levels. Two crucial factors in the Canadianization of the petroleum industry have been the National Energy Policy introduced in 1980, and the development of large state enterprises like Petro-Canada and Alberta's Nova Corporation. The latest estimates show Canadian-controlled assets in the domestic petroleum industry jumping from 10.4% in 1971 to 57.0% in 1982. (Petroleum Monitoring Agency Canada, 1983:19). Private enterprise owns somewhere between two-thirds and three-quarters of these assets while the remainder is owned or controlled by crown corporations.

The process of Canadianization has not been confined to the petroleum industry. Other mining industries such as coal, potash and asbestos have played an important role in the rapid growth of Canadian private and public enterprise during the last decade. In the manufacturing sector foreign control declined mainly for resource-related industries such as oil refining and primary metals. Tables III and IV show the main trends.

The Canadian government has provided the legal framework for the process of Canadianization, but the various nationalist policies have benefitted mainly autochthonous private capital. More than thirty large foreign subsidiaries have been bought out since 1970. The purchase list includes many cornerstones of foreign control including Canadian International Paper, Canadian Johns Manville, Kaiser Coal, a dozen medium-sized oil and gas producers, six potash mining companies, and all the largest foreign-controlled real estate developers.

As Canadian firms consolidate their positions in different industries, the new domestic oligopolists are pushed towards multinationalization. During the 1970's the traditional Canadian transnationals like Inco, Massey-Ferguson, Polysar, Brascan and Alcan were joined by newer domestic giants. Among the kinds of industries moving abroad were some of the large oil companies (Petro-Canada, Denison Mines, Hiram Walker Resources and Pan-American Petroleum), the giant mass media enterprises boosted by the nationalist measures of the 1960's (Thompson Newspapers, MacLean-Hunter, Rogers Cablesystems), telecommunications producers (Northern Telecom, Mitel), and real estate developers (Olympia and York, Cadillac Fairview, Trizec, Campeau).

The main host country for these new Canadian multinationals is the United States. Canadian direct investment in the U.S.A. has grown very rapidly; from 1971 to 1981 it increased by 370% while American direct investment in Canada increased by only 123%. Among the nearly fine hundred Canadian corporations active in the United States, Seagrams deserves special mention as the largest foreign investor. Other Canadian companies with substantial investments in the American economy include Alcan Aluminum, Bata Shoes, Amca International (formerly Dominion Bridge), Inco, Massey-Ferguson, McMillan Bloedell, Moore, Northern Telecom, Polysar and Hiram Walker. The "Big Five" Canadian banks

TABLE III: Foreign Assets in Canada
(% of Foreign Assets by Industry 1970 and 1980)

	1970	1980	Difference
Agriculture	13	4	-9
Mines	69	45	-24
Manufacturing	58	48	-10
Construction	16	10	-6
Public Utilities	8	5	-3
Wholesale Trade	27	24	-3
Retail Trade	22	13	-9
Services	22	15	-7
Total, non-financial industries	36	27	-9

Sources: Statistics Canada (1973; 1982)

TABLE IV: Foreign Manufacturing Assets in Canada
(% of Total Assets by Industry, 1970 and 1980)

	1970	1980	Difference
Petroleum and Coal Products	100	70	-30
Primary Metals	43	13	-30
Machinery	75	52	-23
Transportation Equipment	85	71	-14
Wood Products	33	20	-13
Metal Fabricating	47	34	-13
Electrical Products	65	54	-11
Furniture	21	12	-9
Food	37	29	-8
Miscellaneous Manufacturing	51	43	-8
Leather Products	30	23	-7
Paper and Allied Industries	42	35	-7
Knitting Mills	21	15	-6
Chemical Products	81	77	-4
Printing, Publishing	15	12	-3
Rubber Products	93	91	-2
Clothing Industries	13	14	+1
Textile Mills	52	54	+2
Non-Metallic Mineral Products	63	70	+7
Beverages	20	32	+12
Tobacco Products	84	100	+16

Sources: Statistics Canada (1973; 1982).

and the largest Canadian privately-owned media corporations can also be added to this list (Niosi, 1982).

The Canadian state has neither monitored nor tried to reduce this flow of Canadian capital into the American economy, a flow that reverses previous trends; in 1970 there was 6.6 dollars of American direct investment in Canada for every Canadian dollar of direct investment in the U.S.A. while by 1981 this ratio had fallen to 3.8 American dollars to one Canadian dollar. (U.S. Dept. of Commerce, various years)

Canadian foreign direct investment has also become more geographically concentrated in the United States. In 1969 some 55% of Canadian direct foreign investment was in the U.S.A. while ten years later this figure stood at 61% Canadian enterprise is increasingly continental both in terms of market orientation and in terms of investment patterns.

Conclusion

Although the Canadian bourgeoisie is highly divided as a social group, its indigenous element (both Francophone and Anglophone) has succeeded in establishing itself as a ruling class. It directly controls half the state apparatus, namely the crown corporations, in alliance with the senior state elite. This fact provides important empirical support for the instrumentalist viewpoint.

Over the last fifteen years Federal economic policies have promoted Canadianization as a major, but often unadmitted, goal. Canadian-owned private enterprise has responded favourably to these policies and since 1970 dozens of large foreign subsidiaries have come under Canadian control. The strengthening of indigenous business has pushed these corporations towards international expansion, mainly in the U.S.A.

The emergence of continental nationalism as a coherent development strategy lends support to the reproductivist theory. Continental nationalism involves the expanded reproduction of the Canadian indigenous bourgeoisie in its existing and traditional forms: as a mainly financial-commercial and resource-related class. The strategy is *not* intended to alter Canadian technological dependency, to build up our truncated industrial structure, or to make Canada more independent of the American economy. Adherence to this strategy will only continue Canada's role as a supplier of energy, minerals and semi-finished goods for the American market. The only change such a strategy will bring about is that more of the companies producing these primary resources will be Canadian.

Continental nationalism is a development strategy constructed jointly by senior state managers such as Herb Gray and Marc Lalonde, and intellectual leaders of Canadian business such as Walter Gordon and Senator Molson. It has not been *imposed* by the state (something business would not have accepted), nor by business leaders. It is in fact a compromise that has been worked out between the more conservative elements of Canadian business, who want less government intervention, and the more nationalist wing of industry and the upper state bureaucracy, who advocate a full-fledged industrial policy. Those opposed to the strategy include American businesses in Canada and the U.S.A., and larger Canadian corporations including the banks, whose opposition to nationalist economic policies is based on fear of retaliatory legislation affecting their international operations.

The state autonomy viewpoint also helps make sense of the development of continental nationalism during the 1970's. The senior state bureaucracy has played a major role in shaping this strategy by developing and implementing nationalist policies aimed at the Canadianization of many of the important mining, service and manufacturing industries. As a business strategy, continental nationalism represents a compromise between Canadian business leaders and the state.

Continental nationalism is only one of the options open to the Canadian bourgeoisie, and not necessarily the best. As the political climate favours more conservative politicians and businessmen we shall see other strategies take shape. The continental dimension may take precedence over the nationalist aspect and the relations between the comprador and indigenous bourgeoisie will adjust accordingly. Such developments make the Trudeau era an interlude, a short-lived reversal in the dependent development of Canadian society.

Notes

1. It is interesting to note that twenty years before, another detailed account of Marx, Engels and Lenin's theories of the state had arrived at the same conclusion (Moore, 1957).
2. I have examined the internal composition of the Canadian bourgeoisie in a more detailed way in a separate article (Niosi, 1983).

References

Baran P. and Sweezy P., *Monopoly Capital,* New York: Monthly Review Press, 1966.
Block, F., "The Ruling Class Does Not Rule", *Socialist Revolution,* 33: 6-28, 1977.
Boccara, P., *Etudes sur le C.M.E., sa crise et son issue,* Paris: ed. Sociales, 1974.
Bourdieu, P., *La reproduction,* Paris: Miniut, 1970.
Bresser Pereyra, L.C., *Estadô e subdesenvolvimento industrializado,* S. Paulo: Brasiliense, 1977.
Cardoso, J.H., *Autoritarismo e democratizaçao,* Rio: Paz & Terra, 1975.
Chandler, Jr. A.D., *Strategy and Structure,* Cambridge: MIT Press, 1962.
Channon, D., *The Strategy and Structure of British Enterprise,* London: MacMillan, 1973.
Domhoff, G.W., *Who Rules America?,* E. Cliffs: Prentice Hall, 1967.
Domhoff, G.W., *The Higher Circles,* New York: Random House, 1971.
Domhoff, G.W., *The Powers That Be,* New York: Random House, 1979.
Draper, H., *Marx's Theory of Revolution — State and Bureaucracy,* New York: Monthly Review Press, 1977.
Draper, H., *Marx's Theory of Revolution — The Politics of Social Classes,* New York: Monthly Review Press, 1978.
Esping-Anderson, G., Friedland, R., and Wright, E.O., "Modes of Class Struggle and the Capitalist State", *Kapitalistate:* 4-5: 186-220, 1976.
Evans, P., *Dependent Development,* Princeton: Princeton University Press, 1979.
Fox, J. and Ornstein, M., "The Unity of State and Corporate Elites?", Vancouver, Paper to the CSAA Meeting, 1983.
Gold, D.A., Lo, C.Y.H. and Wright, E.O., "Recent Developments in Marxist Theory of the Capitalist State", *Monthly Review:* Oct: 2-43 and Nov: 36-51, 1975.
Habermas, J., *Legitimation Crisis,* Boston: Beacon Press, 1975.
Herzog, P., *Politique économique et planification en régime capitaliste,* Paris: éd. Sociales, 1971.
Hirst, P., "Economic Classes and Politics", in A. Hunt (ed.) *Class and Class Structure,* London: Lawrence and Wishart, 1977.
Hymer, S., *The International Operations of National Firms,* Cambridge: M.I.T. Press, 1976.
Jessop, B., "Recent Theories of the Capitalist State", *Cambridge Journal of Economics,* 1, (IV): 353-73, 1977.
Jessop, B., *The Capitalist State,* Oxford: M. Robertson, 1982.
Knickerbocker, F., *Oligopolistic Reaction and Multinational Enterprise,* Cambridge Mass: Harvard University Press, 1973.

Magdoff, H., *The Age of Imperialism,* New York: Monthly Review Preess, 1970.

Marcuse, H., *One Dimensional Man,* London: Sphere Books, 1968.

Martins, C.E. (ed.), *Estado e Capitalismo no Brasil,* Rio: Hucitec-CEBRAP, 1977.

Milibrand, R., *The State in Capitalist Society,* London: Weidenfeld & Nicolson, 1969.

Moore, S., *The Critique of Capitalist Democracy,* New York, 1957.

Niosi, J., *Canadian Capitalism,* Toronto: J. Lorimer, 1981.

Niosi, J., *Les multinationales canadiennes,* Montréal: Boréal-Express, 1982.

Niosi, J., "The Canadian Bourgeoisie — Towards a Synthetical Approach", *Canadian Journal of Political and Social Theory,* 7, 3: 128-150, 1983.

O'Connor, J., *The Fiscal Crisis of the State,* New York: St. Martin's Press, 1973.

O'Donnell, G., *El estado burocratico-autoritario,* Buenos Aires: Ed. de Belgrano, 1982.

Olsen, D., *The State Elite,* Toronto: McClelland & Stewart, 1980.

Parti Communiste Français, *Traité marxiste d'économie politique. Le capitalisme monopoliste d'Etat,* Paris: Ed. Sociales, 1971.

Petroleum Monitoring Agency Canada, *Report 1982,* 1983.

Poulantzas, N., *Pouvoir politique et classes sociales,* Paris: Maspéro, 1968.

Poulantzas, N., *Les classes sociales dans le capitalisme aujourd'hui,* Paris: Seuil, 1974.

Poulantzas, N., *L'Etat, le pouvoir, le socialisme,* Paris: P.U.F.

Skocpol, T., *States and Social Revolutions,* Cambridge: Cambridge University Press, 1979.

Statistics Canada, Catalogue 61-210, Ottawa, various years.

Therborn, G., *What Does the Ruling Class Do When it Rules?* London: New Left Books, 1978.

U.S. Dept. of Commerce, *Survey of Current Business,* Washington, various years.

III
Capitalist Class Cleavages

The Political Economy of Aborted Development: The Canadian Case

Gordon Laxer

A: Foreign Ownership and Development

On the whole Canadians continue to believe – wisely, I think – that a limited but prosperous national existence is preferable to a pure, poor nationality.

—Michael Bliss, 1970

Foreign investment makes us richer but less Canadian. Advocates of continentalism and laissez-faire economics see the Canadian dilemma in these terms. "Canada cannot meet its capital needs from within its own borders," stated Rowland Frazee (1984), president of the Bank of Montreal; "Unless we want a steady decline in our living standards, there is no choice about importing capital." George Ball, (1968), former U.S. Under Secretary of State and chairman of Lehman Brothers International argued that the free flow of trade and capital threatens Canadian sovereignty:

Canada, I have long believed, is fighting a rearguard action against the inevitable ... Sooner or later, commercial imperatives will bring about free movement of all goods back and forth across our long border; and ... it will become unmistakably clear that countries with economies so inextricably intertwined must also have free movement of the other vital factors of production – capital, services and labour. The result will inevitably be substantial economic integration, which will require for its full realization a progressively *expanding area of common political decision* (emphasis added) (113).

Ironically, the conservative nationalists of old agreed. John A. MacDonald, architect of Canada's National Policy (1879-1930), attempted to create a more independent economy by resisting the economic pull of the United States. In his famous 1881 election speech, Macdonald warned that reciprocity (free trade) with the United States would "endanger our possession of the great heritage bequeathed to us by our fathers ... our tariff (would be) fixed at Washington, with the prospect of ultimately becoming a portion of the American union." But he conceded that free trade would increase Canadian prosperity. "With my utmost effort, with my latest breath, will I oppose the "veiled treason" which attempts by sordid means and *mercenary proffers* to lure our people from their allegiance" (Creighton, 1957: 375; emphasis added).

George Grant, a 20th century throwback to Macdonald's Canada, also posed the alternative in these terms in his landmark *Lament For a Nation: The Defeat of Canadian Nationalism* (1965). The "pure but poor" option was pitted against the "filthy but rich" choice. "Those who want to maintain separateness[1] also want the advantages of the age of progress. These two are not compatible, for the pursuit of one negates the pursuit of the other'' (76). In the age of progress and materialism it was obvious which choice would win. ''Continentalism is the view of those who do not see what all the fuss is about. The purpose of life is consumption, and therefore the border is an anachronism. The forty-ninth parallel results in a lower standard of living for the majority north of it'' (90).

On the ceiling of the Sistine Chapel in Rome, Michelangelo painted a striking picture of God the Creator reaching out to impart life to man the lifeless, inert mortal. There is a commonly held view that in a similar way, American capitalists gave life to modern Canadian industry through their expert management, advanced technology and infusion of risk capital. Without American help, it is argued, Canadians would still be eking out a primitive existence as hewers of wood and drawers of water. We should be grateful. It is almost as if the company that the Rockefellers bought (Imperial Oil) placed the petroleum in the ground for us at Leduc in 1947, Canada's first great oil discovery.

This article examines whether Canada needed foreign ownership and foreign entrepreneurship in order to develop. To do this, I will look at the state of Canadian industry before the influx of American branch plants and at the experience of other countries that developed on their own, from an economic base as backward as Canada's. The cases of Sweden and Japan are of particular relevance. These themes take up the first half of the article. In the second half I investigate whether Canada had the choice of developing on an independent basis. Did geography or powerful external forces determine our fate or was it the peculiar politics and weak nationalism of Canadians that sent us down the path of dependent development?

Canada has more foreign ownership than any other advanced country and the average Canadian enjoys a high standard of living. These facts cannot be disputed. But whether the one caused the other is an open question. The traditional debate about the role of foreign investment has been stated in terms of growth and living standards. I want to shift the focus from growth to economic development.

Canadians were fortunate in wresting control of a huge land mass from disunited and sparsely populated aboriginal peoples. In most other countries, fewer resources had to be shared amongst much larger numbers. When this situation was combined with the dynamic and avaricious culture known as capitalism, bequeathed to us from northwestern Europe, a high standard of living ensured, almost from the day the newcomers set foot on the northern half of North America. Canadians of European descent have continued to enjoy high, though inequitable living standards.

One reason for past prosperity was Canada's unique ability to adjust population size to conditions of growth or decline. The United States provided an outlet for millions of Canadians in hard times. In the hundred years prior to the mid-1950's, as many people left Canada as entered it and most of them were lured to ''Eldorado'' across the border (Marr and Paterson, 1980:178). This meant that Canadians' incomes remained high even when the economy fared poorly. Thus living standards have been relatively independent of development or retardation. It has not often been so in most countries. Usually it is the workers of a nation who suffer along with the decline of their homeland, while capital is free to roam around the globe in search of high returns.[2] Recently however, because of U.S. immigration restrictions, the elasticity of Canada's population has been reduced. From now on, Canadian incomes will be more closely tied to Canada's level of development.

In 1902, when the Canadian West as the last North American frontier, Wilfrid Laurier caught the optimistic mood of Canadians with the prediction that "the 20th century will be Canada's." Forecasts at the time of a Canada with 100 million people seem wildly optimistic to us now. But a quick glance at a globe demonstrates that it was not the size of the country that has placed limits of Canada's population growth. An advanced industrial Canada could easily have supported more people. This is why I focus on development and retardation rather than on the living standards of the small numbers who live in present-day Canada.

TABLE 1
Percentage Distribution of World's Manufacturing Production[1]
1870-1913
(Population in millions in brackets; 1910-11 population in column two)

	1870	1913
Industrialized Countries[2]		
Britain	31.8% (26m)	14.1% (41m)
United States	23.3% (40m)	35.8% (92m)
Germany	13.2% (41m)	15.7% (65m)
France	10.3% (36m)	6.4% (40m)
Belgium	2.9% (5m)	2.1% (7m)
Late Follower Countries[3]		
Russia	3.7% (85m)	5.5% (161m)
Italy	2.4% (27m)	2.7% (35m)
Canada	1.0% (4m)	2.3% (7m)
Japan	[4] (34m)	1.2% (52m)
Sweden	0.4% (4m)	1.0% (6m)

Source: League of Nations, *Industrialization and Foreign Trade* (1948).

1. Includes finished products, semi-manufactured products such as unworked metals, sawn wood, pulp, coke, fertilizers, and cement, as well as manufactured foodstuff such as flour, bread, sugar and canned goods. Classification is based on International (Brussels) 1913 classification, which differs from the revised S.I.T. classification in current use.

2. Excludes Switzerland because of lack of data.

3. This table does not include Czechoslovakia, the Netherlands or Australia. See endnote 4 for explanation

4. 0.6% in 1896-1900, the earliest period when such information was available.

B: Canada in a Comparative Context:
Life Before Foreign Investment

In the world of the late 19th century, Canada was surprisingly developed. It was the eighth largest manufacturing country at the time of Confederation (1867) and by the 1890's had increased its share of world industrial production by 40% (League of Nations, 148:13). This was before the first major entry of American branch plants to Canada between 1900 and 1917 (Marshall *et al.,* 1976: 21). Ambitious development options did not seem unrealistic.

Canada did well in the older production techniques of wood and wind, possessing the third largest merchant marine in the world in 1867, if Prince Edward Island's and Newfoundland's fleets are included. As well, Canada was advanced in the newer technologies of finished steel production. Agricultural implements were Canada's forte in the days when farmers constituted a major portion of the market. Designed and made in Canada in domestically-owned firms, Canadian harvesters, mowers and ploughs were exported to over 40 countries, with Britain, Germany and France buying almost two-thirds of the total in 1900. Exports of these items more than equalled imports (Canada Year Book, 1901: 228; Denison, 1948: 95).

A handful of other countries were in the same phase of "initial industrialization"[3] then. These were the "late follower" countries that began the industrial revolution in the late 1800's, a century after England. Canadian manufacturing compared favourably[5] with that in the other late follower countries: Russia, Japan, Sweden and Italy. In fact, Canada was ahead in the *per capita* value of manufacturing production and was a respectable third in absolute terms, behind much more populous Russia and Italy. Japan and Sweden trailed.

Canada did not make the transition via domestic ownership to the "high tech" industries of the time — the internal combustion engine, chemicals and electrical goods industries. These were precisely the areas where American branch plants gained early dominance in Canada. Why were other, equally "backward" countries able to take the leap into the "second industrial revolution" on their own while Canada was not? It had to do with the politics of economic development.

Reared on the idea that politics are mildly diverting but basically irrelevant antics, this is not an easy answer for most Canadians to accept. But a look at Canada from the perspective of the development of other countries reveals that Canada had more options than Canadians realized and that our peculiar social and political milieu stood in the way of a fuller and more independent development.

To understand what happened and what did not happen in Canada, it is useful to provide some perspective. If Canadians had opportunities and did not know it, I want to know why. To aid our understanding of the Canadian case I am adopting a comparative approach, which is like a natural experiment. In a controlled experiment, scientists take care that the conditions in two cases are identical in all respects except the one that is being tested. If results differ, they know it is the variation in this factor and not in another that is the cause. In human history, of course, it is not possible or desirable to replicate a controlled experiment. We cannot play God. But we can come close to experimental conditions if we can find societies that were similar in respects which are important to the study. If these societies diverged in their development at a later stage we can then pinpoint the factor or factors which led to the divergence. I will go through such an exercise in this chapter. If I seem a long way from Canada at times, bear with me. The object is to increase our understanding of the Canadian case.

Late Follower Development

During his first year in office, U.S. President Ronald Reagan offered some advice for the underdeveloped countries of the world. It went like this: the best path to prosperity is to be found through free trade and private investment. No nation had ever been less developed that the fledgling United States of America and look how far it had come through economic freedom (*The Atlantic,* January 1982:7). The implication was obvious. Citizens of poor countries should stop complaining about the ubiquitous power of the multinational corporations and the unfairness of international institutions such as the World Bank, and follow the example of the sturdy American pioneer: work hard, save, and the economy will develop through the "magic of the marketplace."

With his ability to recount homespun American truths, President Reagan is undoubtedly "the great communicator." But he is no historian. The prescription to follow the American *laissez-faire* way is even more utopian today than it was 100 years ago when the late follower countries began their own industrial revolutions. They too wanted to join the exclusive club of developed countries. But the way to get there was not by copying the "least government is the best government" models of early industrializing Britain and the United States.[6]

That way was blocked by the very success of the pioneering countries. England underwent the great transformation to an industrial society first, and so for a moment in world history was "its only workshop, its only massive importer and exporter, its only carrier, its only imperialist, almost its only foreign investor" (Hobsbawn, 1968: 13). The loneliness of the pioneer was soon broken when a handful of other countries — France, the U.S.A., Belgium, Switzerland and later Germany — joined the march toward a society where for the first time it was possible to envision a life for the multitudes free from the dreary burden of poverty. (The reality for most was quite different from the promise in these class-divided societies.) Within a century of the first great inventions of the late 1700's, a world economy had been created. But it involved very unequal players: On one side were a half dozen rapidly developing countries which monopolized over 80% of manufacturing production for the world's market place. On the other side, were all the rest of the countries, none of whom yet possessed the means to compete against the astounding new technical and social methods of production.

The revolutionary new techniques drastically slashed the prices of many goods. For example, around 1800, cotton yarn, the basic building block for a modern clothing industry, fell to less than one-fifth of its pre-industrial price within the space of 20 years (Deane, 1965:89). Henceforth hand-made methods of production would fall one by one as new machine techniques developed and as a large number of workers were dispossessed from their land or their tools. In the already industrialized countries, new jobs were usually at hand to replace the work in the declining, pre-industrial sectors (This transition was never an easy process as the sorry plight of England's weavers in the early 1800's attests[7].)

For the vast majority of countries, the old jobs were threatened but new industrial jobs were not created to compensate. Modern transportation and communications systems removed the age-old barriers of distance which protected local producers in local markets. Suddenly, whether they wanted to be or not, all societies were part of this new world.[8] For example, Japan's policy of keeping out the "Komo no yabanjin" (red-haired barbarians) from the West, for fear of foreign contamination[9] and control, came to an end in 1853 when American gunboats entered Tokyo harbour and forced Japan to trade on unequal terms with the advanced countries (Norman, 1940:13, 37).

In the rapidly changing context of the late 1800's, the social and technical revolution began to take hold in several other nations. These were the late follower countries. Being a follower had its advantages and disadvantages. On the positive side, it was possible to import advanced technology, capital and management and to obtain supplies of skilled and disciplined labourers, whose ties to the land had been broken already. On the other hand, shortages of domestic capital, the withering effects of foreign competition and a myriad of internal social and political problems bedevilled the followers. It was certain that the late followers could not take the slow, *laissez-faire* path to independent industrialization.

Follower countries usually had social and political structures that were different from the industrial pioneers. Indeed, that is why they developed later. They either had archaic class structures that were ill-adapted to the creation of a free wage-labour force or else they belonged to areas of the world where large nation-states had not yet formed. Some countries, notably Italy, shared both problems at the same time.

In the older societies, those with "feudal"-like structures, the process of removing people from the land and of breaking up rigid social hierarchies had to be greatly accelerated. In the already developed countries of the late 1800's, the social and political revolutions had taken place *before* industrialization. But in the late follower countries, pressures of international competition and imperial threats to sovereignty forced the pace. The social revolution had to occur simultaneously with the economic revolution (Gerschenkron, 1962). New settler societies, such as British North America, largely avoided the problems associated with outdated social structures, but the pace of their development was forced as well. They had to establish independence and national unity at the same time as economic development. In either case of late follower development, therefore, political and social questions loomed large.

Capital Shortage

Late follower countries did not possess enough of their own capital to finance rapid industrialization easily. It had been different in England during its initial phase of industrialization. Costs had been less, and supplies of domestic capital more plentiful. For example, in cotton, the leading industry of the late 1700's, it cost only 6 pounds to equip a 40 cotton spindle shop.[10] One hundred years later, when finished steel products such as guns, sewing machines, typewriters, locks and farm machinery were the dynamic sector, costs of starting up such industries were much higher (Hobsbawm, 1968:175). By this time however, England was not short of domestic capital. When "Britain rule the waves," profits from international trade surged through the whole economy. Returns to industry were also abnormally high in the first seven or eight decades of British industrialization because Britain faced no rivals.[11]

Thus capital was amassed for British industrialization through short-term loans from commerce and through the reinvestment of manufacturers' profits. This was the *"laissez-faire"* path to capitalist progress, considered by most economists then and by neo-conservatives today as the "normal" course of development. These means had been more than sufficient for England. In fact, 60 or 70 years after the industrial revolution began, British capitalists were so bloated they became the great financiers of other countries' economies.

Late follower countries were in a different situation. They had not been the major trading nations of the world and had no history of slowly amassing capital within industry. Because the costs of starting up industry and transportation had risen and pressures to develop quickly had increased, the *laissez-faire* path was not possible. They faced two alternative models of financing development: (1) the independent route of reducing costs through "planning" and raising funds by tapping pools of domestic capital that lay outside of commerce and the fledgling industries, or (2) the dependent route of importing massive quantities of foreign capital to do the job.

Dependence would be temporary and not as severe if the foreign capital was borrowed — provided it was paid back. But if part of the foreign funds came in the form of ownership capital, as in multinational corporations, dependence could become permanent. In that case, the value of the external debt would continue to grow as the foreign companies built up their assets inside the country, without injecting new infusions of capital. Political sovereignty could also be jeopardized as foreign capital became an internal political force, and the threat of its sudden withdrawal enough to dissuade all but the most sanguine governments from attempts to reassert domestic ownership and control.

Regardless of which route was taken, the state had to play a large economic role in late follower countries, at least in the initial phase of industrialization — because market forces were insufficient. But which way to go? This is where politics as broadly shaped by ideas, national culture, class structure and ethnic homogeneity came into play. Whether the politicians and the public conceived of the development options or not, the state's policies had long-term economic consequences if one or the other path was traversed. Often it was less a matter of conscious choice than of a myriad of short-run decisions made to conform to the premises and demands of important political groupings in each country.

The Route to Independence

The route to independence was taken by all the late follower countries save Canada. It involved not only domestic control of capital in most of the country's productive institutions, but also a fair degree of technological sovereignty. The latter enables a society to generate industries which are in tune with its resource endowments, specialized skills and size of market. The Swedish iron and steel industry is a good example of this. Because Sweden had vast forest reserves but no coal, it continued to make steel on a competitive basis from charcoal, which is wood-based, long after the advanced countries had moved on to coal-using techniques. Then around 1900, Swedish ironmasters pioneered methods of making highgrade steel, using electric forges, powered by Sweden's abundance of hydro power. Some coal for steel making purposes did have to be imported, but Sweden had retained and then developed techniques appropriate to its own resource endowments (Milward and Saul, 1973:495). Such are the advantages of a high degree of techno-logical sovereignty.

Technological independence need not be achieved through autonomous inven-tion. Each country cannot expect to develop every product or technique on its own. But copying and adapting others' technologies within domestically-run companies can also lead to technological sovereignty. (It is sometimes called industrial espionage or just plain stealing but is a time-honoured practice.) Japan and Italy used these means successfully (Landes, 1965:172; Quinn, 1969).

In contrast, technological dependence is incurred when techniques are imported and not adapted to local conditions. Subsidiaries of transnational corporations are the classic case, buying machinery and techniques from head office, often at exor-bitant prices. Licensing inventions from other countries is a compromise position and the eventual outcome can go either way. It can be a stepping stone to in-dependence. In 1907, Kawasaki purchased the right to manufacture ship turbines from American Curtis and soon Japan was developing its own ship engines (Ando, 1966: 125). But licensing can also be the first stage towards takeover. In the same year, the McLaughlin carriage works of Oshawa, Ontario, which had branched out to auto production around the turn of the century, entered into a joint venture with Buick and soon was absorbed into the General Motors empire (Naylor, 1975 Vol. II:58). Thus technological sovereignty is often intricately related to capital sovereignty.

How did Sweden, Japan, Italy and czarist Russia[12] avoid the pitfalls associated with capital shortage and technological backwardness in late follower development? The answer, in a nutshell, is that by making institutional changes they preserved economic independence.

Shortages of domestic capital were overcome in two ways: 1) by reforming the system of financing industrialization through modifications to banking and by direct government expenditures for development and 2) by reducing the level of capital needed for development by a primitive form of government "planning". In these endeavours, an interventionist state was central to finding solutions to domestic capital shortage. This is where politics entered the picture.

Banks were crucial to financing new industry as well as the transportation and communications systems needed to connect markets, move workers to jobs and reach resources. Most countries began with a variant of British banking. During the early stages of the industrial revolution, merchants required more capital than manufacturers. So for the most part, banks were geared towards the short-term financing of trade. Some bankers' and merchants' credit reached the in-dustrialists, but usually for short periods to facilitate the movement of their wares (Crouzet, 1972). Capital for long-term investment usually was not forthcoming. Sharply increased costs of industrial start-up made this arrangement unsuitable for late follower development. All of them either modified their banking systems or else had the state step in to play the role of industrial financier. All, that is, except Canada.

Facing some of the same conditions as the late follower countries, Germany was first to be successful at a new type of investment banking that broke from the British tradition (Tilly, 1966)[13] German banks were much more oriented to the long-term capital needs of manufacturing and railway construction. Not only did they lend money more readily to industrialists who were just starting out, but they sold the stocks of struggling as well as established companies. When banks financed and sold stocks for small manufacturers, a whole new source of domestic capital became available to industry. Small investors, who otherwise would not have touched anything as speculative as industrial stocks, were reassured by the commitment of the large banks. Thus, it was through an institutional change, and not by the accumulation of more capital, that a new pool of domestic capital was opened up to industry. Politics determined whether or not this new kind of banking system would be allowed (Laxer, 1981).

By encouraging the creation of the building blocks necessary for an industry's success, investment banks often planned the development of whole new sectors of the economy. This sort of activity was illustrated in the Swedish electrical generating business. The Stockholms Enskilda Bank (SEB), a *de facto* investment bank owned by the Wallenbergs, the "Rockefellers of Sweden", took over the financing of the giant engineering firm ASEA by 1898. The company had developed electrical generators but could not sell them because there was little demand for electricity. The Stockholms Enskilda Bank did this for its client by becoming heavily involved in "the building of power stations, the purchase of waterfalls, the promotion of urban electrification, including tramways, and the establishment of suitable industries to use the electricity generated" (Potter, 1963:67). This was planning, not by the state, but by a privately-owned Swedish bank (Gasslander, 1962:212).

Banks were not the only means to finance and promote industry. The state itself could overcome the shortage of domestic capital and thus avoid the prospect of branch plant industrialization. Japan's Meiji government financed industry in the 1870's because domestic banks were too small, whether reformed or not, to start Japan down the road to industrialization quickly enough.

Japan was in a race against time; it was a question of developing rapidly on its own or becoming another China, humiliated and colonized by the Western powers. Except for the silk industry, which evolved largely under private auspices, virtually all modern Japanese industries had their beginnings as government enterprises. The state provided the capital, trained the first managers and skilled workers by importing foreign engineers for short periods, and brought in the latest equipment from abroad.

Later, the state relinquished much of its economic role when it sold most of its modern industries at fire sale prices, thereby virtually creating a small group of monopoly capitalists including Mitsui and Mitsubishi. The peasants were the unwilling financiers of capitalist industrialization, paying over half the value of their produce in taxes to the state (Smith, 1965).

In czarist Russia and in Italy, the state took a lesser but still important part in financing and aiding industrialization. Governments in both societies paid for much of the railway systems and used their influence over the railways and the military to procure supplies from domestically-based and domestically-owned companies (Cafagna, 1973:318; Crisp, 1976:31-2, 162). Again, the unfortunate peasant was the source of much of this state largesse. Late follower Sweden was a less backward country, so a reformed banking system was better able to plan and finance industry during the initial phase of industrialization (1870-1914). Nevertheless, Sweden's trunk rail lines were built and operated by the government.

Another sort of state "planning" was equally important for the independent route to industrialization. If the costs of the early part of the process could be lessened, while domestic funds for development were still meagre, the temptation to rely on foreign capital would be reduced. Much of the shortage of domestic capital was accounted for by the enormous costs of building a modern transportation and communications system. This was especially true for railways which are of little use when only partly built. It was imperative, therefore, to build the lines as cheaply and quickly as possible and to avoid duplication. Above all, England's *laissez-faire* example must not be copied.

By the 1830's, after Britain had been industrializing for half a century, its problem was a glut of capital, not a shortage. Eric Hobsbawm (1968: 113) describes the consequences of a capital surplus in Britain:

Because there were vast accumulations of capital burning holes in their owners' pockets (they had to find an outlet for their investments). Most of it was sunk into the railways and much of it was sunk without a trace ... much of it was rashly, stupidly, some of it insanely invested. Britons with surpluses, encouraged by projectors, contractors and others whose profits were made not by running railways but by planning or building them, were undeterred by the extraordinarily swollen costs of railways, which made the capitalization per mile of line in England and Wales three times as high as in Prussia, five times as high as in the USA, seven times as in Sweden.

Comparative estimates of railway costs for Italy, Japan and Russia during initial industrialization (1870-1914) are not readily available but they could not have been as high as Canada's. Many Canadian railways were built according to the British standard and price, some of it by the very same British contractors. Duplication of lines was rampant (Glazebrook, 1964). What had been a benign folly in Britain, took on quite a different character in Canada. The size of the country, the small population and the lateness of development, magnified the consequences of such extravagance. In contrast, Japan built relatively few lines even when its island character is considered. For example in 1907, when Japan launched the Satsuma, the world's largest battleship, fitted with Japanese-built Curtis turbines, the country had only quarter as many miles of railway as Britain (Ike, 1955: 226).

The paucity of lines was the only means by which Japan saved on railway expenditures though, for Japanese railways are said to have been "badly planned, poorly constructed and inefficiently managed" (Hirschmeier, 1965:230). When the private lines were nationalized in 1906, the government paid "about twice as much as the amount of their capital", thus continuing the tradition of state munificence to the newly created capitalists, via taxes obtained from the peasants (Halliday, 1974:60). For all the inflated costs though, the low overall mileage more than compensated. In Japan, capital expenditures were held down in other areas of the economy too. In road and bridge work, and in housing, labour intensive, premodern construction methods continued to be used (Ohkawa and Rosovsky, 1965:149).

Italy and Russia were not noted for strenuous efforts to reduce capital needs through careful railway planning. In fact costs were pushed up in both countries by government procurement programmes that encouraged high cost, domestically-made products (Lyashchenko, 1949: 543). As well, military and national unity considerations[14] increased the costs of railway construction. But neither were railway expenditures wildly extravagant. Although greater Russia had the largest railway mileage of any European country by 1914, its immense size and population meant that it had the fewest miles on both an area and *per capita* basis (Milward and Saul, 1977: 541). Italy was close to the European averages in these respects but the state avoided much duplication from an early point by dividing the country into four non-competing networks (Clough, 1964).

Building railways to bind a national community together for the first time was therefore not a constant in every country, either in terms of costs or the effects on the economy. It depended on the circumstances and how it was done. Perennially short of cash at first, late follower countries had a tendency to adopt less wasteful methods than England. This was especially true of Sweden, which built railways to an exacting standard but managed to do so at a drastically reduced cost per mile (Hedin, 1957). To some extent this was counteracted by the stress on "development" railways, which, as in the new world, were built ahead of settlement in order to facilitate growth. But the pattern of low cost railways in Sweden held nevertheless. Duplication of lines was usually reduced in late follower countries if construction was centrally planned.

Most late follower countries spent extravagantly on defence. For example, when debt servicing costs are removed, Russia spent almost half its budget on the army and navy between 1866 and 1885, on the eve of its industrial spurt (Von Laue, 1963:22). Other countries were less spendthrift on defence; Japan spent about one sixth of its revenue on the armed forces in roughly the same period (Smith, 1955:71), but military expenditures could still accentuate the need for foreign capital. With its miniscule armed forces, Canada stood in contrast to these countries. But as we shall see, while defence costs tended to increase reliance on foreign *loans,* they also provided the strongest motive for blocking foreign *ownership* of industry.

To sum up, most late follower countries dealt with shortages of domestic capital by 1) changing the banking system so that new sources of funds would flow into industry, 2) direct state aid for economic development and 3) state "planning" to lessen the amount of shortage. In these ways, the need to resort to capital imports was lessened. But they were not entirely removed in all cases. Sweden borrowed a great deal of foreign capital to finance its railways but did not allow much external ownership (Fleetwood, 1947; Kuznets, 1955). Czarist Russia blocked foreign ownership in certain strategic sectors, but encouraged its investment elsewhere. The threat of branch plant industrialization was only removed when the Bolsheviks wiped out all foreign indebtedness in 1918 by refusing to recognize the bourgeois obligations of its predecessors (Lewery, 1923).

Japan and Italy made very little use of external capital, partly because foreigners did not find them particularly attractive investment prospects. The absence of natural resources was one deterrent. Another was state indebtedness incurred during the difficult social and economic transformation, resulting in high inflation and the temporary inconvertibility of their bank notes. Neither condition was very enticing to the foreign investor. But of equal importance to low levels of capital imports were the domestic barriers erected to keep out foreign investment, particularly in the case of Japan (Halliday, 1974:55).

Why did other late follower countries actively block foreign ownership investment while Canada did not? It is logical to discuss this together with the question of technological sovereignty because both are related to the military-strategic issue.

Defence and Economic Independence

The late 1800's was the age of classical imperialism. The major Western powers entered into a mad scramble to plant their flags, carve up the globe and administer new colonies for their own benefit. Even the United States joined this largely European game with the occupation of Cuba and the Philippines and the artificial creation of the country of Panama. Most of the action was in Africa and Asia but the backward Western countries were not immune to the threat of foreign tutelage.

Industrialization changed the nature of warfare. It had been a grandiose duel, fought at a leisurely pace and confined to aristocrats and professional military men, operating according to strict codes of honour such as observing the "Truce of God" on the sabbath. It became total war, involving sneak attacks aimed at exterminating civilian populations, mobilization of mass conscript armies, and national efforts to coordinate industrial output and railway timetables (Pearton, 1982: 19-35). Gone were the days when the main military problem was to build a large enough war chest to hire mercenaries (eg, Swiss Guards). Securing the latest technologies of destruction became the principal concern. It was modern industry which could turn out longer range and more accurate guns, stronger armour and the means to transport men speedily to battle. No longer could economically backward nations be on an even military footing with the advanced countries.

This fact was brought home to Russia when it won the war but lost the peace against Turkey in 1877-8. In its historic drive for access to the Mediterranean and caught up in pan-Slav nationalism, Russia defeated Turkey in the Balkans, only to lose most of the spoils at the negotiating table with Britain in Berlin (Taylor, 1954: 228). Russia had to back down because its antiquated army was matched by undeveloped industry.

The Japanese "economic miracle" of which there has been so much talk of late was built to a great extent on a base of military industries. The Japanese learned the hard way that they could not remain in splendid isolation unless they constructed a fortress guarded by Western-style industry. The Japanese expressed this in the slogan "fukoku-kyohei" – rich country, strong army (Jansen, 1968:155). The reaction to Commodore Perry's intrusion in the 1850's was a modernizing revolution "from above", by part of the elite, whose cry was "Revere the Emperor, expel the foreigner". Their way of expelling the foreigner was to embrace Western technology and industry so closely that its output could be turned against the predatory Western powers. Herbert Norman, the son of a Canadian missionary in Japan and a great scholar of Japanese history, characterized the thinking of the Meiji government (1868-1911) in these terms:

What do we most need to save us from the fate of China? A modern army and navy. On what does the creation and maintenance of modern armed forces depend? Chiefly on heavy industries, engineering, mining and shipbuilding, in a word strategic industries (1940: 118).

It is difficult not to marvel at the successful effort of the Mito clan in constructing a reverbatory furnace for making iron in 1855. They had never seen a working model, had great difficulty in securing suitable materials and built it by following the instructions of Dutch textbooks. This was typical of the early Japanese armaments industries in the 1840's to 1860's.

The Western powers seemed able to recognize the status of only two kinds of countries: subject nations or victorious empires. There would be no halfway house of simple independence for Japan. The way to end the humiliating unequal treaties and extra-territorial rights imposed by the West, was to demonstrate that Japan was a Great Power. As Foreign Minister Inoue put it "We have to establish a new, European-style empire on the edge of Asia" (Jansen, 1968:175). This was done by defeating China and then Russia at war around the turn of the century. Once Japan was victorious, the Western powers ceased interfering in her internal affairs (Norman, 1940:198-201).

In Sweden and Italy, the military question was not as strongly related to economic development and national independence. But it was a factor. Sweden has a well-deserved reputation as a peaceful country. It has not gone to war since 1815, refuses to join military alliances and was the birth place of Alfred Nobel, dynamite king turned peace philanthropist. Yet Sweden had not purchased its neutrality and independence by renouncing all arms. The Swedish consensus during this century has been: "no adventure, no conquest, but plenty of arms for self-defence" (Scott, 1977:326).

In the 17th century, Sweden was one of Europe's major powers, controlling the Baltic Sea and able to push its armies deep into Europe. The cry "The Swedes are coming" was enough to terrorize people from the Alps to the Ukraine (Pauli, 1942:19). Sweden was a large munitions manufacturer and exporter, making 20,000 muskets in 1629-30 alone (Scott, 1977:189). Even after Sweden had fallen from great power status in the next century, defence continued to be a major preoccupation. The state lavished funds on the strategic industries – iron and ship-building (Samuelsson, 1968:102). Although Sweden was at peace between the Napoleonic Wars and the First World War, it came close to war in the Crimea, against Prussia over the Danish issue, against Norway in 1905 and was constantly apprehensive of Russian intentions (Scott, 1977:326). Thus the defence question continued to influence state policy and the direction of economic development. For example, Saab, the auto company, developed as an offshoot of the firm that built planes for the Swedish air force.

In the late 1800's, Italy struggled for recognition as a great power. National prestige was undoubtedly one of the motives, but liberating areas where Italians lived under foreign rule was another. Thus the military question in Italy had similarities to that in Japan. Italy pushed the Austrian Empire out of northwestern Italy with the help of France and then occupied Rome when French troops withdrew from that city to fight in the Franco-Prussian War (Taylor, 1954: 108-21).

Once national unification was achieved, Italy still had to develop a modern armed forces to safeguard its newly-won independence. As a country almost surrounded by water, Italy concentrated on sea power and by 1885 had the world's third largest navy. An effective navy, though, needed more than an intelligent command and mere numbers of ships. It needed technical superiority. Hence the state's interest in developing modern strategic industries that were located in Italy and thus under its control. To do this, the state fostered the steel and munitions works inland at Terni and imported up-to-date technology by licence arrangements and joint ventures with British munitions companies (Clough, 1964: 87; Pearton, 1982: 115).

Thus the late follower countries emphasized the creation of independent armaments industries to support modern armed forces. This involved the establishment of a domestic engineering sector that – coincidentally and largely without foresight – went a long way towards the general development of the technologies of the second industrial revolution: the internal combustion engine, chemicals and electrical goods. Once generated, these industries produced for civilian as well as military purposes. The benefits for economic diversification under domestic control were not generally planned, but they occurred because of the strategic logic of the late follower countries.

Strategic Industries and Foreign Ownership

We saw earlier that it was precisely in the new industries of 20th century technology that American manufacturers came to dominate Canadian industry. The creation of an independent armaments and engineering sector was not a strategic requirement, because Canada did not develop its own armed forces to an appreciable level before World War One. This was one of the main reasons Canada encouraged the branch plant route to technological imports while the other late follower countries tended to reject it.

Canadian Confederation (1867) occurred around the same time as the Unification of Italy (1870), the modernizing Meiji Restoration in Japan (1868), the emancipation of the serfs in Russia (1861) and the abolition of the noble estate in the Swedish Parliament (1865-6). On the surface, it looked like all the late follower countries were establishing modern, unified states in the same era. But Canada had a state with a difference. Although Confederation was partly a response to a military threat from the United States at the time of its civil war, Canadian foreign and military policy remained under British authority. This position was not foisted on Canada by the British Empire; in fact, the predominant opinion in official London was that Canada was a burden and a nuisance; the quicker it stood on its own, the better. Despite this, Canada opted for "dominion" status at Confederation, a mid-point between colony and full-nationhood.

It is true that after Confederation, British regular forces left Canada (1871) and a voluntary militia of moderate size was raised, but Canada continued to rely on protection behind the British shield. By 1900 or so, Canada's former enemy, the United States, had come to be seen as an additional guardian. Prime Minister Laurier summed up the view that Canada need not protect itself:

You must not take the militia seriously, for though it is useful for suppressing internal disturbances, it will not be required for the defence of the country, as the Monroe doctrine (proclaiming American military hegemony in the Americas) protects us against enemy aggression (Stacey, 1940:68).

By the First World War, even Australia had a navy, while Canada did not. When Britain declared war on Germany on August 4, 1914, Canada was automatically at war as well.

Canada's voluntary position as a dependency of the Empire (until near the end of the First World War, when Canadian generals were finally put in command of Canadian soldiers), coincided with the period when the industrial structure was established in its branch plant mould. The result was clear: no strategic logic, no compelling motive to block foreign ownership.

It was different in the other late follower countries. In the 1870's to 1890's, not only did Japan forbid direct foreign investment in its industries, but, during a period of extreme capital shortage, even refused the borrowing of foreign capital. Foreign mines and shipping investments were repatriated. The strategic question was the main factor. Bismarck, the architect of a militaristic and autarchic Germany, had advised a visiting Japanese mission of just such a policy in the early 1870's (Halliday, 1975:55). Furthermore, Japan had seen Turkey and Egypt lose autonomy after defaulting on foreign debt repayments (Norman, 1940:116). Strategic industries remained in state hands after most of the publicly-owned companies had been sold to private business. It was only after Japan was on the road to becoming a great power in the late 1890's that restrictions on foreign investment were eased. But they were never lifted entirely and foreign ownership did not come to play a big part in the Japanese economy (Halliday, 1975:305; Landes, 1965:96).

Military strategy did not push the Russians as far as the Japanese in restricting foreign investment. But then, unlike Japan, Russia had not been marked out for colonial status by the Western powers. The temptation to overcome the extreme shortage of domestic capital was great, and about half the capital employed from the 1870's to 1916, in early Russian industries, including mining, came from abroad. Development was undoubtedly speeded up by the process (McKay, 1970), but this did not mean that the military question was of no importance. It affected the character and nationality of foreign investment in Russia.

Germany rose to industrial prominence in spectacular fashion along with the Americans in the late 1800's. Consequently, like the Americans, German industrialists began to look abroad for scarce resources and new markets. Germany established subsidiaries in neighbouring countries, just as the United States did in Canada at the same time. Early German branch plants were remarkably similar to the American ones: they tended to be 1) wholly owned subsidiaries directed by the parent company 2) assembly operations which imported parts and machinery 3) in the same fields of new technology — electrical equipment, metal working and chemicals (McKay, 1970: 34, 172, 201; Marshall et al, 1976: 12-15). For Germany, the main location was Russian-occupied Poland, on their eastern border. An immediate reason for this was the 1868 Russian tariffs which blocked German exports to the area.

It appeared as if czarist Russia was starting down the road to branch plant industrialization and endangering its strategic independence at the same time. Foreign technology and foreign engineers played an overwhelming role in early Russian industrialization. The foreign entrepreneurs assumed, as they tend to do everywhere, that what was good at home was good abroad too. Thus Russian conditions of having plentiful supplies of cheap but unskilled and undisciplined labour, typical of most underdeveloped countries, did not affect the design of plants (McKay, 1970:119). Massive imports of fully developed technologies was the result.

But the push factors emanating from Germany[15] were not the only ones that counted. The czarist state was ambivalent about foreign ownership, as were the politically important classes in Russia. On the one hand, there was unabashed praise for the benefits of foreign capital by Count Witte, Finance Minister from 1891 to 1903. *"The inflow of foreign capital is, in the considered opionion of the Minister of Finance, the only way by which our industry will be able to supply our country quickly with abundant and cheap products"* (McKay, 1970: 11). But the actions of the state belied this open-door policy in important respects. In 1899, Witte disapprovingly enumerated Russian restrictions on foreign investment:

In Russia a foreign company can be opened only by a special decree of the Committee of Ministers ... Russian joint-stock companies in which foreigners are shareholders are permitted to have only a minority of foreigners on their board of directors. In ten provinces of Poland, in eleven provinces of the western regions of Russia, in Turkestan, the steppe regions, and the Amur district, neither foreign companies nor Russian companies with foreign participation are permitted to acquire property or exploit natural resources ... In permitting the activities of foreign companies in Russia, the government retains *the right to revoke at any time that permission and to demand the liquidation of any company.* (quoted in Van Laue, 1963: 180-1)

He could have added that foreign-owned companies did not receive equal treatment[16] with domestic ones regarding government contracts, including the state's railways, and with respect to loans from the state bank and receivership legislation (McKay, 1970: 284).

Preservation of Russian independence was a major factor in these restrictions (Feis, 1930: 212-13). It was not a coincidence that Russia permitted the establishment of German branch plants in strategic-related industries at a time when Russia and Germany were allies in the League of the Three Emperors (Taylor, 1954).

As relations with Germany soured in the 1880's and a Franco-Russian alliance blossomed, the pattern of foreign investment altered. Russia struck at German branch plants in 1887 by insisting that shareholders of joint-stock companies outside towns in Russian Poland, where the largest portion of German investment was situated, must be Russian. In response, many German entrepreneurs accepted Russian nationality (Crisp, 1960).[17] It is difficult to assess how much this affected German investment in all of Russia, because German capital continued to expand in Russian corporations until the First World War. However, Germany fell from the leading to the third largest foreign investor in Russian industry between 1890 and 1900 (McKay, 1970:32).

One of the first hints of an impending alliance with France came when Russia floated a loan in Paris in 1888 and soon after bought a large number of French rifles (Taylor, 1954:326). France was at pains to make Russia an effective ally by hastening its development through infusions of French capital, technology and know-how (Pearton, 1982: 102-4). As the alliance deepened, French investment, often taking the guise of Belgian capital, replaced German as the predominant source of foreign investment in the two decades prior to the First World War (Crisp, 1960: McKay, 1970).

French and Belgian investment was of a different character than German and implied more industrial independence. First, 85% of French capital in Russia was invested in bonds of a public nature (Crisp, 1960:90). Second, even though French ownership capital was preponderant in mining, metallurgy and engineering in south Russia and French capitalists controlled several powerful industrial investment banks, the relationship was not usually that between parent and subsidiary. Most French-owned companies were founded specifically for activity in Russia. This was true of British and Belgian-owned firms as well (Lewery, 1923: 3-5). Thus there was less foreign technological and managerial control than is usually the case with branch plants.

Russia paid the price of making large foreign loans: it lost some degree of sovereignty. For example, when Russian attempts to borrow funds in Paris failed, Russia reluctantly agreed to build a strategic railway that their French allies deemed advisable. Suddenly the loans became available (Feis, 1930:219).

Foreign direct investment in industry also compromised Russian economic and technological independence. But we do not know whether Russia would have followed the Canadian route toward branch plant industrialization if the 1917 revolution had not intervened. It is significant that czarist Russia was moving away from economic dependence on the even of the First World War. In Canada, early foreign investment was largely portfolio (loan) capital while later, direct (ownership) investment predominated. In Russia, during initial industrialization under the Czars, the character of foreign capital was moving in the opposite direction: from direct to portfolio investment. Furthermore, Russian investment banks took the lead in managing and lending to industries in Russia after 1908, muscling out the role of foreign banks in several instances (McKay 1970: 286-9; 368-85).

Anti-foreign investment opinion, often mixed with anti-Semitism, was strong amongst industrialists, the nobility, the intelligentsia and the *petite-bourgeoisie*. It affected government policy. The strategic question, and nationalism, were the bases for restrictions placed against foreign ownership in pre-revolution Russia. A much more significant institutional change, of course, came after 1917, when the Bolsheviks led the country in an autarchic direction, after the expected inter-national socialist revolution failed to materialize.

In Sweden, foreign ownership was less a strategic than a nationalist and economic issue. From 1870 to 1914, Sweden's developed neighbours revealed their predatory interest in her strategic resources, particularly iron ore. German and British rivalry for economic and military hegemony rose as the First World War approached; resources were a key element in this race. Sweden grappled with the issue of foreign ownership of its northern mines throughout this period.

In the boom years of the early 1870's German and English firms began to buy Swedish iron mines, ironworks and forests on a fairly large scale. This was at the beginning of Sweden's transition to an industrial economy and anxiety became sufficient to launch a Riksdag (parliamentary) investigation. Fleetwood (1947: 30-1) summarizes the views expressed in the Riksdag upon the sumbission of the investigation's report in 1874:

It was pointed out that if this movement (foreign acquisitions) was allowed to continue, a large part of Sweden would gradually be bought up by rich foreign firms and companies, because of Sweden's peculiar economic position in relation to other countries, i.e. because it was in the first phase of economic development, with practically untouched natural resources and a scarcity of capital ... Welcome as the capital these foreign firms and companies brought with them was, it could be obtained at too high a price, namely if all the profit of Swedish industry was to go abroad.

Thus as early as the 1870's, Swedish parliamentarians had the prescience to recognize that foreign ownership would bring growth in the short-run but economic retardation over the long term. Profits, the creator of new jobs in capitalism, would flow abroad to the owners of Swedish resources. To guard against this, a law was passed modifying the conditions under which foreigners could buy Swedish land and resources (Fleetwood, 1947: 29-31; Flinn, 1954: 34-8).

But the issue did not end there. A new steel-making technique[18] was developed in the late 1870's, making Sweden's iron ore, with its high phosphorus content, particularly desirable. In the mid-1880's, a British consortium of railway, steamship and smelter companies began to export Swedish iron ore to England, causing a major political storm in Sweden. Revived conservative nationalism, expressing itself in agriculture and industrial protectionism, joined forces with the vociferous opposition of central Swedish ironmasters to the export of iron ore. The state responded by nationalizing the British-owned railway in 1891 and forcing the British group out of the iron ore fields (Flinn, 1954: 36-40; Jonsson, 1969: 367-9).

Another attempt on Swedish iron resources was made in 1901, this time from the German companies of Krupp and Thyssen. Shares of two Swedish firms had been acquired surreptitiously and when word leaked out from Paris, another storm brewed. This time it was the political left, representing the working class and middle strata, which led the campaign for nationalization. By 1907 they were successful and the government assumed half the ownership of the two largest ore companies and full ownership of a number of the smaller ones. Foreign capital could no longer take over Swedish iron ore (Jonsson, 1969).

Although the military importance of iron had been a consideration in these skirmishes, the battle for control of Swedish iron ore had been fought mainly for reasons of economic nationalism. During and after the First World War, the strategic question came to the fore regarding armaments, resources and the primary manufacturing of iron. In 1916, during the First World War, a law was passed that prevented foreign entries into iron and steel, wood products and pulp, and mining. Six years later, the large Fagersta Bruks ironworks, acquired in 1907 by German interests, was bought by a company financed by the State-owned Riksbank and created on the joint initiative of the government and a private bank. In 1935, the newly elected Social Democrats ended German control over much of the Swedish armaments industry — an aircraft factory and the great Bofors armaments works. The Prime Minister stated that the objective was to "eliminate foreign interests wholly". Krupp lost control of Bofors and the airplane factory was closed (Braatoy, 1939: 88-9; Johansson, 1968: 82).

Thus, although Sweden's powerful neighbours cast an acquisitive eye in her direction, many of the initiatives were resisted as a matter of policy. This is one of the reasons foreign direct investment has never predominated in any sector of the economy (Johansson, 1968). Sweden's amazing technological inventiveness and the development role of its investment banks were also important in Sweden's avoidance of branch plant industrialization.

The Politics of Branch Plant Industrialization:
Economic Policies and Agarian Political Strength

John McKay (1970: 21), an historian of Russian development before the revolution, wrote: "If the choice must be between either foreign domination with rapid growth, or national integrity with slower economic progress, few nations will hesitate to pick the latter". Canada it seems, was the exception. Why was this?

Remember that the late follower countries handled their shortages of domestic capital by "planning" reductions in transportation expenditures, by reforming the banking system and by providing state finance directly to industry. Although usually importing loan capital to ease the shortage, the state restricted foreign ownership and favoured domestic investment in strategic industries and resources. Nationalism and defence were the main reasons. Governments also encouraged the development of indigenous technology and entrepreneurship, the latter through legislation or policy allowing for the creation of investment banks. These banks provided expertise as well as capital for their neophyte clients.

Canada did not do these things. Instead it took the easier route of importing most of the factors of production: capital, technology, management and skilled labour. The important consideration in Canadian minds in the 50 years after Confederation was that the job be done quickly because with the many citizens forced to emigrate to find work, Canada was bleeding. This was one of John A. Macdonald's major rationale's for the "National Policy" (1879 to 1930) of moderately higher tariffs, a railway to the Pacific and immigrants to fill the prairies:

We have no manufactures here. We have no work-people; our work-people have gone to the United States. They are to be found employed in the Western States, in Pittsburg, and, in fact, in every place where manufactures are going on. The Canadian artizans are adding to the strength, to the power, and to the wealth of a foreign nation instead of adding to ours ... if Canada had had a judicious system of taxation (a protective tariff) they would be toiling and doing well in their own country. (quoted in Bliss, 1970: 35).

It did not matter whether it was a Canadian or a foreigner who developed industry in Canada, so long as it was done. The Canadian Manufacturers Association revelled in the prospects of foreign businesses coming to Canada:

It is of small moment where the capital comes from that may be employed in developing our industries. When it is invested it at once becomes Canadian capital ... We gladly welcome all American capitalists who desire to join our procession in our march to industrial development and national greatness (quoted in Naylor, 1975 Vol. 11: 71).

The politicians concurred. In the 1911 reciprocity election, some Liberals broke with their party's support for limited free trade and endorsed the Tories' protectionist policies. For example, Lloyd Harris, a Liberal renegade, pointed to the tariff as the inducement for American companies to establish branch plants in Canada:

That is exactly what I want the Canadian policy to do. I want the American manufacturers to be forced to establish plants on this side of the line and provide work for our Canadian workmen if they want to have the advantage of supplying or home markets (quoted in Bliss, 1970: 30).

While Canadians were divided over the merits of free trade, few, it seems, disagreed about the benefits of American branch plants.

Why did Canadians think so differently than others regarding these matters? The standard argument is that Canada lacked a national industrial bourgeoisie which would protect the collective interests of future Canadian capitalists in sectors where there were as yet few domestically-owned firms. In the *Canadian Corporate Elite* (1975: 335), Clement argued that Canada did not have a national *industrial* bourgeoisie as did the U.S.A., Britain, Germany, France and Japan.

Instead, Canada's national bourgeoisie was mainly engaged in *trade and finance*. By implication, if Canada possessed a national bourgeoisie, its economy Instead, Canada's national bourgeoisie was mainly engaged in *trade and finance* (355). By implication, if Canada possessed a national bourgeoisie, its economy could have been as free from external ownership as theirs. This answer, like the argument that tariffs caused foreign investment, is too facile. The real reason is less obvious but follows from our previous discussion.

The idea that Canadian industrialists could have suddenly appeared in strength when modern industry was just beginning, seized the levers of the state and excluded foreign capital, is historical nonsense. It did not happen in other countries — countries that nevertheless managed to ward off foreign economic domination. Nor could it have happened. When the economy was primarily agricultural, as was inevitable in pre-industrial societies, social classes based on farming usually had the biggest influence on state policies. Their power continued into the first phase of industrialization. It was primarily they, not industrialists, who decided on defence issues, railways, banking legislation, immigration, land policies and everything else that affected the direction of economic development.

Thus, if late follower countries managed to guide their way through the shoals of foreign economic domination, it was not their national bourgeoisies who deserved the major credit. Besides, as George Grant (1964: 69-70) wrote, a businessman's main loyalty is to profits, not to nation. It is only when the two coincide in powerful countries, (which the late followers were not, at least in their early phase), that the nationalism of businessmen can be assured.

For some Canadian businessmen, it was more profitable to sell out to a foreign company at a handsome price than to continue to compete. Others limited their ambitions to providing services for the corporate giants who had entered their country. A few, of course, challenged the intruders by establishing successful businesses. But in the resource industries and most of the dynamic sectors of manufacturing, they were the minority. If there was to be exclusion of foreign ownership investment, it was mainly up to other social groups to take the initiative.

This is what happened in the other late follower countries. The ironmasters of central Sweden were important in removing British control over northern ore mines in the early 1890's. But they were by no means the only ones that forced the state to act. In the other moves against foreign investment discussed earlier, Sweden's large independent farmers, working class, urban middle class and old state nobility were more important.[19]

Meiji Japan (1868-1911) was led through the years of early capitalist industrialization by modernizing lower samurai (an aristocratic warrior class of the old order), in alliance with some of the higher aristocracy. It was they, not the "hot-house" industrialists[20] created through state philanthropy, that kept foreign investment of all kinds out of Japan in the 1870's to 1890's.

In czarist Russia some industrialists, especially in the Moscow region and the Urals, opposed foreign direct investment, because they feared the competition. But it was the landed nobility along with their counterparts in the state bureaucracy who were the most strenuous critics of foreign economic penetration. They charged that foreigners were pillaging Russian resources, taking out profits made in Russia, weakening Russian independence and above all destroying the aristocrats' cherished privileges. They carried more weight in government circles than the manufacturers and whatever steps were taken to restrict foreign ownership in czarist Russia can be attributed largely to them (Von Laue, 1963:169, 276; Mac-Kay, 1970:286).

The pattern of political influence regarding foreign ownership also applied to other economic policies affecting industrialization. Manufacturers did not by themselves command great "clout" anywhere in the halls of power during the initial phase of industrialization. Usually it was classes from agriculture—landed aristocrats, independent farmers or revolutionary peasants—who could muster the most influence. Furthermore, if any capitalists exercised political power during this period, it was usually done by commercial businessmen, and not by the emerging industrialists. In a brilliant article written in the 1850's, Karl Marx (1959: 282) noted that a "finance aristocracy"—mainly bankers—controlled the French government in the 1830's and 1840's during early industrialization, while the manufacturers were excluded from the corridors of power. Usually though, commercial capitalists had to take second place to agricultural interests during initial industrialization.

Popular-Democratic Movements in New Settler Societies

What has this to do with Canada which, after all, was a new settler society, free from the intrigues of aristocrats and courts? The same situation held. Despite the tariff of 1879, which contrary to prevailing myth, especially in western Canada, was as much a revenue as a protective tariff[21], manufacturers were not a commanding force in Ottawa until about 1900. Railway promoters, bankers and merchants counted for more when political decisions were made (Clark, 1939). Where Canada and other new settler societies differed from the old world was in the class structure of farming. Independent commodity producers, who owned and worked their land, were the major group involved in Canadian agriculture during initial industrialization (1870-1914). Seigneurs in Quebec, never a real aristrocratic class anyway, were gone, and agricultural labourers were too few in number and too transient to make their voices heard.

Popular-democratic movements developed and swept away the whig elitists in most new settler societies. These movements found most of their voter strength, if not always their leadership, among farmers, farm workers or plantation owners during the early years of industrialization. The United States was the classic case but Australia[22] and New Zealand[23] also conformed to this pattern.

By the time the cotton mills first began to dot the New England countryside and herald a dramatic change away from the frontier agricultural lifestyle of American society, it was already impossible for the Federalists, the old elitist party of Washington and Hamilton, to be elected. Alexander Hamilton, who was very influential in the writing of the American Constitution (1787), is once reported to have intoned that "Your people is a great beast" (Beard and Beard, 1968: 128, 164). Merchants and bankers, who were associated with the old carrying trade of Boston, New York, Philadelphia and Baltimore, along the northern coast, had to give way to the agrarian forces of the interior and the south (Bernhard, 1973:62, 295). Jacksonian democracy predominated in the years when the United States first industrialized, 1828-1860 (North, 1965). Western farmers and plantation slaveowners provided the backbone of these movements and major institutional changes resulted which affected the course of economic development. The old commercial banking system was swept aside and frugality in government spending was instituted (White, 1954). Thus the tendency for classes based on agriculture to influence the state during initial industrialization held in new societies as well as in old.

Again, Canada was the exception. Merchants, bankers, railway promoters and land speculators had the greatest influence on Canadian politics during the transition to an industrial society between Confederation and the First World War. Manufacturers were at first junior partners to the commercial elite and after 1900 or so, full-fledged partners. Popular-democratic movements, however, did not flourish and the agrarian-working class majority had little influence. The fact that the leading politicians openly stated their contempt for the people and yet were still elected gives an idea of the tenor of the times. John A. Macdonald, Conservative federation, also condemned the broad franchise in the United States, where "the minority must be protected and the rich are always fewer in number than the poor" (Whitaker, 1977:45). George Brown, the "Reform" (Liberal) Father of Confederation, also condemned the broad franchise in the United States where "the balance of power is held by the ignorant, unreasoning mass" (Careless, 1967:59).

Why did the ordinary people, amongst whom the farmers constituted the majority, not throw the elitist rascals out and vote in leaders of their own? I will deal with this question shortly. But to assess its relevance, I first want to examine whether it would have mattered to Canada's late follower development if agrarian movements had captured state power at that time. What would the farmers have done if they had run the government during initial industrialization?

Policies Advocated By Canadian Agrarian Movements

The question is hypothetical and since they never were in power, we cannot know for sure. What parties or movements say when they are in opposition is not necessarily what they do in office. But we can ascertain the main outlines of their policies from their class interests and stated grievances, and by looking at similar movements in more powerful positions in other new settler societies.

Broad-based agrarian movements in Canada existed between Confederation and the First World War which had some success at the polls, or else had large enough memberships to make a credible entry into politics. The most significant of these movements were the Patrons of Husbandry (usually known as the Dominion Grange), powerful in the late 1870's; the Patrons of Industry, which won 17 seats in the Ontario legislature in 1894 (and which despite its name was a farmers' party); and the Canadian Council of Agriculture, forerunner of both the Progressive Party and the United Farmers provincial governments after the First World War. The first two movements were based mainly in Ontario. By the time the third movement—the Canadian Council of Agriculture—emerged, the rapid settlement of the prairies had shifted the centre of agrarian dissent ot the west.

Canadian farmers' movements issued a litany of grievances which are familiar to the student of Canadian history. They demanded tariff reductions especially on inputs into agriculture and other primary products, land for actual settlers only, greater democracy and an end to the cruel exactions of the middleman—that swarm of "non-producing, hindering, talking persons"[24] who allegedly raked off much of the farmers' profits. These policies, if adopted, would have affected the course of Canada's late follower development. But more important were two grievances that the farmers also highlighted: the lack of farm credit and "rigid economy" in government expenditures. They bore directly on the problem of shortages of domestic capital for industrialization.

Canadian farmers had a very long history of trying to tear down the restrictive commercial banking system that refused to grant sufficient credit to the farmer. From the 1830's when Reformers in Upper Canada (Ontario) passed legislation establishing a much larger number of banks, only to be disallowed by the British government, to the 1930's when Social Credit in Alberta tried to set up an alternative financial system for farmers and other small businessmen (disallowed this time by the federal government), agrarian popular-democratic movements made numerous assaults against the banking system. All were to no avail.

These attempts were not made because this type of banking thwarted the development of indigenous industry in a late follower country. The purpose was to gain freer credit for the farmer. The motivation[25] had been the same in the U.S., when the Jacksonians destroyed the (second) Bank of the United States in 1836, which had propped up the British (and Canadian) type of commercial banking system in that country (Hammond, 1957). The effect was to usher in a new banking system in the U.S. that was more favourable to the investment of long-term, domestic capital in industry.

Agrarians tended to favour cheap government. They usually had less cash on hand than their urban cousins who lived off the avails of commerce and industry. Canadian farmers were no exception. From the Clear Grits in the 1850's through to the Patrons of Industry in the 1890's, farmers' movements clamoured for "rigid economy in government." Their anger was directed especially against the moneyed interests who bilked the public purse for private ends. In the late 19th century, the railway promoters and speculators raised the greatest ire because of their cozy connections with government.

The Grand Trunk Railway (which later became the Canadian National) was perhaps the most flagrant example. Politicians and businessmen were indistinguishable as they drank at the public trough in the 1850's. George Etienne Cartier, for example, was a solicitor for the Grand Trunk at the same time as he headed the parliamentary railway committee which approved grants to railways. Indeed, according to the American muckrakers, Gustavus Myers (1972: 176): "OF the nineteen Grand Trunk directors, nine were nominated by the Canadian Government for the purpose of safeguarding the public interest. Of these nine, four were Cabinet Ministers, and eight of the nine were really nominees of the English contractors" The contractors[26] had learned in England that there was more money to be made in building railways than running them. The situation was even more enticing in Canada because of government largesse, which came in the form of money grants and the free appropriation of timber, stone and other materials from the public domain. This was the sort of corruption[27] and privilege that angered the thrift-minded farmers (Underhill, 1967).

But the farmers' displeasure and disgust did not lead to an effective political alternative. Canadian elections continued to be characterized by a large amount of corruption well after Confederation. Indeed, Canada's notoriety had spread to the English press. Of the railway scandals in 1891, the *Pall Mall Gazette* declared: "a more sordid spectacle of corruption has never been presented to a free people

. . . it is abundantly clear that the cancer of corruption has eaten deep into Canadian institutions." *The Star,* another English paper, commented on the conduct of John A. Macdonald's government shortly after his death: "for twenty-three years he and his party had maintained themselves in power without a break by a colossal system of bribery . . . whenever a district was wavering in its allegiance to Toryism, Sir John sent a railway into it" (quoted in Cartwright, 1912: 392-3).

Railway politics continued into the first decade of this century, this time under the Liberal government of Wilfrid Laurier. Canada overbuilt its rail system on an enormous scale, and banks, traders, railway-equipment manufacturers, land speculators and railway promoters received the benefits. Government thinking assumed that if one transcontinental railway (CPR) was good, two more would be even better. Neither of the additional lines would have been built without generous aid from the public, but thrift was not a concern of the government. One of the rail lines, the Grand Trunk Pacific, built entirely by the state, was so far north that it avoided contact with Ottawa and Lake Superior. No centre of any size could be found along the almost 2000 kilometre route between Quebec City and Winnipeg (Stevens, 1962:155-7). It was costly to build and was the largest public project of its time, with the exception of the Panama Canal, and yet it was totally useless. As Kenneth Buckly (1974: 52) has said "One traffic bridge over the Canadian shield may have been justified on non-economic grounds, but hardly two and certainly not three".

Railway overbuilding on a colossal scale and often done in the exorbitant British manner was folly for a late follower country with a shortage of domestic capital. The result was a record inflow of British loan capital to finance the railroads. The importation of this amount of capital over such a short period of time had inflationary effects and encouraged the establishment of American branch plants in Canada (Viner, 1975:280).

The agrarian failure in Canada to destroy the commercial banking system, as their counterparts had done in the United States, was equally disastrous. By 1900 Canadian banks were near the point of overcoming the shortage of domestic capital. Did they then use their new found wealth to develop Canadian-owned industries in the new technologies? No, on the contrary, they lent money abroad on a grand scale to finance municipal and national governments, utilities and railways, urban street car lines and coffee plantations in the United States, Central and South America (Naylor, 1975, Vol. II: 218-67). While U.S. manufacturers were establishing branch plants in Canada at a dizzying pace between 1900 and 1917, Canadian bankers were investing Canadian savings abroad. Canadian commercial banks had stayed true to their original nature and did not become involved in industrial investment banking. The only exception to this was in financing the mergers of already-established companies.

Having shown the relevance of agrarian politics for Canada's economic development, we can now return to the question posed earlier. Why were agrarian-based, popular-democratic movements so weak during the period when the country industrialized and the nation-state was established?

Sectionalism and the Weakness of Agrarian Movements

If the 1867 to 1914 period in Canada stood out from the history of other new settler societies in a comparable economic phase, it also contrasted with earlier and later Canadian history. Before the 1837 rebellions in Lower and Upper Canada, farmer-supported, popular movements were powerful under the leadership of Louis Joseph Papineau and William Lyon Mackenzie. With the defeat of the rebellions, however, such movements did not regain their former political strength until after the First World War, when the Progressive Party won 65 seats in the House of Commons and United Farmers parties assumed power in Ontario, Alberta and Manitoba. Canada's economy had altered greatly during the interval. Why the political hiatus of eight decades?

In a word: "sectional conflict" between English and French Canada. The usual politics of class were shunted aside. Rather than a contest based on the conflicting economic interests of farmers (small business class) and commercial business (capitalist class), the main lines of cleavage during the whole period were determined by ethno-national, religious and regional differences. In this context, big business managed to dominate both of the main political parties, while the agrarians and the working class were unable to cross the ethno-national divide.

Differences in outlook between English and French Canada involved very intense, emotional issues. Was Canada a country of one or two language groups? Should political representation be on the basis of equality for the two ethno-national communities or on the basis of population size—Jeremy Bentham's one-man-one-vote principle? Should there be one secular school system or a bi-polar system, one for Protestants and another for Catholics. These issues have continued to divide Canadians, but never was the debate more vehement than in the 1850 to 1914 period of initial industrialization.

The English-speaking business elite found it easier to accommodate the national and religious demands of French Canadians than did the popular-democratic movements in English Canada. By the 1850's English-Canadian capitalists had learned to use the old British formula for accommodation of French Canada, laid down after the conquest of Quebec in 1979. A limited set of national-religious rights were recognized in return for French-Canadians recognizing the right of capitalists to run the economy as they saw fit (Careless, 1970:225).

Popular-democratic movements have always had a more difficult time crossing the ethno-national divide in Canada because their politics have been based more on the principles of equality and democracy than on the pragmatic base of self-interest and economic growth of the pro-business parties. The central problem for popular movements has been the very different meanings of these concepts in the two national communities. For English Canadians, equality and democracy have, for the most part, been seen in classical liberal terms. Every individual has an equal right for self-development and this development can only take place in a capitalist market economy (Macpherson, 1977:1-2). On the other hand, French Canada was a more communal society from the outset and was pushed farther along this road after the Conquest threatened its survival as a national community. When a limited form of English parliamentary democracy was introduced into Lower Canada (Quebec) in 1791, French-Canadian leaders embraced it, not because of their adherence to the enlightenment ideas of individualism and democracy, but because it offered them a legitimate vehicle to preserve their nationality (Ouellet, 1980:386; Trudeau, 1968:105).

After Papineau and Mackenzie were allowed to return from exile in the late 1840's, there were attempts to revive the popular-democratic movements of the

1830's. The "Rouges" emerged in Canada East (Quebec) in 1848, the year of the great liberal uprisings in Europe. Like the revolutionary liberals of Europe, they strongly opposed Church privileges and wanted a complete separation of Church and state. In addition, they pushed for full political democracy (without, of course, advocating female suffrage), and an end to government-granted privileges for the rich. Although most of its leaders belonged to the professions, the Rouges received most of their support from farmers, especially in the eastern townships. A similar, agrarian-based movement in Canada West (Ontario) developed from the remnants of Mackenzie's and Rolph's pre-1837 reformers. They called themselves "Clear Grits," perhaps to distinguish themselves from "time-servers" and those with "false hearts" (Careless, 1959:109). It was natural that the two movements should combine against the corrupt commercial elite who ruled both sections of the colony.

A Clear Grit-Rouge alliance was not to be. During the first year in which the Clear Grit newspaper, the *North American*, was launched, it forecast the future political alignments of Canada. Sectionalism would replace class interests as the basis for political groupings:

We are bound hand and foot, and lie helplessly at the feet of the Catholic priests of Lower Canada who can laugh to scorn all our consulsive efforts for freedom . . . When the civil, political and religious degradation in which we are placed is fully realized, we shall hear very little in Upper Canada of the cry "Tory" and "Reformer." These distinctions will be swept away and another very different organization of parties will be formed" (*North American*, July 2, 1850).

The "French hacks" with their "priestism," not commercial business, became the main enemy of Ontario's agrarian radicals.

The Rouges could not make an alliance with a group that expressed such deep antipathy to Catholics. Despite their anti-clericalism and in some cases their agnosticism, the Rouges "believed in Catholicism as an institution and as a national institution. They rejected its doctrines and beliefs, but they preserved an almost unshakeable confidence in the institutional role of religion" (Ouellet, 1980: 485). Furthermore, the Rouges were a continuation of the pre-1837 *patriote* movement which was intensely natonalist and anti-British. When the Clear Grits were issuing their anti-French anti-Catholic epistles, the Rouges were warning of the threat of assimilation by means of British laws and the English language:

that perfect labyrinth of laws, of manners and of language, which imposes on us a double nationality, so as to render the one necessary, the other useless . . . to make us lose ours and adopt the other . . . We only wish for one thing, the preservation of our language, our laws and our customs (Wade, 1968:262).

The failure of a Clear Grit-Rouges alliance allowed the commercial capitalists to rule, unimpeded. Destruction of the commercial banking system[28] and thrift in government expenditures[29] were not made central issues by either Conservatives or Liberals.

The impossibility of an agrarian movement which could bridge the English-French gap continued through the initial industrialization period. In the 1890's, for example, the Patrons of Industry had a chance to develop a powerful national movement. But ethno-national and religious issues had become so heated with the Riel rebellions, the Manitoba schools question and the Jesuits Estates Act that it proved impossible for the Patrons to remain neutral. Their association with anti-Catholicism could hardly have endeared them to French-Canadians or even to Catholic farmers in English Canada. When the Patrons ran in the 1894 Ontario election, seven of their candidates had already been endorsed by the Protestant Protective Association. The latter aimed to prevent the election of any member of the Roman Catholic Church to political office (Watt, 1979). Meanwhile in Quebec, agricultural associations and co-operatives were organized or controlled by the clergy or the provincial government (Linteau *et al.*, 1983: 421-6).

Thus sectional conflicts between English and French and Protestant and Catholic largely accounted for the peculiar political weakness of agrarian populist movements during initial industrialization. Because of this the reforms that were important for independent, late follower development (and which agrarians, for their own reasons, usually supported), were not carried out.

Weakness of Popular Nationalism and the Military Question

Thus far, I have discussed the political reasons behind Canada's failure to alter its credit system and to reduce the costs of building transportation infrastructure. In other late follower countries, these policies had lessened the need to import foreign capital and thus increased the likelihood of domestic ownership of industries. But there was a more active element in boosting domestic ownership: the actual prevention of foreign direct investment for strategic reasons.

Earlier, we saw that this factor was not operative in Canada because there were no armed forces of consequence in the country during the 1867 to 1914 period. Instead, Canada voluntarily relied on British and American protection. Would great agrarian political influence have pushed Canada in a more independent military direction?

This is a difficult question to answer. In contrast to the banking and state expenditure issues, there is no evidence that farmers' movements wanted a stronger military role. This was another Canadian peculiarity. In the nationalistic and jingoistic age of the late 19th century, agrarians were usually the firmest supporters of defence of the home territory. According to Marx, (1959), the peasants who had succeeded in seizing noble and Church lands in the great French Revolution of 1789 were the main basis for French *gloire* under both Napolean Bonaparte and his nephew Louis Napoleon. Even in the United States, which had a long tradition of opposition to a standing army, it was the western farmers, not the commercial and industrial elites, who pushed for American expansionism in the 19th century. According to William Appleman Williams (1969: 6):

Whether in terms of the drive to possess more land, or in their pressure to protect and expand their position in the marketplace, the Northern as well as the Southern members of the agrarian majority exerted a strong and persistent influence on American foreign policy down through the War of 1812. In the direct sense, they demanded the defeat and expulsion westward of the Indians; they agitated the seizure of Florida, the trans-Mississippi region, and all or part of Canada . . . They were first the harbingers, and then the militant advocates, of America's manifest destiny to lead and reform the world.

Canadian farmers did not display similar views. The way the country was established must have had something to do with it. The pre-1837 popular-democratic movements had combined the beliefs in democracy and nationalism—the desire for home-rule and independence. But after the defeat of the rebellions, they did not lead the movement for Confederation. The whig plutocrats championed the Confederation scheme and made sure that the constitution was not ratified by the people. Alexander Galt, the first member of parliament to propose Confederation to the Canadian assembly, offered this vision of the new country:

It will be observed that the basis of Confederation now proposed differs from that of the United States in several important particulars. *It does not profess to be derived from the people* but would be the constitution provided by the Imperial Parliament . . . (Skelton, 1920: 243; emphasis added).

Confederation was not to lead to an independent country with its own defense policy:

It is in the power of the Imperial Government by sanctioning a confederation of these Pro-vinces, to constitute a *Dependency of the Empire,* valuable in time of peace, and powerful in the event of war—forever removing the fear that these Colonies may ultimately serve to swell the power of another Nation (Skelton, 1920: 241; emphasis added).

This was hardly a vision to arouse widespread popular nationalism amongst the masses. The people were not asked to take part in creating the country. The only province which voted on the issue, New Brunswick, turned it down and had to be cajoled into acceptance by the British. The other provinces took votes only amongst members of their legislatures; there were no general elections on the question. Thus, most of the people did not feel strongly caught up in the creation of the new dominion and few demands were made for an independent foreign and defence role.

Attempts to develop popular nationalism were wrecked on the shoals of English-French differences.[30] In place of the robust nationalism, a more anaemic version was created around narrow economic questions, such as the tariff. Mild economic na-tionalism was the only type that English and French Canadians could agree on. Instead of a strategic logic leading to the build-up of a Canadian-owned armaments and engineering sector, the strategic question in Canada was fought over territory. The CPR was rushed into construction because the American government had explicit designs to annex Western Canada by building railways near the border (Fowke, 1973: 44). In this instance, the nationality of the railway's promoters became a major issue and the public demanded a Canadian-owned line. Such is the logic of the strategic question.

However, in contrast to other late follower countries, the strategic issue had a narrow focus in Canada and did not lead to the widespread fostering of Canadian-owned industry and resources. Failure to create a fully independent country at Con-federation had implications for the direction of economic development.

D: Branch Plants and Truncated Development

Having discussed why Canada was the only late follower country to rely so heavily on foreign ownership and foreign technology, we can now return to the question posed at the beginning of the article. Has foreign ownership made us richer though less independent?

The costs and benefits of foreign ownership in Canada have been debated widely during the past thirty years, but no resolution of the question has been universally accepted. Is the overall impact positive, negative or merely neutral?

A.E. Safarian (1973: xvi-xvii) has argued the advantages of foreign investment for Canada:

Foreign direct investment contributes to (the) sources of expansion to the extent that it supplies capital, and also where it makes available a range of technology, access to markets, and entrepreneurship which are otherwise not available or only at greater overall net costs. These potential gains from increased capital stock and improved technology may appear as one or more of higher real wages rates, fuller employment, lower prices, or better quality of output. An important benefit is the tax payments to various governments from the higher level of output. (xvi-xvii).

On the other hand, Bruce Wilkinson (1980: 74-5) points out some of the negative features:

•The importation of technical and managerial services from foreign parents is . . . becoming one of the largest and most rapidly growing expenses for the Canadian economy.
•A substantial proportion of the capital inflow is for the takeover of existing firms, not for establishing new plants.
•In a number of leading Canadian industries, foreign-owned establishments do not have higher value added per employee .
•Foreign plants . . . are geared to produce too many lines to achieve available economies of scale and have simply added to the fragmentation and inefficiency of manufacturing in Canada.
•Foreign-owned firms have, not infrequently, felt constrained with respect to the degree to which they could enter foreign markets (i.e. they export little) .
•Foreign-owned firms import larger proportions of their purchases than do domestic firms, thus worsening Canada's current-account deficit while simultaneously reducing the market for domestic producers—with the result that achievable economies of scale within the Canadian economy are less than they otherwise might be—and quite possibly aggravating domestic unemployment problems.

Wilkinson lists other points as well, largely concerning the weakness of research and development expenditures in branch plants.

Rather than enter the fine points of this debate, which is mainly about the short-run effects of foreign ownership in the contemporary period, I want to look at the long-run effects. What were the consequences of choosing the dependent or independent route to development during the initial phase of industrialization? How did the other late follower countries fare without the benefit of large-scale foreign ownership? Did they miss the opportunities that foreign firms and foreign capital could have brought them?

If we look at the trade performance in end products, the answer would seem to be no, they did not. The critics of external investment complain that foreign branch plants tend not to export and, on the other hand, import many of their parts and machines. The result is a large deficit in the trade of end products. The way to make up for this trade imbalance is to export raw materials in ever greater quantities.

Let us examine Table II to discover whether Canada and the other late follower countries were able to make end products well enough to be able to export large amounts to other countries and also to satisfy much of the home market. Trade in textiles and clothing has been excluded from this table on the grounds that while they constituted 50% of the world's manufacturing trade in 1899, they made up only 14% of such trade in the mid-1950's.

Notice that Canada's exports of end products was comparable to that in the other late follower countries in 1899, just prior to the first major entry of American branch plants into Canada. (Its imports of end products was larger already, but not disastrously so.) By 1913, Canada was moving backward in a development sense, exporting proportionately fewer end products and importing many more. By 1955, when the other late follower countries were exporting at least as much in the value of end products (excluding textiles and clothing) as they were importing, Canada was doing miserably. It exported only 22% as much in these products as it imported. The record in 1980 was not much better. In that year, even though end-product exports were inflated artificially by the Canada-U.S. auto pact, they stood at only 29% of all Canada's exports (Pollock, 1981: 28).

TABLE II
Trade in End Products[1] Excluding Textiles and Clothing in Late Follower Countries[2], 1899, 1913, 1955

	Exports of End Products in Millions (1913) U.S. $	Imports of End Products in Millions (1913) U.S. $	Exports of End Products as a % of Imports of End Products
1899			
Canada	12	46	26
Italy	23	25	92
Japan	10	30	33
Sweden	13	8	163
1913			
Canada	21	154	14
Italy	65	82	79
Japan	38	58	66
Sweden	50	22	227
1955[3]			
Canada	449	2078	22
Italy	638	476	134
Japan	662	167	396
Sweden	563	554	102

Source: A. Maizels (1963), Tables A 15-19, 20-27, 39, 47-56, 69.

1. "End products" are not the same as "manufactured goods". They do not include fabricated or intermediate goods which require further finishing. "End products" are equivalent to Maizels' definition "finished manufactured goods". See his Appendix A.

2. Not enough information supplied on Soviet Union to include in the table.

3. In 1955 U.S. dollars.

Why does it matter that Canada exports resources and imports end products? First, end-product manufacturing creates five or six times the number of jobs per dollar invested than do resource industries.[32] If Canada produced as much in the value of end products as it consumed, several hundred thousand jobs would be created directly[32] and still more would develop in the service sector.[33] Second, many of our resource exports are non-renewable and increasingly inaccessible. It is certainly preferable to excel in high technology products than to remain "hewers of wood and drawers of water", forever vulnerable to the tastes and demands of others.

Can anything be done now to rectify a century of mis-development? Yes, we can learn from the past that there are no short-cuts to independent development and that we must not leave management of public affairs to elites, foreign or domestic. The intelligent development of Canada requires a citizenry that is informed and concerned, not only about the economy but also about the rights and aspirations of both of Canada's ethno-national communities and all of its regions and minority groups. Canadians must take control over the economy if Canada is to prosper in the future.

Notes

1. Grant was referring specifically to French Canadian nationalism in this instance. But the point applies to pan-Canadian nationalism as well.
2. Thus, workers' interests coincide more closely with "national interests" than do capitalists', whose main loyalty is to profits. For this reason, workers have more "to lose than their chains" if their nation's economy declines.
3. I concentrate on developments during "initial industrialization." This phase begins when secondary manufacturing is carried out in a wide range of industries and ends when manufacturing has become strong enough to overtake the value added of agriculture and other primary sectors. In most late follower countries initial industrialization occurred between the 1870's or 1880's and World War One. It was a crucial period because it had a formative influence on the later structures of these economies.
4. A late follower country is one which began industrialization on a wide scale in the 1870's or 1880's. To qualify it must have had more than 1% of the world's manufacturing production before World War One. Several countries have been excluded from our discussion even though they met the criterion. Czechoslovakia was not an independent country until 1918 and there is not adequate data on manufacturing in the Netherlands prior to 1914 (see Maizels (1963)). Australia excluded on other grounds, although it had barely over 1% of the world manufacturing production. Much of its industry was involved in "primary manufacturing" or the processing of raw materials before exporting. See Laxer (forthcoming) for a discussion of Australian industrial development.
5. International comparisons of industrial statistics present enormous problems regarding different methods applied in calculating national indices, a multiplicity of overlapping national series, a lack of uniform assumptions as to what constitutes manufacturing (prior to the Second World War) and arbitrary currency valuations. The farther back in time we go, the more uncertain the conclusions. Despite the crudeness of the exercise, comparative estimates are crucial to assess comparative development levels.

There are only a handful of comparative studies on industrial levels, and we must rely on these. For estimates of manufacturing output in the advanced industrial countries, there are basically two sets of data that can be used. One is the recent monumental work by Paul Bairoch (1982), which for the first time includes estimates of handicraft production from the Third World. This provides an exciting new view of economic and political relations between the developed and the underdeveloped world since the beginning of the Industrial Revolution in England. Indeed, this is the main purpose of Bairoch's new calculation (see his Appendix A).

The other set of data is older and includes the works of Hilgerdt for the League of Nations (1945), Clark (1960) and Maizels (1963). These studies do not wholly agree among themselves regarding numbers, nor do they involve exactly the same methods of calculation. Nevertheless there is considerable agreement amongst them regarding orders of magnitude and levels of industrial production amongst countries that I am interested in: namely the "late follower" countries, the white dominions (these categories are discussed in the body of the article) and the U.S.A. in the period from 1870 to the 1930's. Furthermore, Simon Kuznet's (1969: 305) work is in general agreement with their estimates as well. He had a high regard for Hilgerdt's study, for instance.

I decided to stay with the earlier sources rather than use Bairoch (for the period before the Second World War for several reasons: 1) Bairoch's estimates for Canada's aggregate level of Canadian manufacturing production in the 1881 to 1913 period is between one-third and two-fifths the level estimated by Hilgerdt. Estimates for the U.S.A. in 1860 and 1880 are also much below Hilgerdt's (and others), suggesting a systematic underestimation of North American manufacturing production at an early point in their industrial development. Bairoch's figures for the later period (starting about 1914 in the case of the U.S.A. and about 1939 in the case of Canada) are very similar to the earlier studies. 2) Bairoch's estimates for Canada do not coincide with what we know about the character as well as the quantity of Canadian manufacturing between 1870 and 1914. The works by Bertram (1962; 1963), Dales (1962), McDougall (1973) and Urquhart (1984) are in general agreement on the question of Canadian manufacturing levels with the earlier sets of comparative international statistics. 3) Bairoch does not reveal enough detail for the reader to make an independent assessment of his sources and assumptions. On the other hand, Hilgerdt, Maizels and Clark have laid out their methods in much greater detail.

6. The United States was less *laissez-faire* than present ideologues would like to admit. The Erie Canal and many railways were built by state governments and Pennsylvania was involved in over 150 mixed corporations in 1844. See Hartz (1948).
7. William Cobbett, an early English radical, wrote of the rapid deterioration of weavers' living standards after the power loom was widely adopted:
It is truly lamentable to behold so many thousands of men who formerly earned 20 to 30 shillings per week, now compelled to live upon 5s, 4s, or even less . . . It is the more sorrowful to behold these men in their state, as they still retain the frank and bold character formed in the days of their independence (cited in Thompson, 1963:314).
8. Marx and Engels made this point 137 years ago in the Communist Manifesto: "The bourgeoisie has through its exploitation of the world market . . . drawn from under the feet of industry the national ground on which it stood. All old-established national industries have been destroyed or are daily being destroyed . . . the bourgeoisie, by the rapid improvement of all instruments of production, by the immensely facilitated means of communication, draws all . . . nations into civilization. The cheap prices of its commodities are the heavy artillery with which it batters down all Chinese walls . . . it compels all nations, on pain of extinction, to adopt the bourgeois mode of production" (1959:10-11).
9. All foreigners and foreign trade were excluded from Japan from 1640 until Commodore Perry's forced entry in 1853. Japanese were not allowed to travel abroad and the size of ships was reduced by decree in order to prohibit international trade. A small window on the western world was kept open however, in remote Nagasaki, where the Dutch (and Chinese) were allowed to trade on a small scale. In the 19th century, scholars learned about western science through "Dutch studies" (Norman, 1940: 13, 28-9).
10. Was cotton or iron the leading industry of the early industrial revolution? Phyllis Deane (1965) argues both were. Hobsbawn (1968: 71) disagrees, pointing out that like coal, iron "did not undergo its real industrial revolution until the middel decades of the nineteenth century or about fifty years later than cotton. Landes concurs: "Not in men, nor capital invested, nor value of output, nor rate of growth could iron be compared with cotton in this period" (1965: 88-9). Although it cost much more to start up an iron company than a cotton firm in the 1700's, the sums involved were not that large. Some large enterprises were established with funds accumulated in "artisan activities" (Crouzet, 1972:166).
11. France was an early industrial rival, but was set back by the revolution and Napoleonic Wars. See Milward and Saul (1973:262).
12. Czarist Russia only very partially avoided the pitfalls of dependent capitalist industrialization. See discussion on Russia below.
13. Under the leadership of the Pereire brothers and their Credit Mobilier (founded 1852), France was actually the first country to experience investment banking. The idea spread rapidly from France to other countries in Europe. But the Credit Mobilier experiment failed in France and the great French banks continued in their security-conscious ways, only slightly altered by the experience. See Cameron (1961). The U.S. also broke away from a British type of commercial banking system in the 1830's, but with small unit banks predominating, only partly moved toward an investment banking system after several decades. See Hammond (1957) and Carosso (1970).

14. According to Witte, about 37 per cent of the railways were built for political and military reasons (Feis, 1930:211).

15. Germany actually held back loan capital to the Russian state in the late 1880's in order to demonstrate German power over Russia. The plan backfired and helped force the Russians into the arms of France (Feis, 1930: 212-14). But there is no evidence that German direct investment in Russian industry was withheld in a similar manner (McKay, 1970: 385-6).

16 Foreign companies received more favourable treatment for a time after 1899-1901. See McKay, (1970: 284).

17. In response, Germany passed a law allowing dual nationality. So the German naturalization movement in Russian Poland may not have been genuine (Crisp, 1960:79).

18. The Gilchrist-Thomson process for the extraction of phosphorus was first developed in 1878 (Pearton, 1982: 105).

19. The politics of Sweden's independent industrialization are discussed in Chapter V of my thesis (Laxer, 1981).

20. Rich merchant families existed in Edo and Osaka before the Meiji Restoration and some were able to make the transition to modern industrialists. I use the term "hot-house" industrialists because the state acted as benefactor to the successful manufacturers. With exception of the silk-reeling industry, the state paid for most of the modern factories and then sold them at very low prices to the existing merchant class. The latter would not have been able to do it on their own. See Thomas Smith (1955: 54-100).

21. Before the era of income, corporate and sales taxes, the tariff was the main means of taxation in Canada. To entice a private company to build the CPR, one of the major components of the National Policy of 1879, the government contributed prairie land and money. Indeed, Finance Minister Tilley listed the need for revenue to finance the CPR as the first reason for introducing the National Policy tariffs. Protection was his second reason.

22. In Australia, a precociously urban society, farm workers were joined by a large contigent of miners and city workers in supporting popular movements for "state socialism" in the latter half of the 19th century. Chartist electoral reforms were instituted between 1856 and 1865, an early period in Australian history. The landholding grazers (the "squattocracy") soon lost their elitist control. See Younger, (1970: 263-88); Rosecrance (1964); Greenwood (1955).

23. Popular democracy came a little later to New Zealand, but then New Zealand became a colony only in 1841. The first rule of a popular party, the Liberals, was in the 1890 to 1906 period when a good deal of pioneering social legislation was introduced. The chief supporters of the Liberals were the farmers and workers. See R.S. Milne (1966).

24. These were the words used by a farmer in 1874 to characterize the "middleman" (Wood, 1975: 74).

25. An urban working class group called the "loco focos" and some New York bankers were also involved in this banking transformation in the 1830's. See Bray Hammond (1957).

26. Peto, Brassey, Betts and Jackson.

27. R.L. Jones (1977: 351) argues that "The Clear Grits were strong in the rural sections of western Upper Canada . . . because they offered a political instrument for throwing the "corruptionists out of office".

28. In fact, a free banking Act was passed in Canada in 1850. But free banks did not flourish because they were saddled with a provision that they tie up their capital in low-yield government securities. The commercial banks, which had been chartered independently of this law, were not subject to this provision (Breckenridge, 1894: 103-6).

29. Alexander Mackenzie's Liberal government (1873-8), was an exception. It stressed thrift. The Liberal Party was still influenced to some extent then by the Clear Grit element (Thomson, 1960).

30. This is discussed in my doctoral dissertation (Laxer, 1981: 450-462).

31. Net capital stock averaged $22,970 per worker in 20 manufacturing industries in Canada in 1974 (current dollars), while it was $77,812 per worker (in 1961 dollars) in 1976 (Wilkinson, 1980: 62. 81).

32. John Orr estimated that an $8 billion trade deficit in end products in the mid-1970's corresponded to a loss of about 400,000 jobs (Globe and Mail, October 26, 1978). Recently, it was estimated that if Canada wiped out its trade deficit in automobiles and auto parts, there would be 19,000 more production jobs, 2,800 more support staff positions and 1,400 more engineering jobs. A U.S. Senate study in 1970 confirmed these estimates. It concluded that the United States had a net employment gain of 500,000 jobs because of American transnational operations in the world. See James Laxer (1981): 124.

33. According to Britton and Gilmour (1978: 71) there were 33 dependent service jobs for every 100 manufacturing jobs in Canada in 1971. As well, many more jobs would be created through the multiplier effect.

References

Ando, Yoshio, 1966–"The Formation of Heavy Industry" in S. Tobata (ed.) *The Modernization of Japan 1*, Tokyo: Institute of Asian Economic Affairs.

Bairoch, Paul, 1982–"International Industrialization levels from 1750 to 1980', *Journal of European Economic History*. Volume 11 No. 2. Spring.

Ball, George W., 1968–*The Discipline of Power*. Boston: Atlantic Monthly Press.

Beard, Charles and Mary, 1968–*New Basic History of the United States*, Garden City: Doubleday.

Bernhard, Winfred E.A. (ed.), 1973–*Political Parties in American History, Volume 1 1789-1828*. New York: G.P. Putnam's Sons.

Bliss, Michael, 1970–"Canadianizing American Business: the roots of the Branch Plant" in I. Lumsden, (ed.) *Close the 49th Parallel Etc.* Toronto, University of Toronto Press.

Braatoy, Bjarne, 1939–*The New Sweden*. London: Thomas Nelson and Sons.

Breckenridge, R.M., 1894–*The Canadian Banking System 1817-1890* Toronto: (no publisher cited).

Britton, John and James Gilmour, 1978–*The Weakest Link: A technological perspective on Canadian industrial development*. Ottawa: Science Council of Canada.

Buckley, Kenneth, 1974–*Capital Formation in Canada, 1896-1930*. Toronto: McClelland and Stewart.

Cafagna, Luciano, 1973–"The Industrial Revolution in Italy 1830-1914" in C.M. Cipolla, *The Fontana Economic History of Europe* Volume IV Part 1. Glasgow: Fontana.

Cameron, Rondo, 1961–*France and the Economic Development of Europe 1800-1914*. Princeton, N.J.: Princeton University Press.

Careless, J.M.S., 1970–*Canada: A Story of Challenge*. Toronto: MacMillan.

Careless, J.M.S., 1967–"The Toronto *Globe* and Agrarian Radicalism 1850-1867" in *Upper Canadian Politics in the 1850's, Canadian Historial Readings* No. 2. Toronto: University of Toronto Press.

Careless, J.M.S., 1959–*Brown of the Globe* Volume I. Toronto: MacMillan.

Carosso, Vincent P., 1970–*Investment Banking in America, A History*. Cambridge, Mass.: Harvard University Press.

Cartwright, Richard, 1912–*Reminiscences*. Toronto: William Briggs.

Clark, Colin, 1960–*The Conditions of Economic Progress* third edition. London: Macmillan.

Clark, S.D., 1939–*The Canadian Manufacturers' Association*. Toronto: University of Toronto Press.

Clement, Wallace, 1975–*The Canadian Corporate Elite*. Toronto: Carleton Library.

Clough, S.B., 1964–*The Economic History of Modern Italy*. New York: Columbia University Press.

Creighton, Donald, 1957–*Dominion of the North*. Revised edition. London: Robert Hale Ltd.

Crisp, Olga, 1976–"Foreign Entrepreneurship and Russian Industry" in O. Crisp, *Studies in the Russian Economy Before 1914*. London: Macmillan.

Crisp, Olga, 1960–"French Investment in Russian Joint Stock Companies 1894-1914." *Business History No. 2*.

Crouzet, Francois, 1972–"Capital Formation in Great Britain during the Industrial Revolution" in F. Crouzet (ed.), *Capital Formation in the Industrial Revolution*. London: Methuen.

Deane, Phyllis, 1965–*The First Industrial Revolution*. Cambridge, U.K.: Cambridge University Press.

Denison, Merrill, 1948–*Harvest Triumphant*. Toronto: McClelland and Stewart.

Feis, Herbert, 1930–*Europe the World's Banker 1870-1914*. New York: Yale University Press.

Fleetwood, E.E., 1947–*Sweden's Capital Imports and Exports*. Geneve: Journal de Geneve.

Flinn, Michael, 1954–"Scandinavian Iron Ore Mining and the British Steel Industry 1870-1914" *Scandinavian Economic History Review* Volume II No. 1, 1954.

Fowke, Vernon, 1973–*The National Policy and the Wheat Economy*. Toronto: University of Toronto Press.

Frazee, Rowland, 1984–"Working Smarter: Improving Productivity in Canada" in G. Lowe and H. Krahn, *Working Canadians*. Toronto: Methuen.

Gasslander, Olle, 1962–*History of Stockholm's Enskilda Bank to 1914*. Stockholm: Stockholms Enskilda Banken.

Glazebrook, G.P. de T., 1964–*A History of Transportation in Canada*. 2 Volumes. Toronto: McClelland and Stewart.

Grant, George, 1965–*Lament for a Nation. The Defeat of Canadian Nationalism*. Toronto: McClelland and Stewart.

Greenwood, Gordon, 1955–*Australia. A Social and Political History*. Sydney: Angus and Robertson.

Halliday, Jon, 1975–*A Political History of Japanese Capitalism*. New York: Pantheon Books.

Hammond, Bray, 1957–*Banks and Politics in America from the Revolution to the Civil War*. Princeton, N.J.: Princeton University Press.

Hartz, Louis, 1948—*Economic Policy and Democratic Thought: Pennsylvania 1776-1860*. Cambridge: Harvard University Press.

Hedin, Lars-Erik, 1957—"Some Notes on the Financing of the Swedish Railroads 1860-1914". *Economy and History* Volume X.

Hirschmeier, Johannes, 1965—"Shibusawa Eiichi: Industrial Pioneer" in W.W. Lockwood (ed.) *The State and Economic Enterprise in Japan*. Princeton, N.J.: Princeton University Press.

Hobsbawm, Eric, 1968—*Industry and Empire*. Suffolk, England: Penguin.

Ike, Nobutaka, 1955—"The Pattern of Railway Development in Japan" *Far Eastern Quarterly* Volume 14, No. 2.

Jansen, Marius, 1968—"Modernization and Foreign Policy in Meiji Japan" in Robert Ward (ed.) *Political Development in Modern Japan*. Princeton, N.J.: Princeton University Press.

Johansson, Harry, 1968—"Foreign Business Operating in Sweden" in M. Norgren (ed.) *Industry in Sweden*. Halmstad, Sweden: Swedish Institute for Cultural Relations with Foreign Countries.

Jones, R.L., 1946—*History of Agriculture in Ontario 1613-1880*. Toronto: University of Toronto Press.

Jonsson, Bo, 1969—"The State and the Ore-fields. A Study in Swedish Ore-fields Politics at the Turn of the Century". Stockholm: Almquist and Wiksell.

Kuznets, Simon, 1955—"International Differences in Capital Formation and Financing" in National Bureau of Economic Research. *Capital Formation and Economic Growth*. Princeton: Princeton University Press.

Kuznets, Simon, 1969—*Modern Economic Growth. Rate structure and spread*. New Haven: Yale University Press.

Landes, David, 1965—"Japan and Europe: Contrasts in Industrialization" in W.W. Lockwood (ed.) *The State and Economic Enterprise in Japan*. Princeton, N.J.: Princeton University Press.

Laxer, Gordon, 1985—"Foreign Ownership and Myths About Canadian Development." *Canadian Review of Sociology and Anthropology* (forthcoming).

Laxer, Gordon, 1981—*The Social Origins of Canada's Branch Plant Economy, 1837-1914*. Doctoral thesis, Department of Sociology, University of Toronto.

Laxer, James, 1981—*Canada's Economic Strategy*. Toronto: McClelland and Stewart.

Laxer, James, 1973—"Introduction to the Political Economy of Canada" in R. Laxer (ed.) *Canada Ltd., the Political Economy of Dependency*. Toronto: McClelland and Stewart.

Lewery, L.J., 1923—*Foreign Capital Investment in Russian Industries and Commerce*. Washington: U.S. Government.

Linteau, Paul-Andre *et al.*, 1983—*Quebec: A History 1867-1929*. Toronto: Lorimer.

Lyaschchenko, Peter, 1949—*History of the National Economy of Russia, to the 1917 Revolution*. New York: Macmillan.

Macpherson, C.B., 1977—*History of the National Economy of Russia, to the 1917 Revolution*. New York: Macmillan

Macpherson, C.B., 1977—*The Life and Times of Liberal Democracy*. Oxford: Oxford University Press.

Maizels, Alfred, 1963—*Industrial Growth and World Trade*. London: Cambridge University Press.

Marr, W. and D. Paterson, 1980—*Canada: An Economic History*. Toronto: MacMillan.

Marshall, H.F., F. Southard and K. Taylor, 1976—*Canadian American Industry*. Toronto: McClelland and Stewart.

Marx, Karl, 1959—"Excerpts from the Class Struggles in France 1848 to 1850" in L. Feuer (ed.) *Marx and Engels*. Garden City, New York: Doubleday.

Marx, Karl and Friedrich Engels, 1959—"Manifesto of the Communist Party" in L. Feuer (ed.) *Marx and Engels*. Garden City, N.J.: Doubleday.

McKay, J.P., 1970—*Pioneers for Profit. Foreign Entrepreneurship and Russian Industrialization 1885-1913*. Chicago: University of Chicago Press.

Milne, R.S., 1966—*Political Parties in New Zealand*. Oxford at the Clarendon Press.

Milward, A.S. and S.B. Saul, 1973—*The Economic Development of Continental Europe 1780-1870*. London: George Allen and Unwin.

Milward, A.S. and S.B. Saul, 1977—*The Development of the Economies of Continental Europe 1850-1914*. Cambridge, Mass.: Harvard University Press.

Myers, Gustavus, 1975—*A History of Canadian Wealth*. Toronto: Lorimer.

Naylor, Tom, 1975—*The History of Canadian Business 1867-1914*, Volumes I and II. Toronto: Lorimer.

Norman, Herbert E., 1940—*Japan's Emergence as a Modern State*. New York: Institute of Pacific Relations.

North, Douglas, 1965–"Aspects of Economic Growth in the U.S. 1815-1860" in H.J. Habakkuk and M. Postan (eds.), *Cambridge Economic History of Europe,* Volume VI, Part II. Cambridge, U.K.: Cambridge University Press.

Ohkawa, K. and H. Rosovsky, 1965–"A Century of Japanese Economic Growth" in W.W. Lockwood (ed.) *The State and Economic Enterprise in Japan.* Princeton, N.J.: Princeton University Press.

Ouellet, Fernand, 1980–*Economic and Social History of Quebec 1760-1850.* (Toronto: McClelland and Stewart).

Pauli, Herta, 1942–*Alfred Nobel. Dynamite King–Architect of Peace.* New York: L.B. Fischer.

Pearton, Maurice, 1982–*The Knowledgeable State: Diplomacy, War and Technology since 1830.* London: Burnett Books.

Pollock, R. Donald, 1981–*Hard Times, Hard Choices. A Statement.* Ottawa: Science Council of Canada

Potter, J., 1963–"The Role of a Swedish Bank in the Process of Industrialization", *Scandinavian Economic History Review* Volume XI.

Quinn, John B., 1969–"Technology Transfer by Multinational Companies". *Harvard Business Review 46.* (November-December).

Rosecrance, Richard, 1964–"The Radical Culture of Australia" in Louis Hartz (ed.) *The Founding of New Societies.* New York: Harcourt, Brace and World Inc.

Safarian, A.E., 1973–*Foreign Ownership of Canadian Industry.* Toronto: University of Toronto Press.

Samuelsson, Kurt, 1968–*From Great Power to Welfare State.* London: George Allen and Unwin Ltd.

Scott, Franklin, 1977–*Sweden: The Nation's Historyh.* Minneapolis: University of Minnesota Press.

Skelton, O.D., 1920–*The Life and Times of Sir Alexander Tilloch Galt.* Toronto: Oxford University Press.

Smith, Thomas C., 1955–*Political Change and Industrial Development in Japan: Government Enterprises 1868-1880.* Stanford, California: Stanford University Press

Stacey, C.P., 1940–*The Military Problems of Canada: A Survey of Defence Policies and Strategic Conditions Past and Present.* Toronto: Ryerson Press

Stevens, G.R., 1962–*Canadian National Railways Volume II.* Toronto: Clarke Irwin.

Taylor, A.J.P., 1954–*The Struggle for Mastery in Europe 1848-1918.* Oxford at the Claredon Press

Thompson, E.P., 1963–*The Making of the English Working Class.* Harmondsworth, England: Penguin

Thomson, Dale, 1960–*Alexander Mackenzie. Clear Grit.* Toronto: Macmillan

Tilly, Richard, 1966–*Financial Institutions and Industrialization in the Rhineland 1815-1870.* Madison: University of Wisconsin

Trudeau, Pierre, 1969–*Federalism and the French Canadians.* Toronto: Macmillan

Underhill, Frank, 1967–"Some Aspects of Upper Canadian Radical Opinion in the Decade before Confederation" in *Upper Canadian Politics in the 1850's.* Canadian Historical Readings No. 2. Toronto: University of Toronto Press

Laue, Theodore von, 1963–*Sergei Witte and the Industrialization of Russia.* New York: Columbia University Press

Viner, Jacob, 1975–*Canada's Balance of International Indebtedness 1900-1913.* Toronto: McClelland and Stewart

Wade, Mason, 1968–*The French Canadians 1760-1967. Volume I 1760-1911.* rev. ed. Toronto: Macmillan of Canada.

Watt, James, 1979–"The Protestant Protective Association of Canada." An Example of Religious Extremism in Ontario in the 1890's" in B. Hodgins and R. Page (eds.), *Canadian History Since Confederation.* Second edition. Georgetown, Ontario: Irwin-Dorsey

Whitaker, Reg, 1977–"Images of the State in Canada" in Leo Panitch (ed.) *The Canadian State: Political Economy and Political Power.* Toronto: University of Toronto Press

White, Leonard, 1954–*The Jacksonians. A Study in Administrative History 1829-1861.* New York: Macmillan

Wilkinson, Bruce, 1980–*Canada in the Changing World Economy.* Montreal: C.D. Howe Institute.

Williams, William A., 1969–*The Roots of the Modern American Empire.* New York: Random House

Wood, Louis, 1975–*A History of Farmers' Movements in Canada.* Toronto: University of Toronto Press

Younger, R.M., 1970–*Australia and the Australians. A New Concise History.* New York: Humanities Press

A "Structural-Rational" Theory of the Functions of Directorship Interlocks Between Financial and Nonfinancial Corporations

R.J. Richardson

Introduction

There are two debates that seem to be among the longest running of any in sociology. The first is: who controls modern corporations? Is it management (Berle and Means, 1932), family capitalists (Zeitlin, 1974), or financial institutions, especially the banks (Kotz, 1978)? The second is: what functions do directorship interlocks serve? Are they mechanisms of financial control, interorganizational cooptation, class consolidation, elite integration or information flow? Indeed, do they fulfill any function at all?

This article examines the intersection of these two debates, asking what functions directorship interlocks between financial and nonfinancial corporations serve. It briefly outlines the propositions of the three most relevant existing theories and proposes a new "structural-rational" theory. Empirical analyses of the present and proposed theories are extensively reported elsewhere (Richardson, 1984). The scope of this article is much more limited. It focuses on the most critical element of corporate performance—profitability—and on the relationship between financial-nonfinancial directorship interlocks and corporate profitability.

The three theories that have the most to say about relationships between financial and nonfinancial corporations are the theories of financial control, finance capital and interorganizational cooptation. The first theory derives from one interpretation of the work of Lenin (1917, 1968), and especially from Hilferding (1910). It holds that monopolistic control of money capital by the few dominant banks in modern economies has given them the power to control virtually the whole range of industry. One way by which this control is implemented is the use of directorship interlocks between financials and nonfinancials. The result of financial control is that nonfinancials operate for the benefit of the financials that control them. Hence, financially-controlled corporations will be more heavily burdened with debt, operated more conservatively, and less profitably than other firms.

The second theory—finance capital—derives from a more widely-held interpretation of Lenin's work. It proposes that modern economies are dominated by a financial-industrial complex which comprises a fusion of financial and industrial

capital, within which neither dominates.[1] This theory holds that directorship interlocks between major financial and nonfinancial corporations provide the "social
cement" for this dominant complex. It also holds that corporations comprising
this financial-industrial complex will be the largest and most profitable ones in the
economy.

The third theory derives from Selznick (1949), who argued that modern corporations try to reduce uncertainty by coopting problematic sectors of their environment. They do this by inviting representatives of the most problematic sectors of
their environment to join their boards. Thus, "corporate interlocks are a cooptive
mechanism" (Burt, 1979: 416). The most generalized and critical resource for nonfinancial corporations is capital. Therefore, the theory holds that nonfinancials
will commonly coopt financials to secure access to capital. Successful use of this
strategy will enhance profits.

These three theories all argue that directorship interlocks fulfill a singular function: financial control in the first case, consolidation of the dominant class fraction
in the second case, and interorganizational cooptation in the last. But other theories
argue that they fulfill entirely different functions, while one theory—that of management control—proposes that they fulfill no function at all. To the managerialists,
directorship interlocks, if formed at all, are formed as a result of the personal characteristics (such as esteem) of the directors involved. The first question this article
addresses, then, is: Under which conditions can directorship interlocks logically
be conceived to fulfill the function of control, class consolidation or cooptation,
or, indeed, any function at all?

I suggest that we can begin to answer this question by taking two simple, logical
steps. First, we need to demonstrate some purposive intent in the formation of
interlocks. Directorship interlocks between dominant Canadian corporations have
an average lifespan of only four or five years.[2] Directors resign, retire or die—and
when this happens, an interlock between a given pair of firms is broken. The broken interlock may have been formed originally because of some personal characteristic of the director involved, or it may have been purposively formed to establish some kind of structural relationship. *Replacement* of a broken interlock can
logically be conceived to indicate purposive intent.

For example, if a broken interlock between corporations A and B is not replaced
by a new interlock between the same two firms, there has been no demonstration
of purposive intent. The original interlock cannot logically be considered a potential mechanism of control.[3] Similarly with class consolidation and cooptation:
replacement is required to demonstrate purposive intent. Here, the replacement
could be either a new interlock between the same two firms (called an "identical
tie"), or by a new interlock from another dominant corporation in the same economic sector (called an "equivalent tie").

The second logical step concerns the *direction* the interlock takes. Surely, to the
financial control theory, there is a vast difference between a banker sitting on an
industrial board and an industrialist sitting on a bank board. In the former case,
the banker participates in the industrial firm's decision-making, while in the latter,
the industrialist participates in the decision-making process of the bank. For the
same reason, the direction of the interlock is crucial to the interorganizational cooptation theory insofar as it specifies the direction of intercorporate influence, and
identifies which is the "cooptor" and which the "cooptee."

Over 100 studies of financial-nonfinancial interlocks have been undertaken.[4]
However, they have produced inconclusive and conflicting results, largely, I suggest, because of inadequate conceptualization. For example, the vast majority of these studies overlook the importance of interlock replacement and direction. Yet, as I hope will become clear shortly, these two concepts are key elements in an adequate theory of the functions of financial-nonfinancial interlocks.

A Proposed "Structural-Rational" Theory

I shall refer to the theory proposed here as a "Structural-Rational" theory. "Structural," because it follows the structural analytic paradigm (sometimes termed network analysis) in emphasizing social structure and process; "rational," because it attempts to attribute instrumentally rational meaning to the actions of the people involved in interlocks. Stated otherwise, relationships between financial and nonfinancial corporations reflect the tension between the purposive, goal-seeking actions of people commanding such firms and the constraints of socio-economic structure which these same people face.

Along with those who adhere to the *financial control* theory one can agree that some interlocks may, indeed, be mechanisms of intercorporate control or influence. However, three qualifications seem to me to be in order. First, only those ties which, when broken, are replaced by what I have termed an "identical tie" can be logically conceived to fulfill this function, at least potentially. Second, just as replaced financial to nonfinancial ties may indicate potential financial control, replaced nonfinancial to financial ties may indicate potential *non*financial control or influence. Third, while the financial control theory argues that financial control (as evidenced by the formation of interlocks) *causes* financially-controlled corporations to become less profitable than those which are not so controlled, I propose the reverse: that the formation of these interlocks is a *result*, not a cause, of unprofitable performance. For example, a financial may demand a seat on the board of a large, particularly unprofitable, and perhaps heavily-indebted nonfinancial as a means of protecting its interests.

The *interorganizational cooptation theory* teaches us that some interlocks may represent attempts by nonfinancials to reduce environmental uncertainty by securing access to capital. I propose some modifications to this theory too. First, just as nonfinancials may coopt financials to secure access to capital, financials may coopt nonfinancials to secure profitable *outlets* for capital. Second, because the cooptee sits on the board of the cooptor and participates in its decision-making process, there is an element of intercorporate influence in every cooptive relationship. Third, this theory ignores the motives of the cootee. But it is necessary to take their motives into account in order to explain such phemonena as large and conservative financial corporations (Mintz, 1979) declining to be represented on the boards of small, unprofitable and risky firms. Fourth, this theory proposes that the formation of interlocks from financials to nonfinancials causes the latter to become more profitable. Again, I propose the reverse: these interlocks are formed as a *result* of corporate profitability.

The *finance capital theory* proposes that the major financial and nonfinancial corporations in the economy form a dominant financial-industrial complex which fuses these capital pools—a fusion implying the dominance of neither. It argues that financial-nonfinancial interlocks fulfill two closely related functions. First, they socially cement this dominant complex. Second, they represent a channel for the flow of valuable information (on capital market trends, industrial performance and expansion plans, etc.). Therefore, these financial-nonfinancial interlocks, whichever direction they take, provide advantages to both parties. I agree, although I think that one qualification needs to be made. While these interlocks seem to provide advantages to both parties, the advantages accrue primarily to the sender, rather than the receiver, of the interlock. This is true for two reasons. First, the sender participates in the decision-making process of the receiver, while the reverse is not true. Second, by sitting on another major corporation's board—which usually contains representatives from several industries—the sender obtains much more information than the receiver.

Which corporation, the financial or the nonfinancial, will be the sender? Exchange theorists (e.g. Emerson, 1962; Jacobs, 1974) propose, entirely sensibly I think, that relationships between corporations will reflect their balance of power and dependency. It seems logical to propose that—among other elements—this power balance is affected by the size, profitability, industrial concentration ratio, and degree of dependence on external capital of the nonfinancials involved. Following exchange theory, the balance of power is reflected in intercorporate influence which, in turn, is indicated by the *direction* of the interlock. However, the power balance, I propose, is a conditional phenomenon, not an immutable one. It can change as a result of many factors, such as changes in the business cycle and in the fortunes of a given industry.

These theoretical considerations may be summarized as follows. Broken interlocks that are replaced can be logically conceived to reflect some purposive, structural intent, whereas those that are not replaced cannot be so described. Interlocks between the dominant financials and nonfinancials in the economy provide advantages (such as the flow of valuable information) to both parties. However, these advantages accrue primarily to the sender, rather than the receiver, of the interlock. The direction of the interlock (indicating which firm is the sender and which the receiver) is a reflection of the balance of power between the corporations involved. This power balance is affected by the relative size of the corporations involved, the capital structure, capital intensity and profitability of the nonfinancial corporations, etc. Therefore, in opposition to the financial control and interorganizational cooptation theories, I propose that financial-nonfinancial interlocks are formed or not formed, and assume the direction that they do as a *result* of the profitability of nonfinancial corporations. Finally, because of the relative conservatism of Canadian financials (Mintz, 1979), and constraints on their executives' time, these corporations avoid representation on the board of small, unprofitable and risky nonfinancials. Thus, financial corporations tend to be unable to send interlocks to the largest, most profitable, and least risky nonfinancials and unwilling to send interlocks to nonfinancials with the opposite characteristics. One exception to this generalization is noteworthy: some financials may demand a seat on the board of a large, but particularly unprofitable and perhaps heavily-indebted nonfinancial as one of several available means of protecting their interests.

Testing the Structural-Rational Theory

Elsewhere (Richardson, 1984) I derived several hypotheses from the structural-rational theory and tested these against pertinent evidence. The hypotheses specify conditions under which replaced ties (taken as indicators of purposive intent) between the major financial and nonfinancial corporations in the Canadian postwar economy tend to be formed and not formed; and, when formed, which direction they will take. I also hypothesized a number of relationships between the presence of specific types of replaced ties and the profitability of nonfinancial corporations.

The comprehensive data base developed by Carroll, Fox and Ornstein (1979; 1981) was used for testing the hypotheses. These data comprise all the directorship interlocks for the period 1946-76 among the following firms:

123 industrial firms (which) were among the top 70 industrials in Canada at one or more of the five year intervals (from 1946 to 1976); 38 financials (which) were among the top 20; 18 merchandisers (which) were among the top 10; 15 property development firms (which) had assets equal to the smallest ranked industrial firms . . . and nine securities dealers (Carroll, Fox and Ornstein, 1981:25).

The project extracts from this data base all of the primary[5] financial-nonfinancial directorship interlocks among these 203 Canadian firms.[6]

These interlock data were then matched against operating, financial and profitability data for this set of corporations. The latter data were obtained from federal and provincial government agencies and from corporate annual reports.

The resulting empirical analysis provided very little support for the financial control theory, and the interorganizational cooptation theory. The majority of the hypotheses derived from these theories was rejected. On the other hand, my analysis provided moderate support for the finance capital theory, and strong support for the structural-rational theory. Of the twelve hypotheses derived from the latter theory, none was rejected; two were partly supported (e.g. for some, but not all of the specific types of ties under study); and ten were fully supported.

Given space limitations, the results of all these empirical tests cannot be reported here. However, it is agreed by virtually all social scientists, whatever their perspective, that the critical indicator of corporate performance is profitability. Therefore, this paper is narrowly focused on the relationship betwen the presence of replaced financial-nonfinancial ties and the profitability of the nonfinancial corporations involved.

The empirical analyses of the relationship between the presence of replaced ties and corporate profitability are conducted by means of multiple classification analysis (MCA)—a statistical technique somewhat similar to multiple regression analysis. The MCA's reported here identify the deviations from the mean for each category of each variable, after adjustment for the other variables in the equation. The strength of each variable is reported as Beta, which measures the degree of association of a given independent variable—again after adjustment for the other variables.

Three measures of corporate profitability are used in this analysis: Return on Shareholders Investment (the most important measure from the shareholders' perspective), Return on Assets (the most widely used measure of the effectiveness of corporate use of capital), and Net and Interest on Assets (an important measure used by the financial community) (Bernstein, 1978; Pennings, 1980). In order to smooth out short term anomalies, I used three year averages for each of these measures of corporate profitability. As might be expected, these three measures of corporate profitability are highly correlated (the correlations are in excess of 0.8). Consequently, I utilized a scale ("PROFITS"), which is the sum of these three standardized variables.

Below I report the empirical relationships between this profit scale and the presence of four conceptually different types of ties:

—broken interlocks replaced by an "identical" tie, i.e. a tie in the same direction and between the same two corporations,

   (a) from financials to nonfinancials, and

   (b) from nonfinancials to financials;

—broken interlocks replaced by an "equivalent" tie, i.e. a tie in the same direction but from a different corporation in the same economic sector,

   (c) from financials to nonfinancials, and

   (d) from nonfinancials to financials.

In each case, these relationships are controlled for the industry of the nonfinancial corporations involved. The results are reported in Tables 1 to 4.

Relationships Between Financial-Nonfinancial Interlocks and Corporate Profitability

The structural-rational theory proposes that, while interlocks between the dominant financial and nonfinancial corporations in an economy provide advantages to both parties, these advantages accrue primarily to the sender. Furthermore, the direction which a purposively formed financial-nonfinancial tie will take reflects the balance of power between the corporations involved. One of the main determinants of relative power is corporate profitability. Thus, the theory hypothesizes that:

The likelihood of the presence of nonfinancial to financial identical ties will increase with the profits of nonfinancial firms.

This hypothesized relationship is strong and statistically significant (see Table 1: 1963 Beta = .28; 1968 Beta = .25; for both years $p < .01$).

In contrast, no hypothesis can be derived from the structural-rational theory concerning the relationship between the presence of *financial to nonfinancial* identical ties and the profits of nonfinancial terms. This is because the logic of the theory suggests that financials might establish identical ties to *two* groups of nonfinancials. The first group would consist of moderately profitable nonfinancials (the most profitable nonfinancials having established identical ties *to* financials). The second group would consist of large, very unprofitable and perhaps heavily-indebted nonfinancials, where financials may establish identical ties in order to protect their investment. The mix of these two groups of nonfinancials is unknown; but given their coexistence, it seems a safe bet that there will be *no* relationship between the presence of financial to nonfinancial identical ties and the magnitude of nonfinancial profits. In fact, I found a negative relationship between these ties and nonfinancial profitability, although the relationship was significant for only one of the two years examined (see Table 1: 1963 Beta = -.11, $p > .01$; 1960 Beta = - .24, $p < .01$). The theory could explain this relationship if the mix of these corporations was weighted in favour of the second group of large and unprofitable nonfinancials. But this is only speculation.[7]

TABLE I
Effect of Identical Ties on Nonfinancial Profits
Dependent Variable: "Profits"

	1963			1968		
(n)	112			108		
R^2	.182**			.325***		
Grand Mean	.06			-.07		
Std. Deviation	2.81			2.90		
Variable and Category	**(n)**	**Adjusted Deviation**	**Beta**	**(n)**	**Adjusted Deviation**	**Beta**
NONFINANCIAL SIC						
Mining	18	1.01		20	1.89	
Manufacturing	52	.16		47	-.62	
Transportation & Communication	7	.64		6	2.32	
Utilities	14	-1.13		13	-.24	
Merchandising	12	.70		11	.27	
Prop. Dev. & Holding	9	-2.61	.35**	11	-2.04	.45**
IDENTICAL TIES:						
FINANCIAL TO NONFINANCIAL						
None	100	.11		91	.29	
1 or more	12	-.90	-.11	17	-1.56	-.24**
NONFINANCIAL TO FINANCIAL						
None	87	-.43		93	-.28	
1 or more	25	1.48	.28**	15	1.74	.25**

** $p < .01$

*** $p < .001$

The theory suggests that the most powerful (profitable) nonfinancials will place their executives on financial boards, while moderately powerful (profitable) nonfinancials will attract financial executives to their boards, and (except for the special circumstances noted above) weak (unprofitable) nonfinancials will be unable to form ties with financials in either direction. The special circumstance of a financial demanding a seat on the board of a large but particularly unprofitable nonfinancial in order to protect its investment would apply only to *identical,* and not to *equivalent* ties. This is because the financial in question would surely be unwilling to have their representative on the board of the weak nonfinancial replaced by a representative of a *different* financial firm (and this is what must happen, by definition, for a financial to nonfinancial equivalent tie to form). Therefore, since financial to nonfinancial *equivalent* ties should be found with only one group of nonfinancials (the moderately profitable and powerful ones) and not with two different groups of firms (as was the case with *identical* ties), the theory hypothesizes that:

The likelihood of the presence of financial to nonfinancial equivalent ties will increase with the profitability of nonfinancial firms.

TABLE 2
Effect of Equivalent Ties on Nonfinancial Profits
Dependent Variable: "Profits"

		1963			1968	
(n)		.72			77	
R²	.134				.380***	
Grand Mean		-.17			-.06	
Std. Deviation		2.85			3.11	
Variable and Category	**(n)**	**Adjusted Deviation**	**Beta**	**(n)**	**Adjusted Deviation**	**Beta**
NONFINANCIAL SIC						
Mining	12	.69		15	1.42	
Manufacturing	31	-.16		35	-.76	
Transportation & Communication	6	1.41		3	4.37	
Utilities	10	-1.06		10	.20	
Merchandising	9	1.00		7	.41	
Prop. Dev. & Holding	4	-2.53	.32*	7	-1.83	.46***
EQUIVALENT TIES: FINANCIAL TO NONFINANCIAL						
None	66	-.14		66	-.37	
1 or more	6	1.59	.16	11	2.23	.32**
NONFINANCIAL TO FINANCIAL						
None	66	-.01		67	-.00	
1 or more	6	.06	.01	10	.01	.00

* p ‹ .05
** p ‹ .01
*** p ‹ .001

This second hypothesis is also supported. The hypothesized correlation is present in both 1963 and 1968, although statistically significant only in 1968 (see Table 2: 1963 Beta = .16, p › .05; 1968 Beta = .32, p ‹ .01).

Concerning *nonfinancial to financial* equivalent ties, the logic of the theory suggests that nonfinancials sending equivalent ties to financials should be among the most profitable when the tie was first formed. However, by definition, the financial must have replaced this tie with a new tie from a *different* nonfinancial in order to form an equivalent tie. This indicates that the original nonfinancial was unable to maintain representation on the financial's board, indicating a decline in its power and profitability. Therefore, it may be hypothesized that:

There exists *no* relationship between the presence of nonfinancial to financial equivalent ties and the magnitude of nonfinancial profits.

In fact, this relationship is found to be non-existent (see Table 2: 1963 Beta = .01 p › .05; 1968 Beta = .00, p › .05).[8]

Inferring Casual Priority

The question of causal priority is of fundamental importance to the present research. The structural-rational theory suggests that nonfinancial corporate profitability is an important determinant of the formation of identical and equivalent ties between financial and nonfinancial corporations. However, the financial control and inter-organizational cooptation theories suggest precisely the opposite causal sequence; that the formation of these financial-nonfinancial ties affects nonfinancial profits. This effect is negative according to the theory of financial control, and positive according to interorganizational cooptation theory. I nonetheless hypothesize that:

Nonfinancial profitability determines the formation rate of replaced ties between financial and nonfinancial corporations.

Inferring Causal Priority with Cross-Lagged Correlations

To this point, I have analyzed simultaneous correlations of the profitability of non-financial corporations with the presence of four specific types of replaced interlocks. These simultaneous correlations are portrayed graphically in Figure 1 as relation-ships A and B. Of course I do not infer causal priority in these two relationships.

FIGURE 1
Inferring Causal Priority with Cross-Lagged Correlations

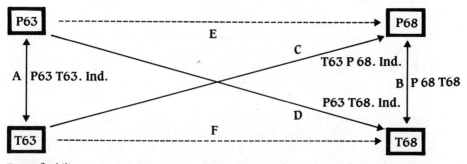

P=profitability
T=the four types of ties (identical and equivalent ties from financials to non-financials and from nonfinancials to financials)
63=1963
68=1968

The use of cross-lagged correlations is a very straightforward and intuitively plausible approach to inferring causal priority. The logic of this method is that a strong correlation between two variables indicates that they are causally related, whereas a weak correlation indicates that they are not. Applying this logic, two variables, I and J, are both measured at two different points in time (t_1 and t_2). Then they are correlated in a cross-lagged fashion. If the correlation It_1 with Jt_2 is found to be substantially stronger than the correlation Jt_1 with It_2, then I can logically be conceived to have causal priority over J. In the present case, these cross-lagged correlations are represented schematically as relationships C and D in Figure 1. The two variables, of course, can also be correlated with themselves when measured at different points in time (see Figure 1, relationships E and F).

Consider now the cross-lagged correlations (controlling for industry) between:

(a) nonfinancial profits in 1963 and the presence of each of the four specific types of replaced ties in 1968; and

(b) nonfinancial profits in 1968 and the presence of each of these four types of ties in 1963 (see Table 3).

TABLE 3
Inferring Causal Priority with Cross-Lagged Correlations
Performance Indicator: "Profits"

Type of Tie	Betas				
Cross-Correlations	Simultaneous Cross-Correlations			Cross-Lagged Correlations	
	P63 T63 Ind	P68 T68 Ind	P63 T68 Ind	T63 P68 Ind	Difference
Identical Ties:					
NF to F	.28**	.21**	.34***	.02	.32
F to NF	.11(-)	.24(-)**	.25(-)**	.01	.23
Equivalent Ties:					
NF to F	.01	.01(-)	.03(-)	.00	.03
F to NF	.16	.31**	.48***	.18	.30

** p < .01
*** p < .001
P=Profits   T=Ties   Ind=Industry (S.I.C.)

The correlation of 1963 profits and 1968 ties is weak and nonsignificant for nonfinancial to financial equivalent ties—just as was found for both years in the simultaneous correlations. However, all of the other three correlations of 1963 profits with 1968 ties are found to be strong and significant. In fact, they are stronger than the simultaneous correlations of these variables. Thus, there is a significant relationship between the profitability of nonfinancial corporations in 1963 and the presence of three specific types of replaced interlocks five years hence. Profitability thus seems to cause tie replacement.

On the other hand, the correlations of the presence of each of these four types of ties in 1963 with nonfinancial corporate profits in 1968 (controlled for industry) are all found to be weak and not significant. There is no significant relationship between the presence of ties in 1963 and corporate profits five years later. Tie replacement thus appears *not* to cause profitability.

This allows us to conclude that the profitability of nonfinancial corporations has causal priority over the formation of three types of ties:
(a) nonfinancial to financial identical ties;
(b) financial to nonfinancial identical ties; and
(c) financial to nonfinancial equivalent ties.

Inferring Causal Priority from Partial Correlations

We can triangulate this attempt to infer causal priority by using a second approach, that of partial correlation.

The logic of the partial correlation approach is that, if nonfinancial corporate

TABLE 4
Effect of Controlling for Prior "Profits" and for Prior Interlocks on Simulations Correlations of "Profits" and Interlocks

Type of Tie	Dependent Var: 1968 Ties Controlling for prior profits		Dependent Var: 1968 Profits Controlling for prior Ties	
	P68 Beta	P63 Beta	T68 Beta	T63 Beta
Identical Ties: NF to F				
T68 P68. Ind	21**		.21**	
T68 P68. Ind, P63	.02	.37***		
T68 P68. Ind, T63			.29**	.14(-)
Identical Ties: F to NF				
T68 P68. Ind	.24(-)**		.24(-)**	
T68 P68. Ind, P63	.13(-)	.17(-)		
T68 P68. Ind, T63			.26(-)**	.08
Equivalent Ties: NF to F				
T68 P68. Ind	.01(-)		.01(-)	
T68 P68. Ind, P63	.05(-)	.20		
T68 P68. Ind, T63			.00	.02(-)
Equivalent Ties: F to NF				
T68 P68. Ind	.31**		.31**	
T68 P68. Ind, P63	.15	.44***		
T68 P68. Ind, T63			.34***	.07(-)

** p ‹ .01
*** p ‹ .001

profits have causal priority over the formation of replaced interlocks, then:

(a) the simultaneous correlation of 1968 profits with 1968 ties will be reduced when controlled for 1963 profits; and

(b) this simultaneous correlation will *not* be reduced when controlled for 1963 ties.

The empirical results meet both of these requirements (see Table 4). In every case when controlled for 1963 profits, the 1968 simultaneous correlation of profits with ties becomes weak and insignificant. In fact, the partial correlation of 1963 profits with 1968 ties is consistently stronger than the partial correlation of 1968 profits with 1968 ties. Furthermore, the strength of the 1968 simultaneous correlation of profits with ties is *not* reduced when 1963 ties are introduced as a control variable. Thus, the profitability of nonfinancial corporations has causal priority over the formation of purposive interlocks between financial and nonfinancial forms, as demonstrated by the use of partial and cross-lagged correlations.

Conclusions

Since two different methodological approaches have allowed us to infer that nonfinancial corporate profitability is causally prior to the replacement of broken interlock tends to occur may be the result of the fact that the nonfinancial is supports the following conclusions.

The identical replacement of a nonfinancial to financial interlock tends to occur among the more profitable nonfinancial corporations. This suggests that, although there appear to be advantages to all nonfinancials in having their executives sit on financial boards, only the more profitable nonfinancials will succeed in their attempts to maintain representation on these boards. The perceived advantages of this relationship will tend to accrue only to the more profitable nonfinancials, thus helping to maintain or perhaps even improve their profit performance and market power.

One situation in which the identical replacement of a financial to nonfinancial interlock tends to occur may be the result of the fact that the nonfinancial is particularly *un*profitable. I suggested earlier that there is normally no reason for a financial executive to choose to sit on the board of an unprofitable or risky firm. Thus, I speculated that this phenomenon might occur as a result of a financial corporation demanding a seat on the board of a large but particularly unprofitable nonfinancial in order to protect its interests. This conjecture was subsequently supported during personal interviews with top executives of three major financial corporations.[9]

The replacement of an equivalent financial to nonfinancial interlock tends to occur among relatively nonfinancial corporations. The preferred access to information and perhaps capital that this arrangement could provide appears to help maintain or perhaps even increase the profit position and market power of these already-profitable firms.

Finally, the equivalent replacement of a nonfinancial to financial interlock has no significant relationship to the profit performance of the nonfinancial corporation. Perhaps this is because in this case, alone among the four types of interlocks investigated, the nonfinancial is unable to maintain a long-term relationship with financial corporations. Perhaps this, in turn, is because the profitability of the nonfinancial corporation declined after the interlock was originally formed. Again, however, this is only conjecture.

All of these conclusions are logically consistent with the proposed structural-rational theory. On the other hand, this inference of casual priority violates the logic of the interorganizational cooptation and financial control theories.

However, the substance of my analysis leads to the conclusion that the inference of causal priority – although logically crucial – may be unimportant in practice. What appears to exist is a circular and self-sustaining process. The profitability of nonfinancial corporations appears to be a causal factor in the formation of financial-nonfinancial interlocks which, in turn, seem to provide advantages (or in one case perhaps disadvantages) which *reinforces* the original profit position. Only in one case (equivalent ties from nonfinancials to financials) does the logic of the analysis not support this self-reinforcing process. This finding suggests that the process is not an immutable one. Rather, it appears to be a conditional process, as I have argued in developing the proposed theory.

On a broader theoretical level these research results also support the finance capital theory, as we have found that the largest and most profitable nonfinancials are the ones most likely to be tied to financial corporations with purposively formed interlocks. This finding is consistent with the finance capital theory's proposition that modern economies are dominated by a highly profitable financial-industrial complex which comprises a fusion of financial and industrial capital.

Notes

1. See Richardson (1982b) for an exposition of these contrasting interpretations.
2. This observation comes from secondary analysis of a data base developed by Carroll, Fox and Ornstein (1979, 1981) of directorship interlocks between the top 156 nonfinancial corporations and the top 47 financials in Canada for the period 1946 to 1976.
3. More specifically, it can *at best* be logically considered a mechanism of short-term ephemeral control.
4. Many of these are described and evaluated in Richardson (1982b).
5. A primary interlock between two corporations is formed by an executive of one corporation sitting as an outside director on the board of the other corporation.
6. Because of its broad coverage of the major Canadian financial and nonfinancial corporations, and especially because it provides longitudinal data for this 30-year period, this data base is ideally suited for the research project. I gratefully acknowledge the kind cooperation of William K. Carroll, John Fox, and Michael D. Ornstein in granting access to this data base.
7. Two other findings give modest support to this speculation. First, the distribution of "Profits" for corporations holding a financial to nonfinancial identical tie (controlled for industry) tends to be bimodal, unlike those without such a tie. Second, for those nonfinancials receiving an identical tie from a financial, there is a substantial number whose "Profit" is more than one standard deviation less than the mean for all nonfinancial corporations (24% of the cases in 1968 and 17% in 1968); and only a small number whose "Profit" is more than one standard deviation *greater* than this mean (6% in 1968 and 8% in 1968). These findings are not statistically significant and could represent only random variations. However, they fit with the speculated mix of highly *un*profitable and moderately profitable corporations.
8. The following empirical result provides some modest support for this logic. Controlling for industry and for corporate profitability in 1968, there is a moderate *positive* correlation between the profitability of nonfinancial firms in 1963 and nonfinancial to financial equivalent ties in 1968 (Table 4: Beta = .20, n.s.). These results, of course, could also be mere random variations.
9. These interviews took place in August, 1983. These executives demanded, and received, assurances of anonymity as a condition of being interviewed.

References

Berle, Adolphe A. and Gardiner, C. Means, 1967. *The Modern Corporation and Private Property* (Revised edition). New York: Harcourt Brace and World.

Bernstein, Leopold A., 1978. *Financial Statement Analysis.* Georgetown: Irwin-Dorsey.

Blalock, Hubert M., 1964. *Causal Inferences in Non-Experimental Research.* Chapel Hill, University of North Carolina Press.

Burt, Ronald S., 1979. "A Structural Theory of Interlocking Corporate Directorates," *Social Networks* 1, 4: 415-35.

Carrington, Peter J., 1981. "Horizontal Cooptation Through Corporate Interlocks," Structural Analysis Programme, University of Toronto, *Occasional Paper Series* No. 1.

Carroll, William K., John Fox and Michael D. Ornstein, 1979. "The Network of Directorship Interlocks Among the Largest Canadian Firms," Department of Sociology, York University, ms.

Carroll, William K., John Fox and Michael D. Ornstein, 1981. "Longitudinal Analysis of Directorship Interlocks." Paper presented to the Annual Meetings of the Canadian Sociology and Anthropology Association, Halifax, May.

Dunca, Otis Dudley, 1966. "Path Analysis: Sociological Examples." *American Journal of Sociology 72,* 1: 1-16.

Emerson, Richard M., 1962. "Power-Dependency Relations." *American Sociological Review* 27:31-41.

Hannan, Michael T. and Alice A. Young, 1977. "Estimation in Panel Models: Results on Pooling Cross-Sections and Time Series." In David R. Heise (ed.) *Sociological Methodology.* San Francisco: Jossey-Bass: 52-83.

Hilferding, Rudolph, 1910 (1970). *Le Capital Financier.* Tr. by Michael Olivier. Paris: Editions de Minuit.

Jacobs, David, 1974. "Dependency and Vulnerability: An Exchange Approach to the Control of Organizations." *Administrative Science* Quarterly 19: 45-59.

Kim, Jae-On and Frank J. Kohout, 1975. "Special Topics in General Linear Models." In Norman H. Nie et al. *Statistical Package for the Social Sciences* (second edition). New York: McGraw-Hill: 368-97.

Kotz, David M., 1978. *Bank Control of Large Corporations in the United States.* Berkeley: University of California Press.

Lazarsfeld, Paul F. and Robert K. Merton, 1964. "Friendship as a Social Process: A Substantive and Methodological Analysis." In M. Berger, T. Abel and C.H. Page (eds) *Freedom and Control in Modern Society.* New York: Octagon Books: 18-66.

Çazarsfeld, Paul F. and Robert K. Merton, 1964. "Friendship as a Social Process: A Substantive and Methodloogical Analysis." In M. Berger, T. Abel and C.H. Page (eds) *Freedom and Control in Modern Society.* New York: Octagon Books, pp. 18-66.

Lenin, V.I., 1917 (1975). "Imperialism, the Highest Stage of Capitalism." In Robert C. Tucker (ed.) *The Lenin Anthology.* New York: Norton: 204-74.

Lenin, V.I., 1968. *Collected Works.* Vol. 39. Moscow: Progress Publishers.

Levine, Joel and W.S. Roy, 1979. "A Study of Interlocking Directorates: Vital Concepts of Organization." In Paul H. Holland and Samuel Leinhardt (eds.) *Perspectives on Social Network Research.* New York: Academic Press: 349-78.

Mintz, Jack M., 1979. *The Measure of Rates of Return in Canadian Banking.* Hull: Canadian Government Printing Centre.

Nie, Norman H. *et al.,* 1975. *Statistical Package for the Social Sciences* (second edition). New York: McGraw-Hill.

Pelz, Donald C. and Frank M. Andrews, 1964. "Detecting Causal Priorities in Panel Study Data." *American Sociological Review,* 29, 6: 836-48.

Pennings, Johannes M., 1980.*Interlocking Directorates.* San Francisco: Jossey-Bass.

Richardson, R.J., 1982a. Perspectives on the Relationship Between Financial and Nonfinancial Corporations: A Critical Review. Structural Analysis Programme, University of Toronto, Working Paper No. 34.

Richardson, R.J., 1982b. "Merchants Against Industry: An Empirical Study of the Canadian Debate." *Canadian Journal of Sociology* 7, 3: 279-95.

Richardson, R.J., 1984. A "Structural-Rational" Theory of Financial-Nonfinancial Directorship Interlocks. Doctoral Dissertation, University of Toronto.

Zeitlin, Maurice, 1974. "Corporate Ownership and Control: The Large Corporation and the Capitalist Class." *American Journal of Sociology* 79: 1073-1119.

The State, The Capitalist Class, and the CPR
Karen Anderson

Since property here exists in the form of stock, its movement and transfer become purely a result of gambling on the stock exchange where the little fish are swallowed by the sharks and the lambs by the stock-exchange wolves (Marx 1970, Vol. III: 440).

Introduction

In 1881 the Canadian Parliament passed "An Act to Incorporate the Canadian Pacific Railway Company" (44 Vic. Cap. 7, 1881, Statutes of Canada). That act granted the right to construct a transcontinental railroad to a group of Canadian, American, British and French capitalists. Efforts to see such a contract successfully passed in Parliament spanned two decades, were instrumental in bringing about the scandalous defeat of the first government of the Dominion, and produced bitter and often ruinous competition among rival groups of capitalists. With the passage of the act in 1881 the first buying and selling syndicates were formed, CPR securities were brought to world markets, and construction was begun on a privately owned transcontinental railroad.

The construction of this long anticipated railroad[1] was financed partly through generous government loans, grants and concessions,[2] and partly through the simultaneous sale of securities on U.S., French, English, German and Dutch markets. This article is concerned with the institutional structures through which private funding was organized and mobilized for the CPR and with the role played by Canadian capitalists in realizing that project. It traces the history of the formation of the successful CPR syndicate, and examines the institutional connections of the members of the first board of directors. Finally, the article offers an interpretation of the general direction of Canadian development during the early post-Confederation period, and the particular role of Canadian capitalists in shaping that direction.

Merchants or Syndicates?

Much of the research on Canadian political economy during the early post-Confederation years concerns the role of Canadian capitalists in shaping the country's development. The most often cited (and criticized) interpretations are associated with the names of Tom Naylor and Wallace Clement.[3] Of the period under consideration in this article Naylor says:

Canadian Confederation and the subsequent National Policy are an unambiguous example of mercantilism in action . . .

Far from being the response of a rising industrial capitalism striving to break down inter-colonial tariff walls, Confederation and the national policy were the work of the descen-dants of the mercantile class which had aligned itself with the Colonial Office in 1837 to crush the indigenous petite bourgeoisie and nascent industrialists (Naylor, 1972: 14, 16).

In short, Naylor is convinced that the economic climate of post-Confederation Canada was strictly mercantilist—concerned with "banking and finance, railways, utilities, land speculation, and so on" (Naylor, 1972: 16) and decidedly hostile to industrial development. These concerns, he contends, represented "the restor-ation of the old mercantile ruling class in a new guise" and relied on "British finance capital and pro-British imperial xenophobia to offset the impact of the branch plant American industry that was a necessary adjunct of the mercantile system they created" (Naylor, 1972: 36).

Naylor's interpretation of this era in Canadian economic history finds support in the work of Wallace Clement. Confederation, Clement argues, produced a "com-mercial state"; a state "which would serve the ends of the dominant commercial ruling class" (Clement, 1975: 62). Clement proposes that the period after confedera-tion was the "age of its (i.e. the Canadian ruling class's) greatest autonomy'', an age in which they allied themselves with the state to "prepare themselves for the extrac-tion, transportation and exportation of Canada's staples." (Clement, 1975: 62). Citing Mel Watkins, Clement concludes that the National Policy was an instrument for "the commercial imperialism of the St. Lawrence merchants . . ." Clement, 1975: 63).

Both Naylor and Clement, then, agree on an interpretation of Canadian econ-omic history which places the direction of the economy in the hands of mercan-tilists *cum* financiers who controlled the Canadian state, and whose actions re-tarded the growth of "nascent industrial capital". According to Naylor important "contradictions exist" between the requirements of merchant and industrial capital, contradictions so profound that the interests of one form of capital are directly antithetical to those of the other. Thus the actions of the merchant capi-talists, who also set state policy, went contrary to the interests of the country's fledgling industrialists. Merchant/financiers drew funds away from Canadian industry and left a gap which American "branch-plant imperialism" quickly filled (Naylor, 1972: 36).

Both Clement and Naylor seem to agree, too, on the sources of capital used by the Canadian merchant/financiers for their so called "mercantile" projects; British "portfolio" or finance capital. According to Naylor (who is cited, approv-ingly, by Clement),

finance capital (sic) emerges not from industrial capital, as is usually supposed, but from merchant capital, through the pooling of merchants' resources and their development of a banking structure, and through the earnings of the entrepot trade. Like merchant capital, it is a low-risk type of venture; but, unlike merchant capital, it is long-term (Naylor, 1972: 13, cited in Clement, 1975: 34).

Using the CPR as a case study, I present a rather different view of Canadian economic history. I argue that, far from being an example of "British mercantilism" in action, of "old mercantile interests in a new guise", the incor-poration of, and raising of capital for, the CPR was at the leading edge of capi-talist development of the time. I seek to demonstrate that the CPR was financed not by British portfolio capital, but by the sale of securities on the world markets. Canadian capitalists were certainly involved in the project, but mainly in the capacity of providing a liaison between the Canadian state (as policy-making, grant-giving body), local financial institutions and the much larger world money markets. I conclude that, in order to make sense of the financing of the CPR, and the role of Canadian capitalists in that financing, it is necessary to analyze these phenomena in the context of world-scale trends in the reorganization of capital. With this in mind, I turn first to an examination of the structure of institutions used to organize the financing of the CPR, and then to events surrounding the chartering of the successful CPR company.

Syndicates and Securities

By 1870, securities floated by investment bankers were seldom less than $1,000,000 per issue.[4] The sheer size and number of issues made in any one year meant that they could not be financed by one individual or even by one financial institution, but had to be disbursed as widely as possible. Syndicates were organized specifically to cope with these problems. The modern syndicate, first used in Europe and the United States in the 1860's (Redlich, 1947:360), provided investment bankers with a series of temporary arrangements through which they could: 1) purchase and sell securities; 2) establish and maintain a stratified system that centralized control in a few large banking houses; 3) tie small banks to a few large firms which actually negotiated the purchase of securities from the companies of issue; 4) temporarily tie together the largest issuing houses, both nationally and internationally; 5) gain access to control over the operations of the companies whose securities they floated; and 6) limit the possibility of losses.

Participation in a syndicate allowed individual investment bankers to diversify commitments, to invest in several undertakings simultaneously, and to develop and strengthen ties to other banking institutions. Moreover, syndicates did nothing to alter existing relations between the issuer and the banker (Carosso, 1970:55). Any given syndicate, organized to dispose of an issue of securities, was actually composed of a number of smaller syndicates, each of which performed a specific function: originating, purchasing or underwriting, banking or selling. Usually each issue was sold to successive syndicates in a chain (Carosso, 1970:25). Control over the entire chain was centered in the hands of the "originator": a large, powerful investment banking house. This house would agree to purchase or underwrite an issue of securities put out by a company (industrial, rail, mining, etc.) or by some government (national or local) for which they already acted as fiscal agents, or for which they gained that position through the agreement to market securities.

The originator purchased or underwrote the securities and then resold them at a profit, usually to a larger syndicate called the "purchase syndicate", and organized for that purpose. A selling syndicate would also be organized at the same time. Much larger than the purchasing syndicate, the selling syndicate's purpose was to distribute the securities to actual investors (Carosso, 1970: 65). The price at which the members of the selling syndicate could sell securities, the number of securities each member of the selling syndicate was allotted (called their 'participation'), and the percentage of profit that each was allowed to keep were all decided by the originator (Carosso, 1970: 60). The most successful syndicates operated internationally, thus assuring a wide placement of securities.

During the 1860's British North America tended to be bypassed as an investment locale in favour of Egypt, Turkey, South America, Italy, India, Great Britain and the United States. These countries all had governments capable of contracting foreign loans to be used to buy materials for railway construction, or to give grants to construction companies.[5] It was not until 1867 that British North America became an independent country capable of floating a large enough loan to make extensive investment attractive. This meant that by 1870, when Sir John A. Macdonald's Conservatives were getting ready to authorize the construction of a transcontinental railroad, a large part of the "new" world had already provided outlets for some form of investment.

The emergence of investment banking in the United States and Germany, and its continued growth in England, France, Holland, Belgium and elsewhere, was coupled with the use of syndicates as the major means of organizing capital. Consequently, after 1870 any investment in the organization of a company on the scale of the proposed Canadian Pacific Railway would almost certainly have to include a large number of financial groups (consortia) operating together, both nationally and internationally, through syndicates. One of the major purposes in organizing syndicates was to prevent competition among investment bankers; competition among different syndicates nonetheless ensued. Competition, however, did not fall along national lines. Because of the structure of the securities market, the most successful syndicates were those with a large number of important *international* banking connections.

While small investors, taken as a whole, often held the largest portion of securities in any given company, they could not maintain control over that company because they were disorganized and scattered throughout the world. The members of the originating syndicate that marketed a company's securities were therefore in a structural position to control any given company by owning more shares than any one other single shareholder or cohesive group of shareholders.

The effects of this form of capital organization on the actions of capitalists are apparent in the events surrounding the incorporation of the CPR. The chartering of the CPR provides a rich source of data, illustrative of the relations between the state, the form of capital and capitalist's actions during the latter decades of the 19th century.

Syndicates and the CPR

When they came to office as the first Government of the Dominion of Canada, Sir John A. Macdonald's Conservatives supported the private construction of a transcontinental railroad. Consequently, on 14 June 1872 they passed the Canadian Pacific Act,[6] providing for the construction of a railway from Lake Nipissing to the Pacific Ocean and offering a land grant of 50,000,000 acres in alternate blocks twenty miles in depth on either side of the road bed and a cash subsidy of $30,000,000. Jay Cooke, one of the most innovative and ruthlessly aggressive of the new American bankers concerned with railroad investment, set out to acquire the contract (Irwin, 1968: 128-9). A few years before, Cooke had been approached by the directors of the Northern Pacific[7] to aid them in raising capital by floating securities. His company contracted to sell $100,000,000 of Northern Pacific 13% bonds (Larson, 1968: 246; Redlich, 1947: 360) and in return, received an option on 60% of the company's stock (Redlich, 1947: 360). The securities were marketed by a method unusual to the United States at the time: Cooke organized the first selling syndicate in America to distribute the issue (Redlich, 1947: 360).[8]

Although able to establish a selling syndicate in the U.S., Cooke failed to interest European houses. This was an unfortunate situation for Cooke & Co. Unable to limit their liability, they were in constant danger of overextending credit to the companies for which they floated securities. This, in turn, made them poor associates for other banking houses. By the time Jay Cooke & Co. were ready to try their hand at financing the CPR they were already in a shaky financial condition.

Vigorous competition from other banking houses, combined with anti-American sentiments among Canadians, made Cooke's projected undertaking in Canadian railroads even more difficult. In order to circumvent anti-Americanism, Cooke resorted to deceit. In 1872 he entered into an agreement with Sir Hugh Allan, a Canadian shipping magnate who had emigrated from Scotland in 1826. Cooke intended that Allan be used to throw a mantle of Canadian respectability over his project. By their agreement, Allan was empowered to negotiate contract terms with the Canadian government, and was authorized to accept an offer of not less than 50,000,000 acres of land and a cash subsidy of not less than $30,000,000 (Irwin, 1968:168).[9] Although all CPR stock would have to be registered in the names of Canadians, it was planned that real ownership would be in the hands of the group put together by Jay Cooke & Co.

Allan's position as intermediary is clearly indicated by his letter to George W. Cass, one of the members of Cooke's group of American financiers:

I have arranged ... that if you will send a certificate of the equivalent of $1,000,000 gold, having been placed by Jay Cooke & Co. to the credit of the Merchant's Bank of Canada, Montreal, in their own bank in New York, I will accept the cheques for the subscription, but no money will pass till the contract is entered into ... (Be) pleased therefore, to send me as early as possible powers of attorney to subscribe the stock, and Jay Cooke & Co.'s certificate above mentioned (*Journals of the House of Commons,* 2nd Session, 1873, Appendix No. 1: 212).

Its connection to Jay Cooke & Co. obscured, the Canadian Pacific Railway Company, with Sir Hugh Allan at its head, was incorporated.[10] On 23 July 1872 the CPR officially applied for the contract to construct the transcontinental railroad. At the same time, The Interoceanic Company[11] was also incorporated and applied for the same contract.[12] The Interoceanic Company had the distinction of being composed entirely of Canadians, including Senator D.I. Macpherson, William MacMaster, E.W. Cumberland and some fifty others (Glazebrook, 1938:243). Although members of the Interoceanic had no links to major sources of capital they did have political connections sufficient to prevent Macdonald from openly granting the Canadian Pacific Railway Company the contract to construct the transcontinental railroad.

Macdonald, returned to power in the election of 1870, tried to effect an amalgamation of the two companies but Senator Macpherson refused, giving as reason Sir Hugh's association with the Americans.[13] A contract finally passed Parliament awarding the right to construct the transcontinental railroad to a company with Allan as president of a board of directors by the Government (Irwin, 1968:193).[14]

Shares were to be allocated proportionately by province.[15] This move was in-tended to silence any criticisms about American control. Shortly after the incor-poration, Allan left for London to look for European partners for Jay Cooke & Company to help market the railroad's securities. He met with complete failure. A few months later the carefully concealed relations between Allan, the Americans and certain key members of the Conservative government became public know-ledge, and the Pacific Scandal broke.

Cooke had forces other than anti-American sentiment ranged against him. Al-though syndicates had emerged partly to prevent competition among investment bankers by drawing them into common interest groups, competition continued among various groupings. We have already seen that Cooke & Co. were in poor financial shape when, through Sir Hugh Allan, they undertook the contract for the CPR. This was due largely to the work of a competing constellation of American and European investment houses that included Morton, Rose & Co., and Morton, Bliss & Co.

Some of the most effective work in preventing Jay Cooke & Co. from finding European participants in their North American railroad ventures was done by Sir John Rose, senior partner in the banking firm of Morton, Rose and Company. Between 1867 and 1869 (when he left to become a partner in Morton, Rose & Co.) Rose acted as finance minister to Macdonald. Both he and his partner, Levi P. Morton (who became Vice-President of the United States in 1889) had extensive political careers. It was largely due to Rose's efforts in London that Jay Cooke was unable to sell Northern Pacific and Canadian Pacific bonds in Europe. In order to prevent their sale Rose advertised the Canadian Pacific as a rival to, rather than an extension of, the Northern Pacific. This was completely contrary to what Cooke had been advertising. When Cooke found out about Sir John's efforts he wrote the following to his partner:

We are astonished to receive your cable about Morton, Rose & Co. It would be unfortunate if the operations in Canada should be interfered with. The American agreement has to be kept dark for the present on account of the political jealousies in the Dominion, and there is to be no hint of the Northern Pacific connection, but the real plan is to cross the Sault Ste. Marie through Northern Michigan and Wisconsin to Duluth, then to build from Pembina up to Fort Garry and by and by through Saskatchewan to British Columbia. At this end Lake Nipissing is the objective point of the Canadian Pacific, to be met there by roads now building from Montreal and Toronto. The Act will provide for building a North shore road to Fort Garry merely to claim public opinion, but it will provide for consolidation with other roads, so that the Michigan portion of the Northern Pacific clear to Duluth can be blended with the Canadian Pacific and the bonds sold as such in London. There will be no forfeiture of anything beyond the completed portion ... Sir Hugh Allan who owns the road from Montreal will consolidate with the Canadian Pacific so that we will have a straight route from Duluth to Montreal. All this is confidential. The parties have now gone to Canada to get the legislation for it, and I think Morton, Rose & Co. will find themselves left out in the cold, except as they may come in with us (Irwin, 1939:172).

As it turned out, it was Cooke & Co., and not Morton, Rose & Co. who were "left out in the cold". Besides their attempts to force Jay Cooke to abandon his in-volvement in the Canadian Pacific Railroad, Morton, Rose & Co., and their American affiliate, Morton, Bliss & Co., worked closely with another banking house, Drexel, Morgan & Co., to discredit Jay Cooke & Co. in another security operations (Redlich, 1947:306; Larson, 1968:394-5 and 408-11).

These tactics proved successful. In 1873 the Northern Pacific was forced into receivership along with another road that Cooke had purchased as a link between the Northern Pacific and the proposed Canadian line (Larson, 1968:401-8). Jay Cooke & Co. itself failed in September 1873.

Public outrage at American involvement in the CPR carried the Liberals under Alexander Mackenzie to an easy victory over the Conservatives. But after one term out of office Macdonald was back. Liberal policy had been to finance the transcontinental railroad as a public venture, out of federal funds. This, in effect, was a policy by default, since no company composed of Canadians could raise the necessary capital on either European or American money markets. The Liberals, committed to giving the contract to "Canadians" (and, preferably, Liberal party supporters) found themselves forced to construct the road, piece by piece, out of available public funds. But with the Conservatives in power once again, government policy was directed toward private, rather than public, financing. In effect, this meant that the Conservatives were willing to allow a certain number of non-Canadians to hold the CPR charter.

In December 1880, the Conservative-dominated Parliament approved a new CPR contract.[16] Banking houses represented on the Board of Directors included Morton, Rose & Co. (London), their European correspondents, Kohn, Reinach & Co. (Paris and Frankfort), and J.S. Kennedy & Co. (N.Y.). Individuals included George Stephen, R.B. Angus and Duncan MacIntyre (Canadian, bankers), J.S. Kennedy (American, banker), Sir John Rose (Canadian resident in London, banker), and J.J. Hill (American, railroad entrepreneur). The name of Donald Smith (Canadian, Chief Commissioner of the Hudson's Bay Company in Canada, MP for Selkirk) was conspicuously omitted from the listing of the first board of directors, most likely because of the role he played in Macdonald's defeat of 1872.[12]

Eight years after it had begun, the struggle between competing syndicates for the CPR contract was finally decided in favour of a group of financial institutions with extensive international connections, as well as connections to governing bodies. Although the attempts to win the contract made by a group of locally-connected Canadian capitalists had brought about the defeat of the Macdonald government, they made little impression on the international scene. Even the Liberal government's move to support the efforts of local capitalists by floating CPR securities on the London money market was blocked. As a result, the Liberals were forced to construct the road out of available public funds. Since neither the Canadian state (in the hands of the Liberals) nor Canadian capitalists, with their limited local connections, could gain access to the stock exchange, any extensive work on the construction of the CPR had to await the re-election of the Conservatives, a political party sympathetic to the interests of international capital. It was only on the re-election of the Conservatives that the competitors from the international scene could, once again, set out to gain their prize.

The institutional affiliations of the members of the first CPR board of directors and their activities in buying and selling railroad securities in Canada and the United States provide useful insights into the extent and complexity of the contemporary international financial arrangements, of which the CPR was only a part.

The men who sat on the first board of directors of the CPR may be thought of as forming an "interest group". Their first experience together in railroads was the reorganization of the St. Paul & Pacific line into the St. Paul, Minneapolis and Manitoba after Jay Cooke had been forced into failure in 1873. They purchased the St. Paul and Pacific for $6,780,000 and received 455.25 miles of completed track and 220 miles of nearly completed track along with a land grant of 3,645,682 acres of land (Pyle, 1968:415-18), and immediately reorganized the company. In December 1878 the Pembina branch of the Canadian Pacific Railroad, under construction by the Liberal government of the day as a publicly-owned road, was connected with the St. Paul, Minneapolis and Manitoba at Winnipeg. The board of directors of this "American railway" was simply expanded to include Morton, Rose & Co., and Kohn, Reinach & Co. to form the board of directors of the Canadian Pacific, incorporated 15 February 1881.

On 29 December 1882 the board of directors of the CPR entered into a "syndicate agreement" with a group of American and Dutch bankers.[18] The organizer of the underwriting syndicate for the first issue of CPR securities was W.L. Scott[19] and the purchase syndicate included J.S. Kennedy & Co. (American), W.L. Scott (American) and Boissevain & Co. (Dutch). One-half of the $30,000,000 in shares was re-assigned to a "subsyndicate in Amsterdam and other European cities".[20] In addition, a number of American-based trust companies were also associated with the sub-syndicate "for the purpose of making the allotment". These trust companies, in turn, were partially controlled by the banking firms of Drexel, Morgan & Co., Morton, Rose & Co., and J.S. Kennedy & Co. Members of these banking firms sat on the trust companies' boards of directors.[21] Other major participants in the syndicate included the American investment banking houses of J.S. Seligman & Co., Kuhn Loeb & Co., Drexel, Morgan & Co., Blake Bros., (U.S. agents for Boissevain & Co., represented on the board of directors of the CPR in 1885), as well as the French banking houses of Cohen & Sons, Ephrussi & Co., and the Banque Parisienne.[22]

This purchase syndicate made its disbursements to a selling syndicate, which, in turn, sold securities to investors. The list of shareholders as of October 1883 shows that 50% of the shares were held in the U.S., 18% in Great Britain, 17% in Canada, 11% in Holland, 4% in France and less than 1% in Germany. Sixteen per cent of all shares were held by the Canadian members of the board of directors, 15% by Morton/Morgan/Rose interests, and 18% by Dutch banking houses and their American correspondent. The single largest shareholder in 1883 was the Netherlandshe Handel-Maatschappij (The Netherland Trading Society of Holland) with 57,000 shares.[23]

One final set of events should be considered: the merging of financing for American and Canadian lines. After the failure of Jay Cooke & Co. in 1873 a German citizen, Henry Villard, organized an investment pool and purchased the Northern Pacific Railroad (Emden, 1937:232). Elected president in 1881, Villard was immediately faced with the problem of financing, and turned to a consortium composed of J.S. Morgan & Co., (London), Drexel, Morgan & Co., (New York), Winslow Lanier & Co., (New York), and Central Trust Co. (New York). This syndicate issued $20,000,000 of Northern Pacific Railroad bonds in January 1881.[24] (It will be remembered that shortly after, these same banking houses issued Canadian Pacific shares.)

Through agreements made with the directors of the Northern Pacific, members of this syndicate of bankers soon came to control the railroad. Villard's presidency was short lived; he was forced to resign in 1883 and the road was reorganized by its bankers (Emden, 1937:232; Redlich, 1947:380). The road was declared bankrupt once more in 1893 and an attempt to merge the Northern Pacific with the Great Northern (formerly the St. Paul, Minneapoils & Manitoba) was undertaken by J.J. Hill. Before undertaking this project, Hill resigned his position on the CPR's board of directors. Stephen, Smith and Angus, however, remained on the Boards of both the reorganized Great Northern and the Canadian Pacific.

When the proposed merger was disallowed by the United States Supreme Court due to a Minnesota law prohibiting the merger of parallel and competing railroads (Holbrook, 1947:128), Hill and the rest of the Great Northern Associates were forced *individually* to buy into the Northern Pacific.

Control of the N.P. was vested in a voting trust including J.P. Morgan, August Belmont and a representative of the Deutsche Bank. James J. Hill and his associates in the Great Northern Pacific acquired $26,000,000 of reorganized Northern pacific stock in order, wrote Hill to Morgan, to bring the two roads "together as nearly as possible in general policy" by "the holding of a large and practically a controlling interest in both companies by the same parties." It was a merger of interests essentially uniting the Northern Pacific and Great Northern, although not an open consolidation . . . The Hill system now moved definitely in the Morgan orbit, J.P. Morgan & Co. becoming Great Northern's bankers in place of Kuhn-Loeb & Co. (Corey, 1930: 207).

Thus, at the turn of the century the boards of directors of the Canadian Pacific, the Northern Pacific and the Great Northern Railroad were well interlocked and all three were financed by the same consortia of investment bankers.

Conclusions

Although Marx wrote little about interest bearing capital and stock companies[25] he was convinced that stock companies represent "the abolition of the capitalist mode of production with the capitalist system itself, and hence a self-dissolving contradiction, which *prima facie* represents a mere phase of transition to a new form of production". Marx went on to explain this statement as follows. The formation of stock companies" . . . establishes a monopoly in certain spheres and thereby requires state interference. It reproduces a new financial aristocracy, a new variety of parasite in the shape of promoters, speculators and simply nominal directors; a whole system of swindling and cheating by means of corporation promotion, stock issuance, and stock speculation. It is private production without the control of private property" (Marx, 1970, Vol. III:438).

When one looks at the events surrounding the chartering of the CPR one can be left with little doubt of either the necessity of "state interference" or of the "swindling and cheating" bound up with inter-syndicate competition during this era. What is equally striking, however, is the extent to which capitalist expansion in post-Confederation Canada required cooperation across international boundaries. The events surrounding the organization of capital for financing the CPR clearly indicates two things: 1) that the project was not the undertaking of exclusively national forces, and 2) those Canadian capitalists involved in the project were not conservative throw-backs to a previous era of mercantilism, but were rather participants in the latest stage of capitalist development.

I have argued that, by the 1880's, the practice of forming syndicates to purchase and sell securities for undertakings throughout the world was well established. But if the structure of these ingenious institutions for organizing and mobilizing capital exploded existing constraints on capitalist expansion, they also established new ones. First, any significant undertaking required the cooperation of financial institutions *across* national boundaries. The absence of such connections among local capitalists meant effective exclusion from participation in the grand new enterprises, be they railroads in North America, land companies in Egypt or banks in South America. (At the same time, the world of high finance opened up to even the smallest of investors, who could risk some money in the hope of gaining returns from an investment in some far off, exotic place.)

The attempts by strictly Canadian-based financiers to mount the CPR project during the Liberal government's stay in office is indicative of these processes. Their attempts failed precisely because they could not gain access, as sellers, to the securities market. Without connections to the ever-growing financial institutions that operated across international boundaries, the aspirations of local Canadian financiers died at the stock market door. It is important to note that, in this instance, the Canadian state under the direction of the Liberal government was ineffective in its attempts to intervene on behalf of those Liberal party supporters who wished to involve themselves in the CPR project.

The relation of the Canadian state to the events surrounding the financing of the CPR requires further explanation. The appearance of syndicates in the mid-19th century depended not only on transnational association, but on the existence of state structures able to exercise coercive power. If a syndicate was unable to secure state protection and assistance it encountered a second constraint on its expansion. At the same time the state did not act independently of the constraints of capital. The case of the CPR clearly indicates that the Canadian state emerged and established its policies in conjunction with the latest development in *international* capital, parallel to the policies of other states of the day, and not merely as a response to the will of capitalists in a single nation. It is more precise to think in terms of a complex of interrelations between political structures, financial structures, and class formations at a transnational level. The events surrounding the financing of the CPR and the formation of three successive governments in Canada following Confederation reflected this complex interrelation.

It is inaccurate to refer, then, to the Canadian capitalist class of the late 19th century as a group of St. Lawrence merchants ensconced in a state structure that held back Canadian economic development because of limited, mercantile interests. Canadian capitalists and the Canadian state (at least under the Conservatives) responded entirely rationally to opportunities afforded by the latest developments in the logic of the reproduction of capital. The successful Canadian capitalists allied themselves with other financiers who operated across national boundaries and who had the institutional means to gain access to vast amounts of capital for investment. Canadian capitalists without alliances to international capital found themselves shut out of money markets, in spite of the backing they were guaranteed by a government friendly to their objectives.

The construction of the CPR depended on the existence of a state structure in Canada, with a government at its helm that was willing to provide favourable conditions in which international capital could operate. This, as we have seen, had certain implications for any capitalist who wanted to experiment with railroad financing. To hold the contract meant to be able to raise the capital. To raise the capital meant to be able to float shares on international money markets. And at this point the way was effectively blocked to all but a few. Competitors lurked in every corner, spying, stealing, blackmailing, issuing false or damning statements to the public or more simply, refusing to give assistance in share offerings. In a world divided into little fish and big sharks, few Canadian capitalists were able to swim far from the shore.

Notes

1. In 1861 Sir Edwin Watkin, working for Baring Bros. and Glyn, Mills, Currie & Co. had the idea that the Grand Trunk Railroad could be saved from its bankruptcy by extending the road to the Pacific (Watkin, 1887:14). Thus began the push for a British North American Transcontinental railroad.

2. On this issue see Innis (1923), Glazebrook (1938), Hedges (1939) and Anderson (1974)

3. See for example Macdonald (1975) and Carroll (1982) for an explication of the errors made by Clement and Naylor in categorizing industrial and mercantile capital.

4. See advertisements in the *Commercial and Financial Chronicler, The Economist,* and *The Times,* for this period.

5. The operation of this system of foreign loans, concessions to railroad companies, and repayment of governmental loans has been discussed by Rosa Luxemburg with reference to the Anatolian Railway Company in Turkey, backed, principally, by the Deutsche Bank.

6. Canada Parliament. "An Act Respecting the Canadian Pacific Railway", Statutes of Canada, 35 Vic. Cap. 71.

7. The Northern Pacific was chartered by the United States Congress in 1864 with a land grant of alternate sections in a belt twenty miles on either side of the track in the states and forty miles on either side in the Terriroties. In spite of this its New England promoters could not attract any financial backing.

8. The securities were marketed in a method unusual to the U.S. Jay Cooke & Co. organized a selling syndicate to disperse the issue. As well an elaborate advertising campaign was organized. The Northern Pacific lands became known as "the banana belt" because of Cooke's outlandish advertisements (Larson, 1936:264).

9. See also Canada Parliament. *Journals of the House of Commons,* 2nd Session, 1873, Appendix No. 1: 216-219, "Copy of list contract between Sir Hugh Allan and his American Associate" (Dec. 1871), and "Copy of Supplementary Contract between Sir Hugh Allan and his American Associates" (March 1872).

10. Canada parliament. "An Act to Incorporate the Canadian Pacific Railroad Company", *Statutes of Canada,* 35 Vic. 1872, Cap. 73.

11. Canada Parliament. *Sessional Papers* 36 Vic. 1873, No. 131.

12. Canada Parliament. "An Act Representing the Interoceanic Railway Company", *Statutes of Canada,* 35 Vic. 1872, Cap. 73.

13. Canada Parliament. *Sessional Papers* 36 Vic. 1873, No. 13: pp. 30-33.

14. *Statutes of Canada* 35 Vic. 1872, Cap. 73. The road had a capitalization of $10,000,000. It incorporators included Sir H. Allan, Sir Edward Kenny, The Hon. James Skead, The Hon. John Albot, The Hon. Asa B. Foster, The Hon. David Christie, The Hon. Gedein Ouimet, The Hon. J.J. Ross, Donald A. Smith, Wm. Nathan the Elder, E.R. Burpee, Andrew Allan, Donald McInnes, Louis Beaubrien, Chas. F. Gildersleve, J.B. Renaud, Ed. Kersteman, and Eugene Chinic.

15. Forty per cent in Ontario, 30.5% in Quebec, 10.5% in Nova Scotia, 8% in New Brunswick, 6% in British Columbia, and 5% Manitoba. The terms of incorporation stipulated that all directors be British subjects, and that the president and a majority of the Board be Canadians. It was further stipulated that no shares were to be transferred during the first six years of the Company's operation without the consent of the Government. The main line was to run north of Lake Superior and be completed by 1881.

16. *Statutes of Canada,* 44 Vic., Cap. 7, 1881. "An Act to Incorporate the Canadian Pacific Railway Company."

17. Smith had refused to support the Conservative Government during the Pacific Scandal when a matter of one or two votes would have kept that Government in office. Beckles Wilson reports: "The

speech of the member for Selkirk (Donald Smith) was delivered amidst intense silence, broken only by hysterical bursts of applause. 'For the honour of the country', he concluded, 'no Government should exist that has a shadow of suspicion resting upon it, and for that reason I cannot give it my support'. ... The House broke up in disorder. In the corridors the members rushed together, cheering and hand-shaking, or reviling and threatening. Suddenly there was a storm centered round Mr. Smith, upon whom Sir John was bearing down. He was held back gesticulating wildly. What he said never got into the blue books. His language was sometimes frequent and painful and free'' (Wilson, 1902: 158). By way of contrast another writer who also claims to be an eye-witness reported that:
''Although Sir John's face was flushed with the realization that the hour of his defeat had come he gave no evidence of his humiliation (Preston 1902:87).
18. Canada Parliament. *Sessional Papers,* 37 Vic. 1884, No. 81.
19. Scott became a member of the board of directors of the C.P.R. in 1883.
20. Canada Parliament. *Sessional Papers,* 37 Vic. 1884, No. 3.
21. See H.V. Poor, *Manual of the Railroads of the United States,* 1885.
22. Canada Parliament. *Sessional Papers,* 37 Vic. 1884, No. 21.
23. Canada Parliament. *Sessional Papers,* 37 Vic. 1884, No. 21.
24. *Commercial and Financial Chronicle,* Vol. XXXII, 1881.
25. For Engels' comments on this see his ''Preface'' to *Capital* Vol. III: 4.

References

Anderson, Karen, 1974—*The Organization of Capital for the Development of the Canadian West.* M.A. Thesis. University of Regina.

Carosso, Vincent P., 1970—*Investment Banking in America.* Cambridge, Mass: Harvard University Press.

Carroll, William K., 1982—''*The Canadian Corporate Elite: Financiers or Finance Capitalists?'' Studies in Political Economy,* 8: 89-114.

Clement Wallace, 1975—*The Canadian Corporate Elite: An Analysis of Economic Power.* Toronto: McClelland and Stewart.

Corey, Lewis, 1930—*The House of Morgan.* New York: A.M.S. Press.

Emden, Paul H., N.D.—*Money Powers of Europe in the Nineteenth and Twentieth Centuries.* London: Appleton-Century.

Glazebrook, G.P. de T., 1938—*A History of Transportation in Canada.* Toronto: Ryerson Press.

Hedges, James B., 1939—*Building the Canadian West.* New York: Macmillan.

Innis, H.A., 1930—*A History of the Canadian Pacific Railway.* Toronto: University of Toronto Press.

Irwin, Leonard Bertram, 1968—*Pacific Railways and Nationalism in the Canadian-American Northwest, 1845-1873.* New York: Greenwood Press.

Jenks, Leland Hamilton, 1927—*The Migration of British Capital to 1875.* New York: Knopf.

Landes, D., 1958—*Bankers and Pashas.* Cambridge, Eng.: Heinemann.

Larson, Henrietta M., 1968—*Jay Cooke, Private Banker,* New York: Greenwood Press.

Macdonald, L.R., 1975—''*Merchants Against Industry: An Idea and its origin'',* in *Canadian Historical Review,* Vol. LVI, No. 3: 263-81.

Marx, Karl, 1970—*Capital, Vol. III.* New York: Progress.

Naylor, Tom, 1972—''*The Rise and Fall of the Third Commercial Empire of the St. Lawrence''* in G. Teeple, (ed.) *Capitalism and the National Question in Canada.* Toronto: University of Toronto Press.

Naylor, Tom, 1975—*The History of Canadian Business 1867-1914.* Toronto: James Lorimer and Co.

Pyle, Joseph G., 1968—*The Life of James J. Hill.* New York: Doubleday Page.

Redlich, Fritz, 1968—*The Molding of American Banking; Men and Ideas.* New YOrk: Johnson Reprint Corp.

Watkin, Sir E.W., 1887—*Canada and the States, Recollections 1851 to 1866.* London: Ward, Lock.

Wilson B., 1902—*Lord Strathcona, The Story of His Life.* London: Metheun.

IV
Capitalist Class Rule

Canadian Capital and the Canadian State: Ideology in an Era of Crisis
Michael Ornstein

Introduction

The renaissance in Canadian political economy has been more concerned with economic than political issues. Attention has focused on the state's immediate role in furthering the accumulation process, on state subsidies to corporations and industries, on direct investments by the Federal and Provincial governments in economic infrastructure which could not (at least when first required) be provided at a profit, and on the legal regulation and at times physical coercion of the working class. This emphasis on the state's role in assuring the reproduction of capitalism as an economic system falls within what has come to be known as the instrumentalist tradition. Less intellectual energy has been devoted to understanding two broader roles of the capitalist state: first, regulation of foreign investment and energy policy; and second, overseeing the reproduction of the entire social formation, at the material, political and ideological levels. There has been a tendency to ignore the aspects of state action that fall outside the instrumentalist problematic and, therefore, potentially give rise to conflict between capital and the state.

Some recent commentary on the National Energy Program (NEP) is a a case in point. From the instrumentalist viewpoint, the NEP serves "to lower the cost of entry by Canadian capital into the oil and gas industries . . . and to encourage the formation of large Canadian-owned petroleum companies." (Pratt, 1982: 28) The problem is then to account for the widespread business hostility to the NEP (Watkins, 1983: 152); Pratt (1982: 29) notes only "by no means all fractions of Canadian capital support the NEP".[1] Sher (1983: 141) takes the argument one step further in asserting that, because of the present economic crisis, "the Canadian bourgeoisie was obliged to develop new economic strategies like the NEP." It is also appropriate to ask how the development of the NEP conforms to the widespread view that Canadian capital and the state are dominated by an alliance of class fractions, one Canadian and

I wish to express my appreciation to H. Michael Stevenson, who collaborated in the design of the survey on which this paper is based. The survey was a part of a larger project entitled "Social Change in Canada" directed by Mr. Tom Atkinson, Bernard R. Blishen, H. Michael Stevenson, and the author. Dr. Darla Rhyne and Mr. David Bates directed the data collection, which was conducted by the Institute for Behavioural Research at York University. The project was supported by a programme grant from the Social Sciences and Humanities Research Council and this article is prepared with the support of an SSHRCC grant to the author. The Council's support is gratefully acknowledged. I thank William Carroll, Penni Stewart, and Robert Brym for comments on earlier versions of this article.

centred in the financial sector and the other foreign-controlled and centred in resources and manufacturing.

One important element of Liberal Party energy policy has been the establishment of Petro-Canada as an alternative to private, capitalist development. Clement characterizes the founding of Petro-Canada as "a move by the Canadian state to look after the general interests of Canadian capitalists, not Canadians in general" (1977b: 245). As its nationalistic advertisements indicate (and Clement notes), the existence of Petro-Canada serves to legitimate the state and an industry that continues under majority foreign ownership; but Petro-Canada plays this role only by coming into conflict with the expressed views of big capital. As commentators have observed, the development of the NEP is not an indication that the state has become anti-capitalist. Nevertheless, the presence of the NEP poses the problem of understanding the nature of conflict between capital and the state, even if these conflicts arise in the course of state attempts to serve the long-term interests of capital.[2]

From a Marxist perspective, the most serious gap in present understanding of the Canadian state and economy concerns economic policies whose implementation offers no short-term gains to individual corporations, industries, or capital (at least, when capital is defined simply as the aggregate of the interests of individual corporations). State efforts to assure the continuity of the accumulation process potentially require policies that run counter to the expressed views of all or a clear majority of capitalists, which favour one capitalist interest at the expense of another, or which cannot be formulated from simple economic calculation. Of course, this problem has long been recognized (Offe, 1974) and its resolution is the subject of recent debates on the capitalist state which are discussed below. In examining the political ideology of the Canadian capitalists and comparing them to state managers, this article deals with one aspect of the problem of understanding the relationship between capital and the state. It is thus a preliminary to analysis of specific policy issues. We address the following questions:

—Is the capitalist class "class conscious"? Fred Block (1977) argues that only state managers are in a position to develop policies that effectively support the reproduction of the social formation, in the sense of fostering the accumulation process while also paying attention to the need for legitimation and control of working class opposition. Block argues that capitalists themselves are only capable of voicing the demands of individual corporations and industries for short run profits and for special favours from government.

—What are the extent, nature and reasons for political conflict between capital and the state?

—Are there important political conflicts between capitalist class fractions which correspond to differences among corporations, for example between the monopolistic and competitive sectors, between domestic and foreign capital, between capitals in different regions, or between an "inner group" and peripheral corporations?

On these fundamental questions, the new Canadian political economy has been largely silent. As our review below will indicate, there is no agreement that conflict between capital and the state exists; indeed, theoretical arguments have been put forward on both sides of the three major questions just advanced. The answers to these questions will serve as a bridge between two important bodies of research on Canadian political economy, one concerned with the structure of Canadian capitalism and the other with the nature of the Canadian state. To address these issues, this article uses the results of a large survey of business executives, elected politicians, senior civil servants, and trade union leaders. Personal interviews lasting an average of about one hour were conducted with random samples of the chief executives of the largest Canadian corporations and of medium-sized firms, and with the senior partners of the largest law firms. In this study the state elites[3] were represented by Members of Parliament, provincial cabinet ministers, and the mayors and city councillors of large cities and, on the bureaucratic side, federal deputy and assistant deputy ministers, provincial deputy ministers, and city department heads. The major concern of this article is to examine ideological differences between capital and the state and differentation within the capitalist class. But it is also important to determine whether the differences that are identified are significant in relation to the overall ideological spectrum in Canadian society. Data on the opinions of union leaders are used to establish a comparative context for the findings concerning the ideology of capitalists and the state elites.

The next section of this article reviews and comments on recent theoretical discussion of these issues, before the presentation of the results of the survey. But, first, a brief comment on the economic conjuncture is in order, since the ideology which is the subject of this discussion is situated at a particular conjuncture and the intention is not to identify universal features of capitalist ideology. World capitalism appears to have entered a period of major restructuring, marked by continuing crisis. Unlike previous cyclical highs of the post-war business cycle, the current recovery has been greeted with little optimism; repeated pronouncements by government officials stress the view that the present high unemployment levels will not be significantly reduced in the next few years. The economic chaos is mirrored in economic theory and policy making. Perceiving a failure of Keynesian policies, some capitalist governments have chosen to stage direct assaults on the working class, with the intentions of raising profits and reversing a supposed decline in bourgeois authority. But the monetarist policies, social programme cutbacks, and wage controls, which are designed to heighten the power of capital, may succeed in weakening the working class *without* curing the underlying economic problems. In the most recent years, the corporatist alternative to these right-wing measures, state-sponsored collaboration between labour and capital, has occupied a more prominent place in political theory than in government practices (Panitch, 1979: 85; Burnell, 1984 11ff.).

There is simply no agreement among bourgeois (or, for that matter, Marxist) economists as to the underlying causes of the current economic crisis. Thus, accompanying the present economic chaos is a crisis in economic policy-making, although their causal relationship is not clear. While there may be something of a consensus between capital and the state on the principles of social service cutbacks and structural reforms to alter the balance of forces between capital and labour, there is much less agreement on which social programmes should be maintained, on how natural resources are to be regulated, on the advisability of an industrial strategy, on the role of government investment, and so on. These disagreements are manifest in the remarkable disparities in the policies of the various capitalist governments, and, in Canada, in Federal-Provincial conflict.

B. Capitalist Ideology in General

Recent Marxist analysis of poltical ideology concentrates on the state, and particularly on its legitimation function, rather than on capital (for example, see

Poulantzas, 1973: 195ff). Capital is what the state is said to be "relatively autonomous" *of*, in a variety of current formulations of the Marxist theory of the state. Theories of the state and ideology are thus implicitly theories of the relationship between capital and the state. The instrumentalist view of the state requires a high degree of ideological and political cohesion between capital and the state.[4] Structuralist theories, on the other hand, suggest more ideological differentiation: the state fosters accumulation, if need be by pursuing policies opposed by some or even all fractions of capital. Poulantzas's (1973: 97-8) formulation is worth quoting at some length:

On a terrain of political domination occupied by several classes and class fractions and divided by internal contradictions, the capitalist state, while predominantly representing the interests of the hegemonic class or fraction (itself variable), enjoys a relative autonomy with respect to that class or fraction as well as to the other classes and fractions in the power bloc. One reason for this is that its task is to ensure the general political interest of the power bloc as a whole, organizing the 'unstable equilibrium of compromise' (Gramsci) among its components under the leadership of the hegemonic class or fractions; the other reason is that it organizes this hegemony with respect to the social formation as a whole, thus also with respect to the dominated classes, according to the specific forms that their struggles assumed under capitalism. This relative autonomy is inscribed in the very structure of the capitalist state by the relative 'separation' of the political and the economic that is specific to capitalism.

Miliband's most recent formulation suggests a still greater separation between capital and the state. Miliband argues that modern capitalist states are moved "by self interest on the one hand, and a conception of the national interest on the other" (1983: 62). He continues (1983: 65),

in short, an accurate and realistic 'model' of the relationship between the dominant class in advanced capitalist societies and the state is one of *partnership between two different, separate forces,* linked to each other by many threads, yet each having its own separate sphere of concerns (emphasis in original).

Miliband (1983: 64) refers to the state elites as a "state" bourgeoisie"[5] whose pursuit of the interests of capital "might well mean refusing to pay heed to capitalist wishes: very often, it was precisely because they wanted to ensure that best conditions for capitalism that they did things which ran counter to the wishes of capitalists." Although he is more explicit concerning the inherent ideological limits of the capitalist *class* (if not the limits of capitalist ideology), Block's (1977: 10) formulation is quite similar:

Those who accumulate capital are conscious of their interests as capitalists, but, in general, they are not conscious of what is necessary to reproduce the social order in changing circumstances. Those who manage the state apparatus, however, are forced to concern themselves to a greater degree with the reproduction of the social order because their continued power rests on the maintenance of political and economic order.

Simply put, Block's argument is that the capitalist class is likely to adopt policies so repressive that they would endanger the social order. Since capitalists are viewed as incapable of taking broader political stands that transcend their narrow concerns, Block concludes that ideological differences between capital and the state need not give rise to political conflicts.

Two parts of the analysis of the interviews with business executives, state elites, and labour leaders bear on the theoretical issues just considered. First, an examination of the extent of ideological conflict between the business and state elites speaks to the question of whether there is a general ideological consensus between capital and the state. Second, a comparison of the amounts of ideological disagreement among the business elites and among the state elites will determine whether the capitalist class is more internally divided than the state.

One aspect of Block's argument should however be dealt with on theoretical grounds, before considering the results of the interviews. At least, his formulations require some "adjustment" to the current poltical and economic conjuncture. Block (1977: 10) believes that state managers "are capable of intervening in the economy on the basis of a more general rationality" that is absent from the capitalist class. Furthermore, Block views increased state intervention as a "rational" strategy for capital—even when the interventions encounter capitalist opposition. The policies of Thatcher, Reagan, and Premier Bennett, however, throw Block's arguments into doubt, for they have adopted policies that replace legitimation (as least as conceived by Block as the extension of state social programmes) with a harsh reassertion of the prerogatives of capital. There are thus no logical grounds for supposing state managers are inherently more co-optive than capitalists themselves, even if that is the tendency in most conjunctures. In certain conjunctures, furthermore, very repressive social policies (often in combination with direct coercion) may effectively serve the legitimation function. Offe (1974) and O'Connor (1973) are similar to Block in viewing cooptation and increased social welfare programmes as the essential means of maintaining capitalist legitimacy.

Poulantzas, Miliband and Block all suggest the possibility of systematic political differences between capital and the state. In fact, Miliband and Block challenge the "relative autonomy" formulation with arguments that lean towards giving the state a still more autonomous political role. While Miliband sees the state as still fundamentally attached to capital, Block (1980: 230) places still greater distance between them:

state managers pose a potential threat to other classes, particularly those classes that control substantial resources. The possibility exists that state managers, to improve their own position, will seek to expropriate, or at the least, place severe restrictions on the property of dominant classes. This threat is the root of the emphasis in bourgeois ideology on the need to prevent the emergence of a Leviathan state that swallows civil society.

Block's analysis may, in part, reflect his American context, in which capitalist fundamentalism plays a far more prominent role than in Europe (Wolfe, 1981).

C. Some Canadian Arguments

Leo Panitch (1977: 17, 18) provides a formulation of the relationship between capital and the state that is quite at variance with the theoretical arguments presented above:

It has been the very lack of relative autonomy of the state, the sheer depth of its commitment to private capital as the motor force of the society, which, when combined with a weak indigenous industrial bourgeoisie and a strong financial bourgeoisie cast in the mould of an intermediary between staple production in Canada and industrial empires abroad, explains the lengths to which the state has gone in promoting private capital accumulation not only for the domestic bourgeoisie but for foreign capitalists as well.

What has been least developed, however, is the state's legitimization function.

More generally, I believe it is fair to say that the Canadian left has tended to take the instrumentalist view, stressing state action at the direct behest of capital. Wallace Clement's work falls within this instrumentalist tradition; his article on "The corporate elite, the capitalist class, and the Canadian state" (Clement, 1977b) is a catalogue of personal ties between the corporate and state elites, the ineffectiveness of state regulation of capital, and bourgeois domination of the political parties. Clement cites Dennis Olsen's work in arguing that there are extensive ties between business and state elites. But Olsen does not actually find that the state elite is dominated by bourgeois personnel and he must therefore confront the clear limitations of instrumentalism (Olsen, 1980: 122, 125):

the state elite's claim to represent the large Canadian working class is not as plausible because there are so few members of the elite with working-class backgrounds. . . . The low level of upper-class representation also makes it difficult to argue that the state is, in any immediate way, only an instrument of the dominant class (p. 122). The elite contains within it various classes and ethnic categories in an unstable alliance (p. 125).

One serious limitation of the instrumentalist tradition lies in the assumption that the state is a captive of its personnel. In turn, the social background of these personnel determines the policies of the state. Clement's (1975; 1977a) focus on the backgrounds of business elites is similar in building an analysis of capitalist economic development from the personal characteristics of capitalists.[6] Similarly, Olsen (1980) lacks a structuralist insight into the character of the capitalist state. Hutcheson's (1973: 174) nationalist view is no less instrumentalist, "The Canadian state is now in the control of the dominant section of the ruling class in Canada—the U.S. corporations."[7]

Koula Mellos's "Developments in Advanced Capitalist Ideology" (1978) approaches these issues from an entirely different viewpoint, but her conclusions are remarkably similar to those reached by proponents of the instrumentalist view. Drawing on the theories of Habermas and Marcuse, Mellos (1978: 860) describes "emerging cooperative norms which appear increasingly to pervade the structure of advanced capitalism". On the basis of her reading of public statements by prominent businessmen and a small number of personal interviews, Mellos divines a "highly integrated rapport" among capital, the state, and organized labour which, in advanced capitalism, must cooperate in defining "an economic policy of expansion." The major elements of the ideological consensus include corporatist political norms, the view that profits serve "the collectivity as reinvestments in the expansionary programmes of economic growth and development," (Mellos, 1978: 845), the acceptance of economic planning, the replacement of beliefs in the virtues of competition by justifications of monopoly, the acceptance of state intervention in the economy, and the belief in the benevolence of science and technology.

As Paul Stevenson (1983) indicates in a recent review of studies of the Canadian state, instrumentalism is presently the dominant perspective in Marxist treatments of the Canadian state. What other interpretation may be placed on Clement's (1977b: 233) statement that "The importance of these direct and kinship ties between the economic elite and the state system cannot be overemphasized" or Finkel's (1979: 176) view of social reforms in the 1930's that "the specific actions were taken only with the encouragement of large sectors of the bourgeoisie''? A number of the essays in Leo Panitch's (1977) edited volume demonstrate a more subtle understanding of the relationship between capital and the state than is apparent in the instrumentalist accounts just discussed. However, the non-instrumentalist accounts are generally confined to descriptive issues rather than directly addressing the predominant, instrumentalist theory.

Political Fractions of the Canadian Capitalist Class?

The discussion has so far treated the ideologies of capital and state managers as coherent wholes, but in both cases there may be serious internal conflicts. Thus, in the context of ideological conflict between capital and the state, a "fraction" of capital may control or form an alliance with the state managers. The state managers may also be split. For example, the recurrent federal-provincial conflicts in Canada often involve a mixture of ideological conflicts and more clearly territorial and institutional interests. The nature and extent of ideological differentiation within the capitalist class has been one major concern of theorists. The survey data provide the basis for an extensive analysis of this differentiation. This section reviews the theoretical issues.

In analyzing capitalist class fractions, theorists usually begin with Marx's distinctions, in the third volume of *Capital*, between industrial, money-dealing, and commercial capital and his scattered comments (also in *Capital*) regarding competition between big and small capital. Lenin's insights into imperialism and the international character of capitalist development then set the stage for Marxist analysis of accumulation on an international scale. We owe a debt to Kari Levitt (1970) for rekindling serious interest in these issues in the Canadian context and to Wallace Clement (1975, 1977a), Tom Naylor (1972), and Jorge Niosi (1978, 1981, 1982) for elaborating them. The question to be addressed here is whether the concept of class fractions offers insights into the *political* organization of the Canadian bourgeoisie. The concept of class fractions has been employed largely as a descriptive tool so that changes in the strength of different fractions are seen to reflect the process of capitalist development. The debate over the historical role of conflict between merchant and industrial capital is one context in which the relationship between economic fractions and politics has been raised.

Like any other group, business executives are subject to a great variety of experiences that serve to create ideological differences and we should not, therefore, expect to find complete political unanimity within the capitalist class. The more important issue, however, is whether the existing political differences coincide with structural divisions that would prevent the development and expression of a coherent capitalist viewpoint. For example, conflicts between the business executives living in different regions are likely to find expression through provincial business organizations. It should be emphasized that this article is concerned with more general aspects of ideology and not government policies that affect only single corporations or industries. The instrumentalist approach is perfectly adequate for understanding efforts by corporations to stave off bankruptcy or obtain special favours and efforts by industries to procure tax concessions or protective tariffs.

Monopoly and Competitive Capital

The division between "monopoly" and "competitive" capital figures importantly in Marxist analyses of capitalism. In the historical context of continuous increases in the average size of corporations and a tendency toward oligopoly (if not actual monopoly), conflict between large and small corporations results from price competition in consumer goods and conflict over the prices of producer goods. Large corporations are tempted to use their market strength to extract superprofits, that is, profits above the average rate of profit.

In this context, the state plays a critical role. At the most immediate level, anti-trust policies (in Canada, chiefly their absence) determine whether big corporations are fully able to take advantage of their size. Second, state regulation of the labour process, including hours and intensity of work, occupational health, minimum wages, and accident compensation, and the legal structure of labour relations do much to govern the conditions under which big and small capitals compete. Third, the level and state expenditure influence the tax burden on business and (by means of the levels of unemployment insurance, daycare, welfare and other programmes) the labour supply and bargaining power of workers. State policies exercise a particularly strong influence on workers whose pay levels are closest to subsistence and who figure disproportionately in the numbers of competitive sector workers. Finally, the state is empowered to decide the level of protection from foreign competition that is provided to domestic capital, at least within the constraints of the international economic order.

In light of these conditions small business should favour anti-trust legislation, strongly anti-union labour relations policies, and protectionism. The impact of social expenditures is more complex. These expenditures lower the cost of labour power by providing services to workers who would otherwise have to pay for them. But the resulting high tax burdens may prove more of a threat to small business than to big capital which, by virtue of its oligopolistic position, is better able to pass additional costs on in the form of higher prices.

On the issue of state investments, small capital may have less of a stake than big capital. Those investments tend to involve very large establishments which are likely to compete with large, private corporations and not small business. Furthermore, small business executives are more likely to be nationalistic, since they may fear new foreign competition and have nothing to gain from the reciprocal rights of Canadian capitalists to invest in other nations.

It is common to view small business as the heir to a legacy of right-wing capitalist rhetoric, while big capital is able to live with and exert influence over the modern liberal state. The above arguments show the issue to be more complex. Small business may seek state protection from competition and may favour state expenditures. It is also possible that corporate ideology corresponds partly to short-run economic imperatives and partly to rhetorical considerations that serve the long term interest of capital in maintaining ideological hegemony.

This discussion raises the issue of whether big capital is actually monopolistic, or at least oligopolistic, in the sense of having the ability to extract superprofits. Willi Semmler's (1982) recent article surveys the very large literature on this subject in conventional economics. He concludes that the "monopolies" do not have the ability to obtain superprofits on any continuing basis. This conclusion has negative implications for monopoly capital theory. So far as Marxist economics is concerned,

Semmler's conclusion has the great virtue of leaving intact the law of value, because if genuine monopolies dominate the capitalist economy, the political power of corporations and state policies (rather than any economic laws) determine prices and profits.

Industrial, Financial, and Commercial Capital

The role of conflict between industry and finance in the history of Canadian capitalist development is the subject of hot debate. However, there appears to be a consensus that the tension between industrial and financial capital has been attenuated by their integration in "finance capital." Clement nevertheless (1977a: 291) see the influence of this division lingering until the present time, and he argues that

An economy dominated by financial capitalists, particularly ones whose business is mainly in long-term interest-bearing investments . . . will not strongly resist state ownership of particular sectors such as transportation and utilities because they can still extract their surplus by investing their capital in those enterprises, regardless of ownership.

It is therefore appropriate to employ the survey data to see whether capitalists in the financial sector are presently major supporters of foreign investment.

Foreign Control and Capitalist Class Fractions

Clement (1977a: 25) defines class fractions on the basis of foreign ownership and size of corporations. There are three main fractions: the *dominant indigenous* fraction, "very active in finance, transportation and utilities, to a lesser extent in trade, and much less in manufacturing and resources"; the *middle-range indigenous* fraction "active mainly in relatively small-scale manufacturing and not international in scope"; and the *dominant comprador* fraction, "active in manufacturing and resources, both national and international . . . located in the branch plants of foreign-controlled multinationals [the capitalist class may be] further subdivided by source of control." Elsewhere, Clement (1977a: 26) notes that in the United States, while there is a middle-range fraction, "there is no need to make a distinction based on economic sectors because U.S. control dominates in them all." This statement implies that, aside from size, *only* nationality of ownership defines class fractions. Returning to the issue of whether these fractions act at the political level, Clement (1975: 117) notes that "it remains to be demonstrated that they exist as distinct social groups." Clement appears to define social groups in terms of their social class origins or ethnic backgrounds.

The conclusion of Niosi's (1983) most recent discussion of the structure of the Canadian capitalist class is similar to Clement's. Niosi sees Canada as occupying an intermediate position in the international division of labour which causes the Canadian capitalist class to fragment into the comprador and national bourgeoisies. In terms of the objectives of this article it is significant that Niosi (1983: 142) links this fragmentation to ethnic differences in the character of capital and then to the political party structure and to development strategy:

On the political level these two cleavages have important effects: the Liberal Party of Canada (representing French-Canadian and Jewish capital plus several nationalistically-minded WASP mavericks) is much more nationally oriented than the purely Anglo-Saxon Conservative Party, in which [the] comprador bourgeoisie is well represented.

A better understanding of this country's ruling class can be derived from an acknowledgement of the existence of a fragmented bourgeoisie with a solid autochthonous fraction as the hegemonic partner. I call the development strategy of this hegemonic fraction "continental or rentier nationalism". This type of nationalism is concerned more with changing the ownership and control pattern of the Canadian economy than on altering its industrial structure. Present-day nationalism is only buying back foreign subsidiaries without destroying dependency.

A different aspect of ownership is raised by the presence of the state in the ownership of capitalist enterprises. The extent of state ownership is often said to be a distinctive feature of the Canadian state. Niosi's (1981: 117) detailed analysis of this state capital concludes with the argument that "the economic instruments of the state do not serve the 'monopoly' sections of the Canadian bourgeoise exclusively, but ensure the reproduction of all the dominant classes." Niosi identifies the roles of state capitalism as strengthening Canadian ownership, supplying monopoly services (such as hydro-electric power and telephones), and building the power bases of provincial governments. Niosi finds that the boards of crown corporations are dominated by executives from the private sector, although there is some representation of state bureaucrats. All of this lends substance to the view that, at least to a limited extent, the managers of state enterprises should differ politically from their private enterprise counterparts, in the direction of being more sympathetic to state intervention at the general economic level—and perhaps also in other aspects of state intervention.

An "Inner Group" of Canadian Capitalists?

Corporate directorships are very unequally distributed. Among the directors of 113 dominant Canadian corporations (in 1972), Clement (1975: 167) found that the 6.5 percent of directors with four or more positions accounted for over one fifth of all the directorships. In a series of papers about American corporate elites, Michael Useem (1978, 1978a, 1979b, 1981) has elaborated this observation that power is concentrated in the hands of a minority of corporate directors into the concept of an "inner group" of capitalists. Members of the inner group are distinguished from other directors in two respects: (a) inner group members have more influence on university boards, charitable organizations, and other voluntary organizations; and (b) the members have more frequent contact with and influence on government. Block (1977) makes similar arguments.

In light of their more frequent and diverse relationships with corporate executives, voluntary organizations and government, Useem (1978: 237ff) predicted that members of the inner group would have more cohesive political views and that they should be more sympathetic to state intervention than other, less cosmopolitan capitalists. Surprisingly, Useem's (1978) only empirical test of these propositions, which employed data from a large survey of university board members, failed to confirm either hypothesis. Inner group members actually proved less supportive of state intervention and they were no more united in their political views than other members of the capitalist class. These arguments are worth testing in the Canadian context.

Forces Producing a Cohesive Capitalist Class

At the most general level, the common class position and experiences of capitalists are the fundamental basis of capitalist class cohesion. Concretely, a number of structural features of the capitalist class serve as mechanisms to enhance its ideological unity. First, a great variety of business organizations serve as vehicles for expressing the collective needs of capital, from trade associations through the Chamber of Commerce and the Canadian Manufacturers Association to overtly political organizations such as the Fraser Institute. Second, the dense network of interlocking directorates which connects the boards of the largest Canadian corporations constitutes an arena for personal contacts within the capitalist class (Clement, 1975, 1977; Ornstein, 1976; Carroll, Fox, and Ornstein, 1982).

The third unifying force is economic. Divisions within the capitalist class are less likely to develop if corporations operate in competitive markets in which individual corporations and industries enjoy no special advantages. As noted above, Semmler concludes that competition is prevalent. Recent research on industrial segmentation also bears on the question of whether structural differences divide corporations into groups that could serve as bases for political conflict. About 1970, a number of economists put forward the argument that modern capitalist economies are "segmented" into two or more sectors. Corporations were divided among the sectors on the basis of their size, profitability, level of technology, and so on (Averitt, 1968; Bluestone, 1970; Edwards, Reich, and Gordon, 1973). The "core" firms were said to be large, oligopolisitic, profitable, and technologically innovative. As a consequence, core firms paid higher wages, tended to support (or least not oppose) efforts to improve working conditions, and supported government intervention. Peripheral firms were said to be smaller, competitive, relatively unprofitable, employ simple technology, and pay low wages; their resistance to government intervention was based on its increasing their costs (O'Connor, 1973).

Very recently, a body of empirical research has challenged the fundamental assumptions of segmentation theory, by showing that the American economy cannot be divided into discrete segments (Oster, 1979; Kaufman, Hodson, and Fligstein, 1981; Hodson and Kaufman, 1982). Larger, technologically advanced industries, it was found, did not necessarily pay higher wages; economic concentration was not strongly associated with greater profitability; and so on. If the recent American findings of limited economic segmentation apply to Canada, the lack of appreciable segmentation should encourage the development of political consensus within the capitalist class.

D. EMPIRICAL METHOD
The Samples of Respondents

Whether or not the survey results reported here actually represent the ideology of capitalists and the state managers depends critically on the design of the samples employed. This section describes the main features of the samples. Further details are given in Appendix A. The samples were designed to represent various sectors. Unlike samples of the general public, the "populations" from which samples were selected for this project were populations of organizations, rather than individuals. The sample of big business executives actually consisted of the executives from a sample of big businesses. For each sector included in this study, different structural criteria were employed in the sample design. Also in contrast to population surveys, the samples of executives, state managers, and labour union leaders selected for this study reflect judgements on the part of the researchers. While it is reasonably clear who should be included in a sample of non-institutionalized adults (at least once there is a definition of an adult), this is necessarily a large element of judgement in defining "large" corporations, "large" trade unions, and "high level" civil servants.

Complex internal divisions within the corporate sector and the state complicate the design of representative samples. In this study, the internal divisions were dealth with by subdividing the corporations and state into more homogeneous subgroups and developing separate, representative samples in each subgroup. The three categories of capital are labelled "big business," "small business," and "lawyers." The "big business" respondents were chief executives of the largest five hundred Canadian corporations, as listed in the 1980 Financial Post ranking.

The small businesses averaged about 40 employees, so their owners are not "petty bourgeois." Only a fraction of the labour in those businesses could have been carried out by the proprietor or family members. Although the term "small business" is commonly applied to businesses with fewer than one hundred employees, the reader should be mindful of the relatively large size of the companies included in this study. In order to reduce the costs of the interviews, the sample of small businesses was confined to the twelve largest metropolitan areas in Canada. The number of small businesses selected from each metropolitan area was made proportional to its population. Within each metropolitan area, the sample of small businesses included approximately equal numbers of manufacturers, randomly selected from a business directory and businesses suggested in response to our inquiries by local Chambers of Commerce.

The lawyers were senior partners of the largest Canadian law firms, ranked by size. The practice of these law firms is largely corporate law and they are certainly unrepresentative of Canadian law firms as a whole. The sample of lawyers was designed with the intention of concentrating on lawyers who were most likely to represent large corporate clients. In terms of income, these lawyers are comparable to all but the highest paid corporate executives. It is therefore appropriate to think of the sample of lawyers as representing a segment of the bourgeoisie engaged in making legal arrangements for large corporations.

The sample of state elites was subdivided into six different categories, based on the conventional distinctions between elected politicians and civil servants and among three levels of government. Because of the very large number of municipalities in Canada, the selections of state politicians and civil servants at the municipal level presented a unique problem. Following the logic of the sample design for small business, the sample of municipal elites was restricted to the twelve largest metropolitan areas. In each of the six state sectors further practical decisions were required before the samples could be drawn. At the Federal level, the elected officials were simply drawn from all the Members of Parliament. At the Provincial level, the sample was restricted to cabinet ministers, in an effort to exclude elected officials with relatively little influence at the national level. At the municipal level, the sample included mayors and, in cities where the positions existed, "controllers" or other elected representatives above the rank of ordinary council members (otherwise, city council members were selected). The civil servant populations were defined as including Federal deputy and assistant deputy ministers, but only deputy ministers at the Provincial level. The omission of Provincial assistant deputy ministers was based on the same reasoning that led us to restrict the sample of Provincial elected officials to the cabinet level. At the municipal level, the sample included the heads of municipal departments, who are given the title "commissioner".

The sample of trade union officials was subdivided in order to represent the various influential positions in the labour movement. The sample included the presidents of the largest trade union locals in Canada (ranked by membership), Labour Council presidents in the twelve largest metropolitan areas, and top executives of the provincial labour federations and national centrals.

The overall response rate for the survey was approximately 75%, somewhat better than would be expected in a standard population survey. In some sectors a substitute was interviewed when the selected respondent was not available. For the large corporations, for example, other top executives were allowed as substitutes for the chief executive officers who were initially selected; not permitted as substitutes were public relations personnel, executive assistants, or other employees who were not top level executives. Concern that these substitutes and the initially selected respondents might take different ideological positions led us to undertake a statistical analysis of the differences between them, using data from an earlier survey of elites. It failed to turn up any significant differences.

Defining and Measuring Ideology

There is no agreement over the definition of the term "ideology" or, for that matter, over its specific content and role in the determination of classes in contemporary capitalism. The term is used in this article to denote an ensemble of political attitudes which, taken together, define the relationship among capital, the working class, and the state.[8] Larrain (1978: 14) makes the useful distinction between the definition of ideology in the negative sense, as false consciousness, and ideology taken in the positive sense as "the expression of the world-view of a class . . . as the opinions, theories and attitudes formed within a class in order to defend and promote its interests." The study results presented in this paper deal with a limited number of aspects of bourgeois ideology. Limitations in the data gathering process and in the space available in this paper force us to concentrate on certain aspects of ideology. This paper deals with four aspects of ideology, relating to: (a) the relationship between capital and labour; (b) state policies on civil liberties and social programmes; (c) state regulation of and intervention in the economy; and (d) political party support, at the federal level. Tables 1 to 6 deal with individual questions from the survey and are self explanatory; Tables 7 and 8 deal with scales created by adding the responses to a number of items. Appendix B contains full descriptions of the scales.

Using Survey Data to Investigate Ideology

The use of survey data to address the questions raised here is somewhat unusual, so it is appropriate to consider a number of objections which are raised against this strategy. The most common objection to surveys concerns validity. Instead of giving their actual opinions perhaps the respondents, particularly business executives who are more accustomed to exercising their influence in private, might choose to adopt what they believe are the most socially acceptable positions. At the most general level this argument is irrefutable, since almost any evidence, and certainly all the evidence practically available, may be dismissed. Behind this general concern about validity lurks the suspicion that executives will demonstrate an exaggerated liberalism (especially in interviews conducted with or sponsored by university researchers). The data presented in the tables below confronts this latter objection. The opinions expressed by the corporate executives in the interviews are very conservative and are perfectly in keeping with the conservative opinions regularly expressed in current business publications.

A related objection concerns the usefulness of general attitude surveys of elites, as opposed to studies of actual policy making. Even when expressed candidly, general opinions may involve a rhetorical element, in the sense that they are unlikely to lead to action. In the unlikely event that political action is taken, respondents' general opinions must be modified to deal with the particular situation. This criticism is entirely reasonable if the objective is to analyze the development of particular policies, but misses the point of this study, which is to analyze ideology. Studies of ideology and political action are distinct and complementary, a point made by structuralists when they distinguish between the ideological and political "levels".

A final objection to the survey approach applies equally to policy studies and other empirical research. Any political conflicts within the capitalist class or conflicts between capital and the state that are identified might be interpreted to mean that the surveys ask the wrong questions. This objection would follow from the arguments that the Canadian state is a capitalist state and it is inconceivable that leading capitalists and the top state officials would not be united in their basic assumptions about private property. These observations are correct but irrelevant to the present study. Conflicts over social, energy, and fiscal and monetary policy are no less real because capital and the state share certain assumptions. An understanding of these conflicts is still an essential element of any analysis of the ideological order of modern capitalism.

E. SURVEY RESULTS

Tables 1 to 6 give the distributions of responses to twenty items from the questionnaire, grouped on the basis of subject matter. Two theoretical questions inform the discussion of these tables: (a) Are there significant political differences between capital and the state?; and (b) is the capitalist class "class conscious," in Block's sense of upholding an ideology that constitutes a viable plan for class rule, as opposed to a rhetoric lacking a readiness to accommodate the working class and therefore likely to lead to unmanageable class conflict.

Labour Relations Issues

Table 1 indicates that the trade unionists are politically isolated from the state elites and capital on three issues directly involving the power of trade unions: the right of employers to hire strikebreakers, the passage of legislation to decrease the power of trade unions, and the prohibition of strikes by postal workers. A ban on strikebreaking was supported by 26 percent of the big business executives, 8 percent of small business proprietors, and 29 percent of the lawyers, compared to between 32 and 59 percent for the six categories of state respondents, and 94 percent of the labour leaders. Generally the pattern of responses to these labour relations issues may be summarized as follows: (a) trade unionists were isolated on the left; (b) state elites were significantly to the left of business executives, but closer to business than to labour; and (c) proprietors of small businesses were considerably to the right of big business executives and lawyers.

The state elites and labour leaders had similar positions on the question of whether workers should be represented on corporate boards; about 60 percent of each group

TABLE 1. Opinion on Labour Union Issues by Group

	Prohibit hiring of strikebreakers			Legislation should be used to decrease the power of unions			Prohibit postal workers from striking			Employees should be represented on corporate boards			Number of Cases
	Agree	Neutral	Disagree	Agree	Neutral	Disagree	Agree	Neutral	Disagree	Agree	Neutral	Disagree	
Corporate													
Big Business	26	7	67	51	25	24	70	5	25	13	18	69	217
Small Business	8	10	82	69	18	13	79	5	16	38	14	48	80
Lawyers	29	8	63	42	23	35	78	10	12	29	16	55	53
State Politicians													
Federal	32	13	55	42	14	44	54	2	44	79	12	9	57
Provincial	38	7	55	37	19	44	52	15	33	54	15	31	59
Local	51	2	47	51	13	36	49	9	42	48	4	48	46
Civil Servants													
Federal	38	6	56	40	18	42	40	5	55	60	22	18	81
Provincial	37	7	56	46	21	33	54	6	40	53	18	29	108
Local	59	2	39	51	21	23	51	12	37	55	17	28	43
Trade Unionists	94	2	4	6	0	94	13	4	83	60	22	18	139

approved. The small business proprietors were fairly sympathetic to worker representation, but opponents of the measure outnumbered supporters, by five to four. Of course, the small business proprietors would not themselves be much affected by a law calling for worker representatives on their boards (even without the likely exemption of small business from such legislation). The boards of small businesses usually have a nominal role, rather than intervening in actual management.

More than two-thirds of the big business executives opposed worker representation on corporate boards and more than half of the remainder were neutral rather than approving. Thus, while big business executives were more liberal than small business proprietors on trade union issues, they were more conservative on the issue of board representation. In light of the Canadian labour movement's general disinterest in the strategy of co-management, the labour leaders' support for board representation is surprising. Attempts by government to move in this direction will certainly be met by strong opposition from big business.

Civil Liberties Issues

Four civil liberties issues are dealt with in Table 2: legislation to protect homosexuals from job discrimination, the elimination of existing provincial boards of censors, abolition of the War Measures Act, and civilian review of complaints against the police. Compared to the labour issues, the differences among the survey groups were relatively small, although the relative positions of the groups remained unchanged. On all four civil liberties issues, labour took the leftmost position; business was on the right; and the state elites were in between. There were substantial differences in the overall level of support given to the four proposed measures. Two-thirds or more of each category of respondents approved civilian review of complaints against the police. Only the lawyers and provincial civil servants do not give majority support to protecting homosexuals. Just over one-third of the business and state elites would eliminate censorship. Abolition of the War Measures Act received the least support; only the labour leaders gave it majority support.

It would be surprising to discover a perfect relationship between the views expressed in this survey and public policy, but the finding that there is majority support for legislation to protect homosexuals and civil review of police complaints is worthy of comment. Neither measure is embodied in existing legislation. Widespread public debate did not succeed in placing sexual preference in the protections afforded by the Charter of Rights and, despite calls for such a reform, provinces and municipalities have generally failed to institute any civilian review of police.[9] In both cases, strong pressures from the right have succeeded in preventing reform.

Social Welfare and Redistribution

On social welfare issues as well, the opinions of state elites were more or less midway between business and labour. For example, unqualified support for a guaranteed annual income was voiced by about 15 percent of the business respondents, about 45 percent of the state elites, and 71 percent of the labour leaders. Of particular interest are the responses to the following general question:

Do you think governments in Canada have cut back too much on social expenditures that these cuts have been justified but there should be no further cuts, or that further cuts should be made?

TABLE 2. Percent Supporting* For Policies Regarding Civil Liberties by Group

Group	Legislation to protect homosexuals from job discrimination	Elimination of existing provincial boards of censors	Abolition of the War Measures Act	Civilian review of complaints against the police
Corporate				
Big Business	53	44	21	71
Small Business	51	38	17	69
Lawyers	40	28	17	66
State				
Politicians				
Federal	61	47	47	77
Provincial	44	30	35	82
Local	64	33	30	70
Civil Servants				
Federal	70	55	28	80
Provincial	61	38	24	84
Local	65	35	10	84
Trade Unionists	84	60	61	87

*Including qualified approval, as stated spontaneously by the respondent.

Fully 71 percent big business endorsed further cuts (just one percent believed that cutbacks had gone too far), compared to 54 percent of small business and 47 percent of the lawyers. For all six categories of state elites, the largest group of respondents took the view that the social welfare cutbacks already carried out were justified, but that there should not be further cuts. Disregarding the supporters of the status quo there were more supporters of further cutbacks than state elites who believed that cuts had gone too far. At all three levels of government civil servants were much more supportive of cutbacks than the politicians; but there was relatively little variation among the levels of government. The trade union leaders were totally isolated on this issue: 58 percent believed that cutbacks had gone too far and only eight percent favoured further cutbacks.

The responses to the specific question of whether health and medical care efforts should be cut back were quite different: an overwhelming majority in each of the three business sectors, between 64 and 79 percent supported the status quo and among the remainder, the supporters of more expenditure clearly outnumbered those endorsing further cutbacks. Thus, when the question was less rhetorical and more specific about which social service is involved, business respondents tended to support the status quo and not further cutbacks. Additional analysis (not reported in a table) of support for spending on education, workers' compensation, and other social programmes

TABLE 3. Opinion on Social Welfare Issues by Group

	View of cutbacks by government in social programmes			Support for guaranteed annual income				Government effort for health and medical care			Agree that there is too much difference between rich and poor (percent)
	Too great	No more	More cuts	Yes	Yes, qualified	No, qualified	No	More	Same	Less	
Corporate											
Big Business	1	28	71	10	17	9	65	12	79	9	22
Small Business	4	42	54	12	10	9	69	29	64	7	31
Lawyers	6	47	47	16	8	4	71	19	74	7	32
State											
Politicians											
Federal	30	37	33	42	12	5	40	46	49	5	55
Provincial	26	40	34	46	12	5	37	32	66	2	57
Local	19	50	31	40	5	7	48	36	62	2	45
Civil Servants											
Federal	15	45	40	41	16	2	41	17	82	1	53
Provincial	13	52	35	39	14	7	40	14	78	8	50
Local	10	57	33	46	19	5	30	37	61	2	51
Trade Unionists	58	34	8	71	15	3	11	76	24	0	83

TABLE 4. Opinion on Foreign Investment and Economic Relationships with the U.S., by Group

Group	Assessment of overall effect of foreign investment on the Canadian economy				Approve of negotiation of continental energy pact			Approve of free trade between U.S. and Canada			Approve of passage of FIRA		
	Mostly good	Some good	Mixed	Some/Mostly bad	Yes	Neither	No	Yes	Neither	No	Yes	Neither	No
Corporate													
Big Business	59	31	8	2	47	12	41	60	13	27	31	13	57
Small Business	46	28	16	10	71	10	19	66	7	27	68	10	22
Lawyers	60	27	11	2	61	10	29	57	16	27	42	6	52
State													
Politicians													
Federal	28	31	23	18	31	5	64	37	20	43	70	4	26
Provincial	38	25	20	17	49	13	38	51	16	33	50	11	39
Local	27	38	22	13	55	9	36	50	14	36	71	3	26
Civil Servants													
Federal	25	33	26	16	26	9	65	41	13	46	78	8	14
Provincial	33	39	24	12	43	14	43	37	20	43	66	16	18
Local	24	40	24	12	67	9	24	64	14	22	79	14	7
Trade Unionists	11	22	34	33	59	6	35	47	10	43	93	3	4

revealed similar patterns. Business should therefore not be classified as supporting wholesale deterioration of social services. Small business proprietors were more likely than big business and lawyers to favour increases in health care spending: 29 percent of the small business respondents took this view, compared to 7 percent wanting to cut spending; but the majority of small business, 64 percent, supported the status quo.

Foreign Investment and Relations with the U.S.

The strongly pro-foreign investment views of big capital and the lawyers associated with big corporations are readily apparent in Table 4. An astonishing 57 percent of big businessmen disapproved of the Foreign Investment Review Act (FIRA), 31 percent approved, and 13 percent were neither in favour nor opposed. These responses compare to 68 percent of the small business proprietors, between 50 and 79 percent of various state groups, and 93 percent of the labour union leaders that approved of FIRA. Assessments of the overall impact of foreign investment on the Canadian economy follow a similar pattern. On two current issues, a continental energy pact and free trade between Canada and the U.S., the respondent groups are far less distinct in their views and there is less consensus within each sector. Still, 60 percent of big business, 66 percent of small business, and 57 percent of the lawyers approved free trade. On this issue, the trade unionists are nearly evenly split, as are a number of state elite groups. Big business was nearly evenly split over the continental energy pact, while the small business proprietors and lawyers favoured it by large majorities.

Not surprisingly in light of government policy, the federal state elites strongly opposed the energy pact and free trade with the U.S. The provincial elites are somewhat more enthusiastic, but the extent of federal-provincial differences is relatively small when considered in the light of recent political conflicts over these issues.

Government Economic Policies

In Table 5, the simplest pattern of responses is for the general questions about government investment and question about nationalization of a part of the potash industry. In both cases, the big business executives were very strongly opposed and the views of the lawyers were quite similar. The small business respondents also opposed government investment and the potash takeover by a strong majority, but their views were still more liberal than the two other business groups. The state elites are split on the potash takeover, with a complex pattern of differences among six groups. Only the trade union leaders favoured the measure, and they did so by a sizeable majority.

Of the ten groups of respondents, only the municipal elites, and then by just a small margin, gave majority support to the use of wage controls to combat inflation. Most opposed were big business, followed by the trade unionists! Small business and lawyers were also strongly opposed to controls. Big business and lawyers gave the greatest support to the use of tight money policies to combat inflation; five-sixths of each group approved. The opinions of the small business proprietors, 68 percent of whom approved of tight money, were in the range defined by the various state groups; between 54 and 71 percent of the latter voice approval.

TABLE 5. Opinion on Anti-Labour Policies to Combat Inflation and Government Investments in Industry, by Group

Group	Approve of wage controls to combat inflation			Approve of tight money to combat inflation			Approve of government investments in industry			Approve of Sask. Gov't potash takeover		
	Yes	Neither	No	Yes	Neither	No	Yes	Neither	No	Yes	Neither	No
Corporate												
Big Business	9	4	87	84	8	8	6	6	88	7	6	87
Small Business	29	9	62	68	15	17	22	11	67	12	18	70
Lawyers	21	7	72	84	10	6	17	2	81	14	10	76
State												
Politicians												
Federal	13	12	75	67	11	22	46	7	47	40	11	49
Provincial	36	8	56	54	11	35	42	6	52	34	12	54
Local	47	13	40	55	17	28	33	13	54	31	9	60
Civil Servants												
Federal	28	18	54	71	9	20	45	10	45	44	23	33
Provincial	30	18	52	66	16	18	44	7	49	44	18	38
Local	47	13	40	74	16	10	42	23	35	33	16	51
Trade Unionists	19	4	77	30	18	52	67	12	21	73	10	17

Federal Party Support

Finally, Table 6 shows the distribution of party support. Big business supported the Conservative Party over the Liberals, two to one.[10] The lawyers were 41 percent Conservative and 47 percent Liberal, and small business was 45 percent Conservative and 51 percent Liberal. The state elites gave some support to the NDP, and all but the provincial civil servants supported the Liberals to a far greater extent than the Conservative party. Not surprisingly, 57 percent of the Federal civil servants supported the Liberals, compared to 20 percent for the Conservatives and 16 percent for the NDP. Two-thirds of the trade unionists supported the NDP, one quarter supported the Liberals and 10 percent supported the Conservatives.

TABLE 6. Federal Political Party Support, by Group
Federal Party Support
(percentage distribution)

Group	Liberal	Conserv- ative, Social Credit	NDP	Other Party	No Party	Total
Coporate						
Big Business	31	62	1	2	4	100
Small Business	51	45	0	1	3	100
Lawyers	41	47	4	4	4	100
State*						
Politicians						
Local	57	20	16	0	7	100
Civil Servants						
Federal	44	20	13	1	22	100
Provincial	22	44	11	1	22	100
Local	55	33	16	0	8	100
Trade Unionists	23	10	62	2	3	100

*Federal and Provincial politicians are omitted from this Table because their party affiliations are public and the distribution simply reflects the sample characteristics.

Summary and Discussion

These data demonstrate the existence of significant ideological differences between capital and the state. The differences are large enough to affect the creation of policies and are in keeping with the recent history of conflicts over energy policy, foreign investment, and social programmes that have characterized capital-state relations. The political terrain defined by these data has the labour leaders located on the left, business on the right, and the state elites somewhere in between, their actual locations being a function of the issue at stake. There are significant differences among the three sectors of capital, but the divisions are not as large as those dividing captial as a whole from the six groups of state personnel. Relative to the enormous ideological gap between capital and labour, the differences among the three business groups are small.

The ideology of business revealed here may be characterized as involving strong opposition to increasing the power of trade unions and state investment in business, weaker opposition to the cooptation of labour, a "middle of the road" position on civil rights issues, and right-wing views on social welfare issues posed in a general way (but supportive of the status quo on specific programs). Business favours foreign investment and economic continentalism, Fiscal conservatism and the Conservative Party in Federal politics. In keeping with the predictions of Clement and Niosi, the small business proprietors were less opposed to government investment and more critical of foreign investment than big business. Small business was more anti-union, but less conservative on social welfare issues than big capital. There are differences of degree—a majority of the small business respondents, for example, opposed the Saskatchewan potash takeover. Small business proprietors proved substantially more likely to support the Liberal Party than big business, a finding which is entirely in keeping with their lesser concerns about government intervention. Compared to big capital, small business is more fearful of the organized working class, but more supportive of state programmes that reproduce the working class.

While some of the ideological characteristics of small business demonstrated in this study suggest that small business proprietors' main concern is the threat from monopolistic corporations, these anti-monopolistic sentiments are combined with the view that the trade unions are anathema and are set in the general ideological context that is conservative in comparison with the state elites, and very far to the right of the trade union leadership. This does not make small business a very good candidate for membership in an "anti-monopoly alliance," especially if this alliance has social democratic or trade union leadership.

Finally, let us consider the question of whether big business may be regarded as "class conscious" in the sense of being able to formulate a viable political project of capitalist rule. The positions reflected in responses to the questionnaire are certainly no more right-wing than the official government policies being implemented in some major capitalist nations, one of which, Britain, has a far stronger working-class tradition than Canada. For this reason, the Canadian capitalist class cannot be said to lack class-consciousness. Canadian capital has a distinct ideology, which would give rise to policies distinctly to the right of those presently pursued by the state.

Further Analysis of Sectoral Differences in Ideology

The interpretation of Tables 1 to 6 is straightforward because the differences among the groups are fairly large, especially in the context of socio-economic and other differences in the political attitudes of the Canadian population as a whole (Johnston and Ornstein, forthcoming 1985). Still there is some degree of unreliability in any analysis based on individual questionnaire items, mainly because of the limited range of responses provided for each question, the tendency for respondents to interpret the questions in slightly different ways, and the fact that the questions are asked in rapid sequence, which may discourage reflection on the part of the respondent. One alternative to the analysis of individual items is to form scales combining the responses to various questions—so that problems noted above, which contribute to random error, become less important. The remainder of this article is based on eighteen multi-item scales, which are precisely defined in Appendix B. Compared to the individual questionnaire items, these scales offer a considerable gain in statistical precision, but there is some compensating loss in the specificity since each scale combines the results of a variety of items concerning a topic. The scales are calibrated so as to indicate the relative positions, rather than the absolute positions of the various groups of respondents.

The eighteen scales are all scored in the same manner. The mean score for the state elites, considering the six separate groups together, is set to zero. So the mean scores for the three business groups and labour are therefore relative to the position of the state elites. In addition the standard deviation of each scale is set equal to one hundred times the standard deviation of the responses of all the state elites (again considering the six groups together). Thus, if a group has a mean score of +75 for one of the scales, the mean of that group is three-quarters of a standard deviation (i.e. 75 one-hundredths) above the mean for the state elites. Assuming the scale is normally distributed, the average score for that group is greater than the response given by 73 percent of the state respondents and lower than the response given by 27 percent of state respondents.

Table 7 gives the mean score on each scale for the ten categories of respondents. It may seem surprising that the six state groups do not have mean scores of zero, but that is because the six state groups *taken individually* do not have mean scores identical to the mean of respondents for all six groups combined (which is what was set to zero). The six columns of mean scores for the different groups of state respondents contain no number above 40 or below -50, which indicates that the variation among the state groups is relatively small. By comparison, all but four of the scores for labour are *outside* the range from -50 to +50. Most of the scores for the three capitalist groups are also outside this range.

The issues on which there is the most conflict between capital and the state are those for which the mean scores for the three business groups are most different from zero. Those issues involve government investment in industry, foreign investment, and policies designed to reduce the role of government in society; close behind in terms of conflict are social welfare programmes, labour policies, and foreign policy; relatively little conflict between capital and the state is evident over government programmes to subsidize business (endorsed by small business and mildly opposed by big business and lawyers), lowering personal taxation, and a generalized belief that the structure of Canadian capitalism is responsible for economic problems the country is facing. The conflict between labour and the state is greatest over labour policies and social welfare programmes.

The small business proprietors proved significantly more liberal than big business on a variety of issues, including support for government investment in industry (where the small business proprietors were not far from the mean of the state elites), support for decreasing the size of government, support for socialized medicine, support for government social welfare programmes taken as a whole, the belief that the structure of the economy causes serious problems, and support for foreign investment. In addition, small business proprietors were significantly more federalist. The conflicts between big and small capital all involved the role of the state: small business proprietors were far more willing to accept an interventionist state which makes some investments in industry and supports a broad range of social welfare programmes. These findings bear little resemblance to the reactionary labels commonly attached to small capital. For the most part the lawyers held opinions very close to those of

TABLE 7
Means* of Various Political Attitude Scales, by Group

Political Attitude Scale	BUSINESS			POLITICIANS			CIVIL SERVANTS			Labour
	Big	Small	Law	Fed	Prov	Local	Fed	Prov	Local	
Support for government social welfare programmes	-88	-38	-91	36	18	19	-27	-18	2	145
Support for decreasing social programme support levels	68	28	15	-25	-35	-22	11	20	27	-132
Support for socialized medicine	-73	-20	-79	-3	-20	-15	11	5	13	92
Support for affirmative action and structural aid to minorities	-49	-21	-96	22	-19	3	13	-6	-17	59
Support income redistribution	-33	3	4	29	-11	-13	6	-8	0	48
Belief economic problems are due to structure of economy	-64	-6	-69	30	-8	26	-26	-19	39	90
Belief economy suffers from too much government power	47	69	50	4	16	42	-48	-4	27	20
Belief economy suffers from power of capital	-36	13	-38	31	3	5	6	-20	-12	-12
Support for decreasing size of government	110	32	77	11	-15	-8	2	1	7	-81
Support for government policies to weaken labour	62	90	40	-16	-17	12	7	-1	22	160
Support for labour movement	-89	-66	-31	19	2	7	-7	-8	-2	101
Support for government subsidies to business	-25	57	-23	16	-3	25	-20	-11	20	-80
Support for lowering personal taxation	46	63	20	0	5	17	-22	-1	20	33
Critical of foreign investment	-102	-54	-90	16	-20	-19	15	-11	30	71
Support for government investment in industry	-134	-32	-102	13	-26	-7	15	-11	26	87
Support for government undertaking research efforts	-77	-7	-31	27	3	11	-19	-19	34	52
Increase the power of Federal relative to Prov. gov'ts.	0	51	-16	28	-46	12	31	-29	29	75
Support for more left-wing foreign policy	-73	-40	-62	-4	-4	-11	1	12	-9	98

*All the scores are 'standardized'. For the six state sectors, taken together, the mean is zero and the standard deviation is one hundred. For example, a score of -25 for a gropu indicates that the mean for the group is .25 (25/100) of a standard deviation below the mean for the state.

TABLE 8 Variance of Various Political Attitude Scales, for Business Groups and Labour

Political Attitude Scale	Business		Law	Labour
	Big	Small		
Support for government social welfare programmes	96	107	117	111
Support for decreasing social programme support levels	87	85	101	102
Support for socialized medicine	80	91	90	93
Support for affirmative action and structural aid to minorities	109	107	118	66
Support income redistribution	82	90	83	85
Belief economic problems are due to structure of economy	98	107	114	90
Belief economy suffers from too much government power	76	88	98	119
Belief economy suffers from power of capital	106	132	155	119
Support for decreasing size of government	71	96	85	72
Support for government policies to weaken labour	84	98	106	100
Support for labour movement	105	109	108	94
Support for government subsidies to business	105	97	100	135
Support for lowering personal taxation	97	89	118	105
Critical of foreign investment	90	100	87	91
Support for government investment in industry	105	113	111	87
Support for governemnt undertaking research efforts	103	93	91	52
Increase the power of Federal relative to Prov. gov'ts.	95	138	111	164
Support for more left wing foreign policy	77	74	77	107

*All the scores are 'standardized'. For the six state sectors, taken together, the standard deviation is one hundred. For example, a score of 125 indicates the standard deviation.

big business, but the lawyers were less anti-union, more supportive of social programmes (but opposed to socialized medicine), and marginally less opposed to government intervention in the economy.

Table 8 carries this analysis further by examining variation within the capitalist groups and labour, again relative to the variation within the state elites. A score of 100 on the scale indicates there is as much internal division within the group as within the state elites, taken as a whole. This analysis reflects the assumption that the ability of a group to act politically is not only a function of its average position, but also of the amount of internal unity. The results in Table 8 may be very simply summarized: the variation within the three capitalist sectors is approximately equal to the variation within the state elite.

On a small minority of issues there are demonstrably higher levels of dissensus within the categories of business respondents. Among the small business proprietors and lawyers there is a great deal of dissensus over whether structural problems of the economy (such as the industrial structure and the extent of foreign control) are the cause of current economic difficulties. In addition, small business is divided (to a greater extent that other groups) over the appropriate division of powers between the federal and provincial governments and the lawyers are divided over affirmative action, the levels of social welfare spending and whether personal taxes should be lowered.

These data certainly do not support the proposition that capital is too disunited politically to have a collective ideology. Business executives proved to be no more disunited than the state managers who actually formulate policy. This is a further argument against Block's contention that state managers, with their experience in making broad policy decisions, differ fundamentally from big business executives whose ideology, he says, only reflects corporations' immediate interests in increasing their profits.

A More Extensive Examination of Ideological Divisions Within Capital

The ideological divisions within the capitalist class have thus far been considered only in light of the distinctions among big business, small business, and the lawyers. This section considers the internal divisions within the capitalist sector in much more detail. Multiple regression analysis was used to distinguish the effects of a number of different variables on political ideology.

The regressions (not shown) provided comparisons among the major industrial sectors, between crown corporations and privately-owned corporations, between Canadian-controlled corporations and corporations controlled in the U.S. and in other nations, and among corporations with head offices in the different regions of Canada (for foreign-controlled corporations, their Canadian head offices). These measures, of course, all refer to the characteristics of the firms with which the respondents are associated. In addition, the regressions included characteristics of the individual respondents (which are distinguishable from, but may be associated with their corporate associations). The individual-level variables measured the amount of contact between the respondent and the federal, provincial, and municipal governments, membership in private clubs, and the extent of the executives' activities in lobbying organizations, government task forces and advisory boards, and community and charitable organizations. These last measures were intended to distinguish ''inner group'' members on the basis of their extensive contacts with government officials and within the business community.

The previously observed, distinctive ideological features of small business were confirmed by the regression analysis. Therefore, differences between the regions, in the frequency of contacts with government, etc., could not have been responsible for the ideological differences between small business and big capital and the lawyers. Compared to big business, the small business proprietors proved to be more opposed to efforts to decrease the size of government, more supportive of subsidies to business, more critical of foreign investment, more federalist, more supportive of social welfare programmes, and more opposed to labour. Although in terms of the specific ideological dimensions the small business executives are closer to the state, they proved no more likely than big business executives to support the Liberal Party. The crown corporation executives' opinions were very similar to those of the small business proprietors and they are more likely than private corporation executives to support the Liberal Party.

Compared to the ideological distinctiveness of small business and the crown corporation executives, the remaining divisions within the capitalist class are small and not sufficiently consistent to indicate major ideological cleavage. The lawyers and financial sector executives were less likely to support cuts in the size of government than industrial corporation executives. The executives of foreign-controlled corporations differed from Canadian capitalists only with respect to their views of foreign investment and government investment in industry. Otherwise, the comprador bourgeoisie was not ideologically distinctive. Because large foreign investors are often affected by the creation of crown corporations—the CDC is one obvious example—these two ideological differences may be collapsed into one: foreign capitalists are mainly concerned about their own ability to invest. The executives of family-controlled, large corporations were distinctive only in being more critical than average of foreign investment and less opposed than average to government investment.

Contacts with government had virtually no impact on ideology, except for the suggestion that executives who belong to upper class clubs are slightly more conservative than average. There was some regional differentiation in the political ideology of the capitalist class. Quebecers took somewhat more liberal positions than Ontario business executives on social welfare programmes, foreign investment, and government investment, and were more likely to support the Liberal party. Again compared to Ontario, westerners were more conservative on social welfare programmes, government subsidies to business, foreign investment, and government investment, and are more supportive of provincial powers. There was no detectable difference between business executives from Toronto and those from other parts of Ontario, and for only one of the ten independent variables was there a significant difference between Ontario and the Atlantic region. The finding that variables describing the corporation with which each executive was associated (such as its sector, and ownership) were far better predictors of ideology than region and the measures of the respondents personal characteristics, including contacts with government and other organizations, lends support to a ''sectoral'' approach to capitalist class divisions.

Among the executives of industrial firms, those working for corporations with large assets were less likely to support social programmes, more likely to support decreasing the size of government, less critical of foreign investment, and more opposed to government investment. This suggests that the very largest corporations are most likely to oppose economic intervention by the state, even after foreign ownership is taken into account. The regional differences among the largest industrial firms are similar to those observed for the large sample.

The extent of ideological differentiation varied considerably across issues. There was more conflict over foreign investment, government investment, decreasing the size of government, and party support than on other issues. Thus, the conflicts within the capitalist class are largely concerned with the direct intervention of government in the domain of big business rather than with social service issues and other aspects of the state's activities.

Summary and Discussion

The small business proprietors and crown corporation executives proved to be the most politically distinctive fractions of the capitalist class. In fact, these two sectors display a remarkable ideological similarity in being more favourable to state investment, more critical of foreign investment, and less concerned about the size of government than the other groups. Their reasons for taking these positions are likely somewhat different. For example, the crown corporations are sympathetic to government investment which is required for their very existence; while small business tends to be unaffected by government investment in large projects. The two groups are also more hostile to trade unions; while the small businesses fear unionization, the bad labour relations in many unionized crown corporations probably account for the attitudes of crown corporation executives on this dimension.

Although the distinctions have received a great deal of attention from students of Canadian capital, the very limited ideological differences between the executives of foreign and domestic corporations and among industry, finance, and commerce suggest that the classical categories of political economy do not tell us very much about present-day political divisions in capital. The Quebec businessmen betray a greater liberalism and support for the Liberal Party which presumably reflects their political milieu.

The inner group of capital—defined here as the executives with the greatest number of contacts with government and highest levels of participation in the "political" activities of business—is not politically distinctive. If anything, the inner group is slightly more conservative, despite its role as a buffer between capital and the state. Useem's findings, for American corporate executives, are precisely the same.

In general, these data reveal a capitalist class that is ideologically united at its core of large, privately controlled corporations. Monopoly capital theory, broadly understood, does point to a number of the differences that did emerge. Wedged between the working class and the monopolists, competitive capital turns to the state for protection. Social welfare programmes are often said to be threatening to small businessmen, who are supposedly least able to pay for them and most worried that high unemployment benefits and other social benefits will decrease the supply of labour and raise wages.

F. Conclusions

The data analysis offers unambiguous answers to the questions raised in the introduction. First, there is abundant evidence of ideological conflict between capital and the state. The divisions within the capitalist class are considerably smaller than the differences between capital and the state. Furthermore, these ideological differences extend across a number of dimensions of ideology, including labour relations, social welfare, fiscal and monetary policy, foreign investment, and government investment. State efforts to protect the accumulation process thus give rise to conflicts with capital. It should be emphasized that this does not imply that the state has knowledge of the most effective policies; its pursuit of specific policies reflects no more than a belief that they will work.

The corporate executives could hardly be classed as liberal. Their political views are clearly on the right of the political spectrum, even when that spectrum is defined only by issues that have had some public debate. Nevertheless, the executives are not so far to the ideological right that they could be said to differ from the policies of the present Conservative Party. In addition, there is no more ideological disunity among the corporate executives than there is among the state managers themselves. The data do not support the conjecture that corporate executives are unable to formulate policy alternatives to present state policies. In Block's terms, the corporate executives are class conscious, although the translation of their ideology into policy would certainly involve far less of an attempt to co-opt the working class, and far more of an effort to secure overt ideological hegemony compared to present state policies.

It is apparent that big capital is relatively united ideologically and that the capitalist class fractions defined by the political economists, largely in the context of explaining historical developments, have relatively little utility in pointing to present-day divisions within big capital. However, this analysis suggests that small business proprietors and the executives of crown corporations (the "state capitalists") may be regarded as two distinct class fractions. Niosi is insightful in pointing to the role of the state and the coalition of class forces that shape state economic policies, but these data provide no support for his conjecture that foreign capital is most strongly represented in the Conservative Party.

Whatever the merits of the economic distinction between core and peripheral firms, O'Connor's arguments concerning ideological differences are completely without empirical support, at least in Canada at the time of our survey. Contrary to O'Connor's prediction, small business proprietors proved to be less worried about state intervention than big capital, and they were more likely to support social welfare measures. This suggests that small business is less likely to be influenced by some version of pure, competitive capitalist ideology than by the network of tax breaks, incentives to expand employment, favourable purchasing policies, manpower development programs, and protection from the predatory policies of large corporations now provided by government.

These divisions within the capitalist class are of considerable theoretical interest, but they should be understood in the more general context of the larger ideological differences between capital, the state, and labour. In that context, the survey provides evidence of a strong ideological consensus within the capitalist class, including big and small capital and the lawyers in the largest firms. The differences among the executives of the largest corporations, who constitute the big bourgeoisie proper, are still smaller. In light of the extremely high level of foreign ownership in the Canadian economy, it is significant that the ideological differences between the "comprador" and "indigenous" bourgeoisies are limited to the issue of foreign ownership itself. There is no evidence, for example, to support Clement's contention that Canadian capital in the financial sector offers less opposition to nationalization than the comprador fraction.

Finally, let us return to the argument which began this article. Canadian political economists have taken the view that the Canadian state is distinguished by its instrumentalism. They are quite at variance with the theoretical views of Miliband, Poulantzas, and Block, which suggest a relatively high degree of state autonomy. The analysis here does not support exceptionalist theories of the instrumentalism of the Canadian state. One implication of these findings is that more attention should be directed towards understanding the role of the Canadian state in regulating the entire capitalist economy and overseeing the reproduction of the social formation.

Notes

1. Pratt is similarly instrumentalist in explaining the apparent contradiction between the central-Canadian ownership of the western news media and their oppositon to the NEP, which he sees as benefitting central Canada. It is simply that "Eastern-controlled newspapers (are) attempting to increase Western circulation" (1982:29). A more plausible explanation is that chain-owned newspapers are allowed to reflect their local managers' political positions, so long as they remain profitable.
2. Economist tendencies are also present in some accounts of the development of social welfare programmes. A good example is Alvin Finkel's (1979:ch.6) argument that the introduction of unemployment insurance in the 1930's has significant support from big business. Cuneo (1979) convincingly demonstrates the central role of trade union pressure in assuring the passage of the first unemployment insurance measures.
3. The term "elite" is used loosely in this paper. There is no agreement in the research literature over just what term should be applied to high-level elected officials and civil servants.
4. This viewpoint is most commonly associated with Miliband's (1968) landmark *The State in Capitalist Society*, although it is quite common to exaggerate Miliband's careful formulations. Two good reviews of recent Marxist theory of the state are Gold, Lo, and Wright (1975) and Jessop (1977).
5. For Miliband this "state bourgeoisie" includes "thousands of people in the upper reaches of the state . . . whom the state provides with high salaries and all that goes with state service at this level, not only in government departments, but also in innumerable boards, commissions, and other public bodies . . . Their first concern is naturally with their jobs and careers" (1983: 63). Unfortunately this reduction of the state managers to a fraction of the bourgeoisie seriously undercuts Miliband's otherwise cogent arguments concerning the relative autonomy of capital and the state.
6. Clement follows Porter (1965) in emphasizing the role of social backgrounds in understanding capital. A very considerable body of American scholarship, most closely associated with G. William Domhoff, is similar, but tends to place more of an emphasis on social institutions of the capitalist class such as clubs and policy organizations.
7. This quotation is cited by Niosi (1981: 118). A nationalist political strategy grows directly out of this assessment of the Canadian state. Hutcheson (1973: 174-5) continues: "For the Canadian people to demand the right to control that state would be a profoundly anti-imperialist action. This would not mean the defence of the present state which daily works in opposition to the interests of the people of this country. It would mean the political possibility of creating a Canadian state controlled by working people which would serve as an instrument of national liberation. The demand for an independent state would itself be a demand for a state in the hands of the people. The capitalists in Canada are well aware of this danger and for this reason work assiduously to undermine the concept of Canadian sovereignty and to assert their right to their own independent state at the same time as they struggle against the policies of the capitalist state in Canada." Writing five years later, Hutcheson (1978) offers no formal statement concerning the Canadian state. He still does not grant a central role to class conflict in Canadian society. In the introduction to *Dominance and Dependency* he argues: " . . . Canadian society is marked by three basic contradictions. There is the bi-national nature of this country, the division between French-speaking Canada and English-speaking Canada. There is the contradiction between the regions, with their provincial governments, and the Confederation with its central government. And there is the fundamental problem which results from the relationship between Canada and the United States" (Hutcheson, 1978: 7).
8. For a brilliant discussion of ideology which focuses on the general problem of analyzing the role of ideology in maintaining capitalist order as a whole, see Poulantzas (1973:195ff). He stresses the

"relational" character of ideology, that is the role of ideology in framing class relations (particularly in legitimizing class domination). Poulantzas makes a sustained critique of "historicist" models of ideology, which emphasize a simple correspondence between ideology and class. The definition of ideology in this paper is clearly open to this criticism of historicism.

9. There has been a great deal of conflict over this issue in Toronto. In response to strong evidence of police brutality, a voluntary organization called the Citizens' Independent Review of Police Activities has been established. Despite strong public pressure, the Police Commission has refused to establish an independent body and has instead set up its own investigative body.

10. The very small number of Federal Social Credit supporters are thrown in with the Conservatives.

References

Averitt, Robert, 1968—*The Dual Economy: The Dynamics of American Industry Structure.* New York: Norton.

Block, Fred, 1977—"The ruling class does not rule: notes on the Marxist theory of the state." *Socialist Revolution* 3:6-28.

1980—"Beyond relative autonomy: state managers as historical subjects." Pp.227-42 in Ralph Miliband and John Saville, eds., *The Socialist Register 1980.* London: Merlin.

Bluestone, Barry, 1970—"The tri-partite economy: Labour markets and the working poor." *Poverty and Human Resources Abstracts* 5:15-35.

Burrell, Gibson—1984—"Comporatism in comparative context." Paper presented at the Conference on Theories of Business-Government Relations, York University, Toronto.

Clawson, Dan, Allen Kaufman, and Alan Neustadtl, 1983—"Which class fractions found the new right." Paper presented at the 1983 annual meeting of the American Sociological Association, Detroit.

Clement, Wallace, 1975—*The Canadian Corporate Elite: An Analysis of Economic Power.* Toronto: McClelland and Stewart.

1977a—*Continental Corporate Power.* Toronto: McClelland and Stewart.

1977b—"The corporate elite, the capitalist class, and the Canadian state." Pp.225-48 in Leo Panitch, ed., *The Canadian State: Political Economy and Political Power.* Toronto: University of Toronto Press.

Cuneo, Carl, 1979—"State, class and reserve labour: the case of the 1941 Canadian Unemployment Insurance Act." *The Canadian Review of Sociology and Anthropology* 16:146-170.

Edwards, Richard C., Michael Reich, and David M. Gordon, 1975—*Labour Market Segmentation.* Lexington, Mass.: Heath.

Finkel, Alvin, 1979—*Business and Social Reform in the Thirties.* Toronto: Lorimer.

Gold, David A., Clarence Y. H. Lo, and Erik Olin Wright, 1975—"Recent developments in Marxist theories of the capitalist state." *Monthly Review* 27, No.6:29-43 and No.7:36-51.

Hodson, Randy and Robert L. Kaufman, 1982—"Economic dualism: a critical review." *American Sociological Review* 47:727-739.

Hutcheson, John, 1973—"The capitalist state in Canada." Pp.153-177 in Robert M. Laxer, ed., *(Canada) Ltd.: The Political Economy of Dependency.* Toronto: McClelland and Stewart.

1978—*Dominance and Dependency.* Toronto: McClelland and Stewart.

Jessop, Bob, 1977—"Recent theories of the capitalist state." *Cambrdige Journal of Economics* 4: 353-373.

Johnston, William, and Michael Ornstein, 1985—"Social class and political ideology in Canada." *Canadian Review of Sociology and Anthropology,* forthcoming.

Kaufman, Robert L., Randy Hodson, and Neil D. Fligstein, 1981—"Defrocking dualism: a new approach to defining industrial sectors." *Social Science Research* 10:1—31.

Larrain, Jorge, 1978—*The Concept of Ideology.* London: Hutchinson.

Levitt, Kari, 1970—*Silent Surrender: The Multinational Corporation in Canada.* Toronto: Macmillan.

Mellos, Koula, 1978—"Developments in advanced capitalist ideology." *Canadian Journal of Political Science* XI:829-861.

Miliband, Ralph, 1968—*The State in Capitalist Society.* London: Wiedenfeld and Nicolson.

1983—"State power and class interests." *New Left Review 138:* 57-68.

Naylor, Tom, 1972—"The rise and fall of the third commercial empire of the St. Lawrence." Pp.1-41 in Gary Teeple, ed., *Capitalisn and the National Question in Canada.* Toronto: U. of T. Press.

1975—*The History of Canadian Business.* (2 vols) Toronto: Lorimer.

Niosi, Jorge, 1978—*Le Controle financier du capitalisme canadien.* Montreal: Les presses de l'Université du Québec.

1981—*Canadian Capitalism: A Study of Power in the Canadian Business Establishment.* Toronto: Lorimer.

1983—"The Canadian bourgeoisie: towards a synthetical approach." *Canadian Journal of Politcal and Social Theory 7,* No. 3: 128-149.

1985—*Canadian Multinationals.* Toronto: Garamond Press.

O'Connor, James, 1973—*The Fiscal Crisis of the State.* New York: St. Martin's.

Offe, Klaus, 1974—"Structural problems of the capitalist state." Pp.31-57 in Klaus von Beyme, ed., *German Political Studies.* London: Sage.

Olsen, Dennis, 1980—*The State Elite.* Toronto: McClelland and Stewart.

Oster, Gerry, 1979—"A factor analytic test of the dual economy." *Review of Economics and Statistics* 61:33-39.

Panitch, Leo, 1977—"The Role and Nature of the Canadian State." Pp.3-27 in Leo Panitch, ed., *The Canadian State: Political Economy and Political Power.* Toronto: U. of T. Press.

1979—"Corporatism in Canada." *Studies in Political Economy* 1:43—92.

Porter, John, 1965—*The Vertical Mosaic.* Toronto: University of Toronto Press.

Poulantzas, Nicos, 1973—*Political Power and Social Classes.* London: New Left Books.

1975—*Classes in Contemporary Capitalism.* London: New Left Books.

Pratt, Larry, 1982—"Energy: The roots of national policy." *Studies in Political Economy* 7:27-59.

Semmler, Willi, 1982—"Theories of competition and monopoly." *Capital and Class* 18:91-116.

Sher, Julian, 1983—"The NEP: patriotism or profits?" *Socialist Studies* 1: 141-150.

Stevenson, Paul, 1983—"the state in English Canada—the political economy of production and repro-duction." *Socialist Studies* 1: 88-127.

Useem, Michael, 1978—"The inner group of the American capitalist class." *Social Problems* 25: 225-240.

1970a—"Studying the corporation and the corporate elite." *The American Sociologist* 14:97-107.

1979b—"The social organization of the American business elite and participation of corporation directors in the governance of American institutions." *American Sociological Review* 44:553-572.

181—"Business segments and corporate relations with U.S. universities." *Social Problems* 29: 129-141.

Watkins, Mel, 1983—"The NEP and the left: a comment on Sher and others." *Socialist Studies* 1: 151-157.

Wolfe, Alan, 1981—"Sociology, liberalism, and the radical right." *New Left Review* 128:3-27.

APPENDIX A: Description of Sample

Sector	Method of Selection
Big business	Chief executive officer of a systematic sample of corporations selected from 1980 *Financial Post* ranking of the 500 largest Canadian corporations
Small business	Chief executives from a. samples from lists provided by the Chambers of Commerce or Boards of Trade of the twelve largest census metro-politan areas (CMA's); the number selected in the CMA was proportional to its population. b. a random sample of manufacturing companies selected from *Scott's Directory of Manufacturing Firms* for 1980; the number of selections was again proportional to the CMA population.
Lawyers	senior partners from all Canadian law firms with twenty or more partners as listed in the 1979 *Canadian Law List*
Federal politicians	random selection of Members of Parliament, stratified by party to assure the parties would be present in the correct proportions

Federal civil servants   random selection of deputy and assistant deputy ministers

Provincial politicians   in each province, cabinet ministers responsible for a pre-selected set of ministries were selected

Provincial civil
   servants   the deputy ministers in the same ministries were selected

Municipal politicians   the mayor, and a random selection of the controllers (where they existed), or of the city councillors

Municipal civil
   servants   heads of the major city departments were selected

Trade union leaders   presidents of the largest trade union locals, as listed in the *Directory of Labour Organization;* presidents of the provincial labour federations; presidents of the Labour Councils in the twelve largest CMA's; and top officials of the national labour organizations

APPENDIX B: Description of Political Ideology Scales

All the scales are formed by summing the responses to the items. Scales are formed for respondents who give valid responses (i.e. not "don't know" or "no opinion" or "depends") to two-thirds or more of the items and missing data are assigned the average of the respondent's valid responses. Items marked with an asterisk are reversed before being added into the scales, because their "direction" is not the same as the other items. The scales are labelled to correspond to the trait common to each set of items. All scales have been checked for unidimensionality and to eliminate non-scale items with factor analysis.

1. Support for government social welfare programmes

Now we would like your answers to a question that we asked of the general public about the effort which government should put into a number of activities. By effort, we mean specifically the proportion of our total resources which is spent in each area . . . The general public was cautioned that putting more effort into one area would require a shift of money from other areas, or an increase in taxes. Could you choose the answer on this card which comes closest to your opinion about the amount of effort which should be put into health and medical care?

The card included the following responses (the scores given to each response are shown in parenthesis)

Much more effort (5)
More effort (4)
About the same effort (3)
Less effort (2)
Much less effort (1)

The following areas were rated using the above scale:

a. health and medical care
b. protecting the rights of native people
c. providing assistance to the unemployed

d. creating more jobs
e. helping the poor
f. building public housing
g. eliminating discrimination against women ·
h. protecting the environment
i. providing daycare
j. helping retired people
k. workmen's compensation
l. decreasing regional inequality

2. Support for affirmative action and structural aid to minorities

Various groups have proposed a number of additions to the protection of civil rights in Canada. Forgetting, for the moment, whether or not these items should be in the constitution, please tell me whether or not you support each of the following proposed changes to the law.

Responses were scored as follows:

Yes (4)
Yes, with some qualification stated (3)
No, with some qualification stated (2)
No (1)

a. legislation to protect the rights of the disabled
b. the right of women to equal pay for work of equal value
c. protection of homosexuals from discrimination in employment
d. programmes of affirmative action to favour the hiring and promotion of women and other minorities in order to redress historical traditions of discrimination

3. Support for decreasing size of government

Now we would like your opinion concerning a number of government policies which have been put forward to deal with inflation. Could you tell me how you feel about each of them using the alternatives on this card? We would like your general evaluation of each policy in principal, not a specific evaluation of the present government's policy. Again, if you have mixed feelings about the state-ment, please use the "neither approve nor disapprove" response. Use the "no opinion" answer if you don't have any views on the statement.

The card included the following responses (the scores given in each response are shown in parenthesis)

Strongly approve (5)
Agree (4)
Neither approve nor disapprove (3)
Disapprove (2)
Strongly disapprove (1)
No opinion (missing)

The policies rated are as follows:

a. restriction of the money supply
b. mandatory government controls on prices
c. mandatory government controls on wages
d. decreased government spending on social services
e. decreased government spending in areas other than social services

Now we would like your opinion of a number of government policies which have not been put forward to deal with unemployment, again using the alternatives on this card (the following items are scored negatively).

a. temporary government employment programmes
b. direct government investment in productive industry
c. government creation of new jobs in social services

4. Support for government policies to weaken labour

This scale involves three ratings in the format of No. 3, above: the first is a rating of "legislation to decrease the power of trade unions" as a policy to lower inflation; the second and third are ratings of "lowering the minimum wage" and "regulations to make it more difficult for able-bodied workers to obtain unemployment insurance" as policies to decrease unemployment.

5. Support for government subsidies to business

This scale involves two ratings in the format of No. 3, above: the first and second are ratings of "incentives for business expansion" and "cuts in taxes on business" as policies to decrease inflation; the third and fourth are ratings of "selective business tax cuts to encourage job creation" and "subsides to businesses which create jobs" as policies to decrease unemployment.

6. Critical of foreign investment

There has been considerable debate about the impact of foreign investment on the Canadian economy. Could you tell me how you feel about the following statements, using the responses on this card (the responses are scored as for No. 3, above)?

a. *Foreign-controlled firms import needed technology into Canada that would not otherwise be available.
b. The return of interest, dividends, fees and commissions by foreign firms to their home bases seriously hurts Canada's balance of payments.
c. *Foreign-controlled firms' failure to carry out research and development in firms in the same industries.
d. Foreign-controlled firms' failure to carry out research and development in Canada injures the Canadian economy.
e. *Foreign-controlled firms benefit Canada by taking risks their Canadian controlled counterparts will not.
f. *Foreign firms are not more likely than Canadian firms to import supplies and parts that could be made in Canada.
g. Foreign ownership results in our producing too many competing products in certain areas and this market fragmentation unnecessarily raises costs to consumers.
h. The economic power of foreign firms has stunted the development of Canadian companies.
i. *Foreign firms import capital that would otherwise be unavailable to Canada.

7. Support for government investment in industry

Using the responses on this card, could you please give me your opinion on a number of present and possible policies intended to decrease foreign ownership (the responses and scored as for No. 3).

a. Passage of the Foreign Investment Review Act.
b. Establishment of the Canada Development Corporation
c. Giving tax breaks to Canadian firms to allow them to grow faster than foreign firms.
d. Sponsorship of crown corporations in critical industries to compete with foreign firms, such as PetroCan.
e. Tax and other incentives to encourage Canadians to take over foreign firms.
f. Directing government spending to Canadian firms to increase their sales.
g. Takeover of some, but not all, of the multinational oil companies by crown corporations.
h. Nationalization of the Canadian operations of large multinational oil companies.
i. Laws to require foreign companies not now in Canada to form joint ventures with Canadian partners if they wish to start a business in Canada.
j. Legislation to force the sale of foreign-owned companies to Canadians.

8. Increase the power of the Federal Government relative to the provincial governments

How do you think powers of the Federal and provincial governments should be distributed in the future in a number of areas?

The card includes a scale from 1 to 5, with 1 labelled "more power to provincial governments", 3 labelled "balance of power should remain unchanged, and 5 labelled "more power to Federal Government".

a. economic policy
b. education
c. immigration
d. energy policy
e. environmental protection
f. communications
g. social assistance
h. labour relations
i. language policy
j. health
k. civil rights

9. Support for more left-wing foreign policy

Now we would like to ask you some questions about foreign policy. Could you please give me your views on each of the following statements, using the responses on Card 4 (scored as for No. 3, above)?

a. *The most important objective of Canadian foreign policy ought to be to resist the spread of communism.
b. Present economic relations between rich and poor countries work largely to the detriment of the poor countries.
c. *At present the Soviet Union is generally expansionist rather than defensive in its foreign policy aims.
d. *International agencies like the World Bank are right to impose conditions that encourage a good climate for foreign investment in borrowing countries.
e. The Canadian Government should prohibit Canadian firms from investing in South Africa.

f. *Canadian commitments to NATO should be strongly increased.
g. Developed nations should allow their foreign aid to be spent where the recipients decide, rather than being tied to purchases in the donating nations.
h. The Western Allies should take stronger action to reduce the proliferation of nuclear weapons.
i. The Canadian government should set and enforce standards of business conduct to prevent Canadian firms from taking unfair advantage of customers and employees in Third World countries.
j. Canada should support socialist movements which overthrow dictatorial regimes.
k. The Canadian Government should prohibit Canadian firms from investing in Chile.

Class Consolidation in Extra-Market Relations: The Case of Toronto General Hospital
Diane Clark and Lorne Tepperman

The Question of Extra-Market Relations

The "merchants against industry" and the alternative "class consolidation" theses of Canadian economic development have been reviewed extensively in this book (see, for example, the introductory article by Brym). Our purpose in this article is to test these competing explanations of the role of the capitalist class in Canadian economic development. Did the Canadian capitalist class consist of two separate groups, financial and industrial, with the former dominating the latter and blocking the growth of industry (Naylor 1972, 1975; Clement 1975, 1977)? Or did merchants and industrialists fuse into one group of finance capitalists, with no one clique clearly predominating (Carroll 1982, Carroll forthcoming, Macdonald 1975, Richardson 1982)? On the whole, our evidence supports the latter interpretation.

Unlike the data used in most studies in this area, ours do not pertain to economic enterprises as such. Rather, we shall examine six Boards of Directors of The Toronto General Hospital. We have chosen to focus on a non-economic institution because the power of the bourgeoisie is not manifested solely in economic domination. As Johnson (1980: 111) notes, the power of the corporate giants "both foreign and domestically based, is greatly enhanced by their close association with government, to say nothing of their ownership and control of the media, university boards of directors, and other aspects of the national ideological apparatus". This relationship has been empirically documented. Axelrod (1982), for example, demonstrates the importance and extent of.capitalist class involvement in the establishment and operation of York University. "Good corporate citizenship", as' demonstrated by involvement in philanthropic social welfare endeavours, should be seen as furthering the interests of corporate survival and dominance (Marchak, 1979: 14), as maintaining and consolidating class power. Just as members of corporate boards of directors are motivated by class interest, members of non-corporate boards of directors also represent class interests.

Proponents and critics of the merchants against industry thesis have paid little attention to extra-market relations among capitalists, those ties to social and political institutions and organizations which link capitalists outside the purely economic realm of the marketplace. But as Carroll, Fox and Ornstein (1982: 45) note:

Numerous extra-market relations among capitalists have developed to serve the instrumental function of co-ordinating distinct capitals and the expressive function of integrating the controllers of large-scale capital into a self-conscious, hegemonic class . . . In an earlier era of capitalism the bourgeoisie was socially organized around kinship ties and informal social relations, as well as participating in such organizations as boards of trade, poltical parties, and the state.

These researchers argue that these extra-market social relations increase in range and intensity as a result of modern corporate concentration and centralization. Moreover, it follows from their argument that the existence of extensive extra-market relations which bind together commercial and industrial capitalists would support the finance capital/capital integration argument as evidence of a "community of *capitalist* interests". Conversely, if commercial and industrial capitalists tend *not* to be linked by extra-market relations, but instead associate only within their respective class fractions, that would indicate the merchants against industry argument should not be dismissed out of hand, as its critics advocate.

Participation in non-economic organizations thus provides an additional benchmark for assessing both the question of class cleavages among the bourgeoisie and the relative power of one fraction over the other. These predictions about the extent and nature of extra-market relations can be empirically tested to shed new light on the merchants against industry debate.

The Case of Toronto General Hospital

Toronto General Hospital developed historically in close connection with the City of Toronto and its ruling elites. The members of the Board of Directors of Toronto General Hospital have included Toronto's leading merchant-financiers and industrialists since the hospital's founding by the Family Compact 150 years ago. From its inception, the hospital has been an important outlet for upper-class philanthropy and its Board has been composed of bourgeois members. Toronto General Hospital's Board of Directors is thus an appropriate organization for consideration of extra-market relations among capitalists. Moreover, given the significance of the hospital as a focus for elite social welfare interest, its lack of clear political or religious affiliation, and the importance of Toronto as a commercial and industrial centre, our conclusions can to some degree be generalized. What is true of the Board members of Toronto General Hospital will be true of the ruling elites of Toronto and, perhaps, of Canada. If we find no division of labour, let alone conflict, between merchants and industrialists on the Board, none is likely to exist in the ruling class as a whole.

Studying Toronto's elite of the 1920s, Richardson (1982) showed an absence of division and conflict between merchants and industrialists in their market relations. In this article, we examine both a later and an earlier period. This allows us to discover whether Richardson's findings can be generalized to extra-market relations, and also to discover historical trends in the data. Naylor's merchants against industry thesis applies particularly to late nineteenth century capitalists.

Some might claim that Richardson, in studying early twentieth century capitalists, failed to study the "right" period. Our data will allow us to judge whether the merchants against industry argument holds in the late nineteenth century subsample and also whether a movement toward class consolidation in the twentieth century (as suggested by the finance capital argument) explains Richardson's conclusions.

Four Boards of Directors of Toronto General Hospital (1872-1921) provide the date from the early period and two Boards (1946-1982), data from the later period. The later boards have nearly twice as many members as the earlier boards because of a progressive growth of Board size starting in 1907 and continuing throughout this century. Thus what began as a board of four very select people in the latter decades of the nineteenth century became a board of more than a dozen in the latter decades of the twentieth century.

We collected biographical and financial information on the 35 early Board members and 69 later Board members. Information could not be found for two of the early members and eight of the later members. Of the remaining members, six to eight of the early members and eight of the later members were members of elites outside the economic sector, typically in education, the judiciary, or government.

Data on the remaining members were coded (following Richardson, 1982) according to their primary economic affiliation as suggested by the staples, Marxist, and finance capital models. These three models define the merchant-financier and industrial categories somewhat differently, thus giving slightly different empirical results. The staples model defines a mercantile economic affiliation as including finance, trade, real estate, transportation and utilities; industrialists are involved in manufacturing and minerals. The Marxist model defines merchants' capital as involved in finance, trade, and real estate; its industrial (or "productive") capital category includes manufacturing, transportation, utilities and minerals. The finance capital model follows the Marxist definition of productive capital but defines mercantile/financial affiliations as involved only in finance (but not trade or real estate).

Members' primary economic affiliation was identified according to the economic sector in which they held directorships. If directorships were held in more than one sector, members were identified with the sector in which they held an officership (or a full-time affiliation) with a specific firm. If they held more than one such position, the first office held was used to identify their primary affiliation. In addition, we identified members as "crossovers" if they were involved in both mercantile/financial and industrial economic activities.

What is most remarkable is how little the results vary from model to model despite their different definitions. The data in Table 1 compare the Board members by model, period and primary affiliation. If the merchants against industry argument were valid, we would find a predominance of either merchants or industrialists on the Board, and an absence of people who are both merchants and industrialists. The majority of Board members in both periods have merchant/financier as their primary affiliation. Industrialists make up one-quarter to one-third of the Board members; thus they are certainly not devoid of contact with members of the other class fraction.

There is also a clear tendency for Board members to be active in both trade/finance and industry; this holds true across periods, models and primary affiliations. Of the twelve entries in the table which test the hypothesis that merchants are distinct from industrialists, only one barely succeeds. Therefore, these data, with the one exception noted, fail to support the "merchants against industry" argument.

TABLE ONE
Proportion of Toronto General Hospital Board Members
Who are Crossovers,
by model, period and primary affiliation
(N in parentheses)

PRIMARY AFFILIATION \ MODEL*	EARLY PERIOD 1879-1921			LATE PERIOD 1946-1982		
	Staples	Marxist	Finance Capital	Staples	Marxist	Finance Capital
Merchant/ Financial	.455 (22)	.600 (20)	.611 (18)	.543 (35)	.677 (31)	.750 (28)
Industrial/ Productive	.600 (5)	.714 (7)	.714 (7)	.800 (15)	.632 (19)	.650 (20)

*As defined in Richardson, 1982

The merchants against industry thesis receives support *only* in the early period by the staples model for those who are primarily merchants/financiers. The staples model is supported because it defines the merchant class most inclusively. By definition, more types of activity, hence more people, are included in the category "merchant". However, for merchants/financiers the merchants against industry argument does not, for the most part, hold in the early period and does not hold at all in the later period.

The merchants against industry theory does best in accounting for the early period; there it should be expected to do best, for it is primarily a theory about nineteenth century Canadian economic development. For this reason, we turn our attention to the early Board members who were both merchants and industrialists, the "crossovers". Were these members marginal to the Board? Were they marginal to the Toronto upper class? Were they only insignificantly involved in both merchant and industrial activity? An affirmative answer to any of these questions would argue for an acceptance of the "merchants against industry" thesis because, while links between merchants and industrialists may have existed, they were either peripheral or unimportant.

On the first question, the answer is 'no'. The list of seventeen members who were crossovers included three of the four Board Chairmen during the early period: Walter Lee, John Blaikie, and Joseph Flavelle. (The fourth chairman, the Hon. Christopher Paterson, was not in the economic sector at all, but a judge of the Ontario and Canadian Supreme Courts.) These three chairmen exemplify a clear commitment to both merchant/financial *and* industrial activities.

Walter Lee, who served on the Board between 1879 and 1902, was a director of the Western Canada Loan and Savings Company, as well as the Dominion Bank and Confederation Life, and was thus clearly a financier. He was also a director of

the St. Lawrence Foundry and the Industrial Exhibition (now the Canadian National Exhibition); he was thus also an industrialist. John Blaikie, a member of the
Board between 1880 and 1904, and its Chairman between 1902 and 1904, was a
director of Toronto General Trusts, the North American Insurance Company, and
several investment companies; clearly a financier. He was also heavily involved in
utilities, as a director of Consumers Gas Company and the Northern Railway. (In
the staples model these are considered merchant/financial activities, but they are
considered industrial activities in the other two models.) Finally, Sir Joseph
Flavelle, who served on the Board from 1902 to 1939, and as its Chairman from
1904 to 1921, was also a crossover. His merchandising and financial activities
included directorships in the Canadian Bank of Commerce, National Trust Company, Toronto Penny Bank and Robert Simpson Company. His manufacturing
and industrial affiliations included a directorship of Canadian Marconi, the
Presidency of William Davis Company (pork packing), and chairmanship of the
Board of the Grand Trunk Railway.

Thus crossovers on the Hospital Board were not peripheral; they were among its
leading members, even in the early period. Nor were these crossovers marginal to
the Toronto upper class or, for that matter to the national upper class. We already
noted that Chairman Christopher Patterson was promoted to the highest courts in
Ontario and Canada. Chairman Joseph Flavelle was knighted in Britain for his
work on the Imperial Munitions Board during the First World War. Other crossovers were members of Toronto's leading families. They included George Gooderham, Cawthra Mulock, Vincent Massey, John Eaton and Sir Edmund Osler.

Finally, it should be emphasized the these crossover affiliations were to be
found in the upper echelons of both merchant and industrial realms. In finance,
we find directorships in the Dominion Bank (three mentions), the Bank of Toronto
(one mention), the Imperial Bank (three mentions), the Canadian Bank of Commerce (five mentions), Toronto Penny Bank (two mentions), the Toronto General
Trust (four mentions), the Trust Corporation of Ontario (two mentions), and Guardian Trust (one mention). Directorships in several insurance companies which
were each mentioned more than once include Confederation Life (four mentions),
Canada Life (two mentions), Mutual (two mentions), and North American (two
mentions). (Five others were mentioned only once.)

Connections to the industrial realm were similarly impressive. They included
directorships in Gooderham and Worts—in the mid-nineteenth century, Toronto's
leading industry—Canadian General Electric (four mentions), Massey-Harris (two
mentions), the Steel Company of Canada (two mentions), Dominion Cable, and a
variety of other manufacturing and construction firms. What is most impressive,
however, is the Board members' involvement in transportation and utilities. (As
already noted, the staples model categorizes such activities as mercantile/fin-
ancial but the other two models—Marxist and finance capital—define them as industrial activities.)

The least important of these directorships are in utilities, which among others
include Toronto Electric Light, Consumers Gas (two mentions), Bell Telephone,
Sao Paulo Tramway, Light and Power (two mentions), Rio de Janeiro Tramway,
Havana Traction, and Mexican Light and Power. Far more remarkable are the
activities of these early crossovers in transportation. In all, seven of these seventeen crossovers were active in railways and three in steamships, and one was

even involved in aviation.

From these observations, one must conclude that, even during the early period, when the "merchants against industry" argument is least likely to be false, it gains little support. The seventeen crossovers on early Boards at Toronto General Hospital are central to those Boards; they are also central to Toronto's upper class; and they are affiliated with weighty enterprises in both the financial and industrial sectors.

The only support these data lend to the "merchants against industry" theory is evidence of the importance of utilities and transportation in the industrial activities of this group. Scholars applying the staples model would deny these were true industrial activities. However, even the staples model definition of industrial activity would only reduce by two the number of crossovers on the Board. Board members who were heavily involved in utilities and transportation tended also to be involved in other types of industrial activity.

Concluding Remarks

To reiterate, our findings would have had to show the following in order for the merchants against industry theory to be judged valid: (1) In at least the early period, the Board would have had to exclude one or another class fraction. We found that it did not. (2) In at least the early period, few members would have had to be engaged in both merchant/financial and industrial activities. This was not found to be the case. (3) In the early period, crossovers, though numerous, would have had to be peripheral to the Board, to the Toronto upper class, or to significant economic activities. They were found not to be so. The "merchants against industry" argument, though in general unsupported by these data, was weakly supported for the early period using a staples model for Board members whose primary affiliation was in the mercantile/financial sector. This, however, hardly amounts to a recommendation that we accept the theory.

Our underlying assumption is that the Board Members of Toronto General Hospital represent the Toronto elite and can therefore be taken as a sample of this elite. This assumption may be invalid. Our findings could be rejected outright if the Toronto General Hospital Board had selected its members *in favour of* crossovers. This would have made the Board precisely the wrong place to look for a representative sample of Toronto elite members.

We cannot dismiss such a possibility. It might reasonably be held that a philanthropic board ought to diversify the types of people it appoints, and these people ought to diversify their economic activities, if they are to reach the largest possible donor audience in the elite community (cf. Granovetter, 1973). But we have no evidence that the Toronto General Hospital Board was diversified in this sense. Some of the most effective and long-lived Hospital Boards, including those chaired by Flavelle (1904-1921) and by Urquhart (1946-1966), were remarkably in-grown; that is, characterized by multiple connections between Chairman and Board member, and between one member and another.

Neither, however, could we find evidence that Toronto General Hospital Boards were composed uniformly of people who mirrored the characteristics of the Board Chairman. This would have allowed the possibility that chairmen who were crossovers tended to appoint people like themselves to the Board. Some chairmen did so immediately, while others let attrition take its gradual course. In the latter case the Board would not have reflected the characteristics of the Chairman for quite a while. But one cannot prove with these data that crossovers like Bell always appointed members to their Board who were other crossovers like themselves.

The presence of crossovers on the Toronto General Hospital Board offers support for the movement toward class consolidation predicted by the capital integration argument. The relative lack of discernible class fractions among Board members suggests the Board encompassed a consolidated capitalist elite in Toronto. To the extent that the Board is representative of Toronto's elite, it reflects a capitalist class which was not fragmented into mercantile and industrialist fractions.

Despite historical changes in Toronto's upper class from the Early Compact to the modern capitalist elite over the hospital's one hundred and fifty year history, the membership of the Board remains consistently upper-class while accommodating shifts within the upper class. For example, the expansion of the Board in the early twentieth century allowed for the inclusion of emerging new elites in the state (provincial government) and academia (University of Toronto). In this sense, the Board's composition reflects changes in both economic and non-economic power structures. More important, however, is the fact that the structure of the Board itself changed to allow for the incorporation and consolidation of these elites in an extra-market relation.

There is a danger in extending this argument for class consolidation too far. It may be that the Toronto General Hospital gives a distorted picture of the degree of capitalist class integration. At a very fundamental level, *all* capitalists (whether financiers or industrialists) have certain common interests in maintaining their class position and hegemony. This community of class interests is perhaps more likely to surface in ideological and cultural realms than in the economic market-place where competition is far from perfect but certainly not absent. While merchants and industrialists *may* have antagonistic interests, in fundamental ideological terms their interests are similar. Thus non-economic organizations may bring class fractions together in a very limited and specific type of consolidation. This is a possibility for the Toronto General Hospital Board members, but a remote one given the evidence of extensive crossovers of members in the economic sector.

It thus seems reasonable to conclude that the "merchants against industry" argument, which highlights divisions among capitalists, is open to very serious question. The finance capital argument, which highlights interpenetrations of class fractions and class consolidation, is broadly supported by our investigation of the extent and strength of extra-market relations among Toronto capitalists.

References

Axelrod, Paul—1982—"Businessmen and the building of Canadian Univerisities", *Canadian Historical Review* LXIII (2): 202-222
Carroll, William K.—"The Canadian corporate elite: Financiers or finance capitalists?" *Studies in Political Economy* 6: 89-114
Carroll, William K.—*Capital Accumulation and Corporate Interlocking in Post-War Canada.* Vancouver: University of British Columbia Press, forthcoming
Carroll, William K., John Fox and Michael Ornstein, 1982—"The network of directorate links among the largest Canadian firms", *Canadian Review of Sociology and Anthropology.* 19 (1): 44-69
Chodos, 1973—*The CPR: A Century of Corporate Welfare.* Toronto: James Lewis & Samuel

Clement, Wallace, 1975—*The Canadian Corporate Elite*. Toronto: McClelland and Stewart

Clement, Wallace, 1977—*Continental Corporate Power*. Toronto: McClelland and Stewart

Granovetter, Mark, 1973—"The Strength of Weak Ties," *American Journal of Sociology*. 78: 1360-80

Hofley, John R., 1980—"Classlessness vs. equality: an agonizing choice," in Harp and Hofley (eds) *Structured Inequality in Canada*. Scarborough, Ontario: Prentice-Hall

Innis, Harold A., 1930—*The Fur Trade in Canada*. New Haven: Yale University Press

Innis, Harold A., 1956—*Essays in Canadian Economic History*. Toronto: University of Toronto Press

Johnson, Leo A., 1980—"The development of class in Canada in the twentieth century" in Harp and Hofley (eds.) *Structured Inequality in Canada*. Scarborough, Ontario: Prentice-Hall

Macdonald, L.R., 1975—"Merchants against industry: an idea and its origins" *Canadian Historical Review*. LVI (3): 263-281

Marchak, Patricia, 1979—*In Whose Interests?* Toronto: McClelland and Stewart

Myers, Gustav, 1975 (1914)—*A History of Canadian Wealth*. Toronto: Lorimer

Naylor, R.J., 1972—"The rise and fall of the third commercial empire of the St. Lawrence" in G. Teeple (ed.) *Capitalism and the National Question in Canada*. Toronto: University of Toronto Press

Naylor, R.J., 1975a—*The History of Canadian Business 1867-1914, Volume I: The Banks and Finance Capital*. Toronto: Lorimer

Naylor, R.J., 1975b—*The History of Canadian Business, Volume II: Industrial Development*. Toronto: Lorimer

Noisi, Jorge—"Who Controls Canadian Capitalism? *Our Generation*. 12 (1): 19-35

Panitch, Leo, 1977—"The role and nature of the Canadian State," in Panitch (ed.) *The Canadian State*. Toronto: University of Toronto Press

Panitch, Leo, 1981—"Dependency and Class in Canadian Political Economy" *Studies in Political Economy*. 6: 7-33

Richardson, R.J., 1982—"Merchants against industry: an empirical debate," *Canadian Journal of Sociology*. 7 (3): 279-295

Ryerson, Stanley B., 1975—*Unequal Union*. Toronto: Progress Publishers

Statistic Canada, 1977—*Canada Year Book*. Ottawa: Statistics Canada

Teeple, Gary, 1972—"Introduction" in Teeple (ed.) *Capitalism and the National Question in Canada*. Toronto: University of Toronto Press.

GARAMOND PRESS BOOKS:

Books on the leading edge of research and debate in Canadian social science and the humanities, written and priced to be accessible to students and the general reader.

- Robert Brym (ed): *The Structure of the Canadian Capitalist Class*
- Peter Li and R. Singh-Bolaria (eds): *Racial Oppression in Canada*
- Jorge Niosi: *Canadian Multinationals*

THE NETWORK BASIC SERIES

Available now:
- Armstrong et al: *Feminist Marxism or Marxist Feminism: A debate* Intro. by Meg Luxton.
- Varda Burstyn and Dorothy Smith: *Women, Class, Family and the State* Intro. by Roxana Ng
- David Frank et al: *Industrialization and Underdevelopment in the Maritimes, 1880-1920*
- David Livingstone: *Social Crisis and Schooling*
- Leo Panitch and Don Swartz: *From Consent to Coercion; The Assault on the Labour Movement*

FORTHCOMING TITLES INCLUDE:
- Howard Buchbinder et al: *The Politics of Heterosexuality*
- Margrit Eichler: *Towards a N̶   ̶ist Scholarship*
- Murray Knutilla: *Theories of t̶ ̶*
- Graham Lowe and Herb Northc̶ ̶ ̶ssure: A Study of Job Stress*
- Robert White: *Capitalism, Law an̶ ̶ ̶Work*

Garamond Press, 163 Neville Park Blv̶ ̶ Ont. M4E 3P7 (416) 699-4845